The
Holy Days
of God,
The
Holidays
of Man

THE HOLY DAYS OF GOD, THE HOLIDAYS OF MAN

HOLLY M. SNEAD

iUniverse, Inc.
Bloomington

The Holy Days of God, The Holidays of Man

iUniverse books may be ordered through booksellers or by contacting:

iUniverse
1663 Liberty Drive
Bloomington, IN 47403
www.iuniverse.com
1-800-Authors (1-800-288-4677)

ISBN: 978-1-4759-5965-9 (sc)
ISBN: 978-1-4759-5966-6 (ebk)

Printed in the United States of America

iUniverse rev. date: 01/22/2013

Contents

DEDICATION

Dedicated, in gratitude, to all who study
longing to know the truth,
live the truth and teach the truth,
and yearn to grow in knowledge.
Dedicated to the continued search for the truth,
wherever it is, whatever it is.

Dedicated especially to
the One who is the Truth,
who will teach us all, if we but listen.

The Time has come;
The Kingdom of God is at hand.
Repent, believe the Good News!

WHAT I BELIEVE

I am assured that the Gospels were written by Jesus' apostles and disciples who lived during Jesus' life and after-death appearances. They recorded the words of those who knew Jesus and witnessed his works. They did not compose their texts from their own beliefs; they wrote what God revealed through his Spirit.

The Bible is inerrant. To understand its words, we must set aside our 21st century, western understanding and learn of the history of our faith, as revealed in Scripture, using 1st century eyes and eastern understanding.

I further believe the entire New Testament was written in the Apostolic Age, before AD 70, before the destruction of Jerusalem. If it was written post-AD 70, they would surely have recorded the destruction of their beloved city and the razing of their Temple. The New Testament gives no hint of Jerusalem's destruction, the slaughter of a million brethren or the burning of the Very Dwelling Place of God.

The Apostle Paul died about AD 67. The Christian community understood Jesus had not returned as they had expected but this did not divert their attention from Jesus' promised return. The Gospels and the epistles had all circulated throughout the faith communities. The infant church had grown into a mature church, prepared for their Lord's return. Assured by their Lord, they knew he would return in their generation.

The 'Tanakh', Old Testament Scripture, speaks of God's miracles which included creation of the world, Adam and Eve, Noah's flood and Elijah ascending to heaven in a 'chariot of fire'. The New Testament records miracles as well: the virgin birth, Jesus healing the sick and raising the dead, his resurrection and his ascension to heaven. Our mortal minds cannot verify these acts, but that does not remove them from the miraculous. We must not believe that if the eye does not see or the mind does not understand, it cannot be. We cannot understand all that is written but we must believe the miracles. Without the miracles of God's love and redemption, we have no reason to study His Word or follow his commands.

I am assured the Tanakh was a shadow of what is revealed in the New Testament. The people in both Covenants were real; the events truly happened. We must be careful as we study Scripture. Acknowledging that Scripture interprets Scripture, we must let God's word guide and teach us so we can know the truth of what it teaches us.

The Bible is an historic book; it does not contradict history or valid scientific study. Research constantly changes; the Bible does not change. The New Testament was written for 1st century Jewish, Greek and Roman readers. Reading the New Testament, we must understand we are reading someone else's mail. Much of what was written was for Jewish readers who were taught by their Lord of the redemption and restoration they would know through God's Grace, through faith, revealed in their Scriptures, through Christ, all to the Glory of God.

Sola Gracia—Only Through Grace

Titus 3:5-7   "He saved us, not because of righteous things we have done, but because of his mercy; he saved us through the washing of rebirth and renewal by the Holy Spirit whom he poured out on us generously through Jesus Christ our Savior, so that having been justified by his grace, we might become heirs, having hope of eternal life."

Romans 11:6   "If by grace, it is no longer by works, if it were, grace would no longer be grace."

Romans 3:23-24 "All have sinned and fall short of the glory of God, and are justified freely by his grace, through the redemption that came by Christ Jesus.

Ephesians 1:5-6 "He predestined us to be adopted as his sons through Jesus Christ in accordance with his pleasure and will, to the praise of his glorious grace which he has freely given us."

Ephesians 2:5-6 "It is by grace you have been saved; God raised us up with Christ and seated us with him in the heavenly realms."

Hebrews 2:9   "We see Jesus, who was made a little lower than the angels, now crowned with glory and honor because he suffered death, so by the grace of God he might taste death for everyone."

Sola Fide—Only By Faith

Acts 15:9   "He made no distinction between us and them, for he purified their hearts by faith."

Ephesians 2:8-9 "It is by grace you have been saved by faith, not from yourselves; it is the gift of God, not of works, so that no one can boast."

Act 26:18   "I am sending you to them to open their eyes and turn them from darkness to light, from the power of Satan to God, so they may receive forgiveness of sins and a place among those who are sanctified by faith.

Romans 3:28   "Man is justified by faith apart from observing the law."

Romans 4:4-5 "When a man works, wages are not credited to him as a gift but as an obligation; to the man who does not work, but trusts God who justifies the wicked, his faith is credited as righteousness."

Romans 4:16	"The promise comes by faith so it may be by grace and may be guaranteed to Abraham's offspring, not only those who are of the law, but also those who are of the faith of Abraham.
Romans 5:1	"We have been justified through faith, we have peace with God through our Lord Jesus Christ.
Romans 9:30	"The Gentiles who did not pursue righteousness obtained it, a righteousness by faith."

SOLA SCRIPTURA—ONLY THROUGH SCRIPTURE

John 8:31-32	"If you hold to my teaching you are really my disciples; you will know the truth; the truth will set you free."
Acts 17:11	"The Bereans were of more noble character than the Thessalonians for they received the message with great eagerness and examined the Scriptures every day to see if what Paul said was true."
Hebrews 4:12	"The word of God is living and active, sharper than any two-edged sword; it penetrates even to dividing soul and spirit, joints and marrow. It judges the thoughts and attitudes of the heart."
Psalm 119:11-12, 15-16	"I have hidden your word in my heart that I might not sin against you. Praise be to you O LORD; teach me your decrees. I meditate on your precepts and consider your ways; I delight in your decrees. I will not neglect your word."
Colossians 3:16-17	"Let the word of Christ dwell in you richly as you teach and admonish one another in all wisdom, as you sing psalms and hymns and spiritual songs with gratitude in your hearts to God."
11 Timothy 3:16	"All Scripture is God-breathed and is useful for teaching, rebuking, correcting and training in righteousness, so that the man of God may be thoroughly equipped for every good work."
11 Timothy 2:15	"Do your best to present yourself to God as one approved, a workman who does not need to be ashamed and who correctly handles the word of truth."

SOLUS CHRISTUS—ONLY BY CHRIST

John 5:39	"You dilligently study the Scriptures because you think that by them you possess eternal life. These are the Scriptures that testify about me, yet you refuse to come to me to have life."
Luke 24:27, 44-47	"Beginning with Moses and the prophets, he explained to them what was said in all the Scriptures concerning himself. He told them, "This is what I told you while I was still with you. Everything must be fulfilled

that is written about me in the Law of Moses, the Prophets and the Psalms. He opened their minds so they could understand the Scriptures; he told them, "This is what is written: The Christ will suffer and rise from the dead on the third day, and repentance and forgiveness of sins will be preached in his name to all nations, beginning at Jerusalem."

John 3:16-17   "For God so loved the world that he gave his one and only Son, whoever believes in him shall not perish but have eternal life. For God did not send his Son into the world to condemn the world, but to save the world through him."

Acts 4:12   "Salvation is found in no one else, for there is no other name under heaven given to men by which we must be saved."

Sola Deo Gloria—All to the Glory of God

Joshua 7:19   "Give Glory to the LORD, the God of Israel; give him the praise.

Psalm 29:2   "Ascribe to the LORD the glory due his name; worship the LORD in the splendor of his holiness.

1 Corinthians 10:31 "Whatever you do, do it all for the Glory of God."

Ephesians 3:21 "To him be glory in the church and in Christ Jesus throughout all generations forever and ever.

Sola Fide Only by Faith
Sola Gracia Only by Grace
Sola Scriptura Only through Scripture
Solus Christus Only by Christ
Sola Deo Gloria Only the Glory of God

INTRODUCTION

W hat do we know of our religious holidays, or our Holy Days? How should we celebrate their truth? To rightly honor and celebrate our Christian holidays, we must learn of the foundation of our faith, as revealed in Hebrew Scripture. To learn the truth of our Holy Days, we must understand Israel's Holy Days. Unfortunately we often rely on ancient scholars and latter Church beliefs that have little or nothing to do with the true time or reasons for the Holy Days we are called to honor.

Biblical study reveals Jesus' birth was not celebrated by the early saints. In AD 313, at Constantine's Edict of Toleration however, the Roman Empire became a 'Christian' Empire, and Constantine determined Christ's birth would be celebrated on December 25th. By AD 354, the Roman church designated this as the date of Jesus' birth and by AD 550 it became the legal holiday.

Jesus was crucified on Nisan 14, at Passover, the Feast where Israel recalled the sacrifice of the lamb and their Exodus from Egypt. The Apostolic faith was closely connected with its Jewish roots and Jesus did not intend for it to be otherwise. His teaching was bound to the Torah. In early Church history, Pascha, our Lord's Crucifixion, was commemorated on Nisan 14. Eusebius believed *"For true biblical unity, Christ's Church should observe our Lord's Passion on this date."* (Ch. Hist. Bk. IV c. AD 324) The Passover lamb delivered Israel from slavery and death in Egypt; Christ's death at Passover delivered us from slavery to sin-death.

Jesus' Resurrection was originally celebrated at First Fruits, the day following the Passover Sabbath. The Apostolic celebration of Jesus' crucifixion and resurrection, fulfillments of Israel's Passover Convocations, were celebrated as the Christian Passover, Pascha, through Jerusalem's first fifteen Jewish bishops, faithful believers, worthy to judge on such matters. Epistles were sent out so Jesus' followers could celebrate as Torah commanded.

At the Bar Kochba revolt in AD 135, anti-Jewish sentiment began to invade the Church. Hadrian had all Jews driven from the land. Apostolic believers were forced to flee, as they still observed the Jewish Holy Days. Greeks, led by Gentile Bishops, convinced Hadrian they were not 'of the Jews' and were allowed to remain.

At the Council of Nicea, in AD 325, Constantine formally prohibited Gentile Christians from fasting or worshiping with 'the odious Jews' or honoring their Holy Days. Christians were forbidden to honor or commemorate Jesus' death and resurrection as a 'Christian Passover'. Ignoring the Hebrew lunar calendar, Constantine separated

Jesus' Passion and Resurrection from Passover's Convocations, severing Christians from their Spiritual connection to Hebrew Scripture and from Israel. Easter was to follow Passover's Convocations. At his word, the 'Sword of the Empire' replaced the 'Sword of the Spirit' in the teaching of Christian doctrine.

Jesus prophesied his 1st century Return; his disciples taught their generation of His Imminent Return, as taught in the Law and Prophets. Futurists, expecting a physical, earthly kingdom, imply he failed to do what he promised, when he promised. Like the evil servant in Matthew 24:48, they deceive their people saying our Master is staying away a long time, giving his enemies occasion to condemn him as a False Prophet.

Jesus condemned the Pharisees for their false worship. Setting aside God's commands, they observed their own traditions. (Matthew 15:9, Mark 7:9) For far too long we have kept our own traditions rather than learning Scripture's truth. Celebrating our Holy Days at the wrong times, for the wrong reasons, failing to celebrate their truth, we miss the Glory of the convocations God has called us to honor. Jesus warned Judah's leaders of their errors because they did not know Scripture nor understand God's power. (Matthew 22:29)

Serious study of the Sinai festivals reveals our Christian Holy Days fulfill God's ordained Holy Days, his 'Holy Convocations', revealed in the Torah. Israel's Holy Days were summoned assemblies, 'miqra qodesh'. Strong's # 4744 'miqra' was 'called out public meeting'; # 6944 'qodesh' was 'holy'. God's 'Miqra qodesh' were 'Holy Convocations', 'appointed feasts'. More than historical celebrations, they were rehearsals for later events, prophetic in intent until fulfilled. After fulfillment, they were to serve as memorials.

Israel' Feast Days were clearly declared by God. Israel knew what each day represented physically and how they were to celebrate in worship to God. They knew from the Torah why they celebrated Passover, Shavuot and Tabernacles. Every feast day was a Great Day of the LORD. They knew they were to take these Feast Days seriously but they needed to understand, and we must understand, their convocations were prophetic rehearsals, spiritual shadows of celebrations they were yet to know. Israel also honored fast days, in particular, Yom Kippur, the Day of Atonement. They understood the holiness of this day and celebrated this Sabbath of Sabbaths fasting in repentance to God in holy reverence.

Forgetting or ignoring God's Miqra qodesh, we celebrate our holidays as the world celebrates, as Rome commanded. We feast not as the LORD commands, in communion with him, but as the world feasts with parties and worldly pleasure. We declare our celebrations honor the holy days we celebrate but we often pretend our celebrations and party just for the sake of partying. Our celebrations give no thought of the true meaning of the Holy Days we are called to honor. We forget or ignore the celebrations God ordained, neither feasting nor fasting in reverence, remembrance or celebration of God's love. We have no true understanding of the Holy Days God calls us to honor.

At Christmas, we buy our children too many presents, forgetting the true celebration. We forget those who need the bare minimum just to survive, eat more in one meal than we would need for a week and forget those who would celebrate if we offered a morsel from our tables.

At Easter, we celebrate with baskets filled with candies. We dress in our finest, not to honor our Lord but to impress our neighbors of how gloriously we celebrate. Whom are we fooling? Certainly we do not fool our Lord. He knows the truth and sees the lies we tell. In truth, we are not celebrating at all.

We are taught that Jesus' Second Coming is still future; he will visibly return, reign in Jerusalem in a physical temple and destroy the evil nations of the earth. The Earth will be destroyed; a New, Physical Earth will descend from Heaven. Only then can we celebrate.

Most Jews rejected God's New Covenant and Kingdom when their Messiah first appeared two thousand years ago. They did not recognize Yeshua's fulfillment of Tanakh's promises; they preferred to hold onto their ancient scholars' beliefs. Unfortunately, we are no different; for two thousand years we have held onto ancient beliefs and practices, believing God's Kingdom will be a physical Kingdom simply because that is what we were taught by all our 'wise and learned scholars'.

Too many churches, both Protestant and Catholic, continue to reject God's New Covenant Kingdom, bringing confusion to our Holy Days. Churches of all denominations teach as doctrine the commandments of man, demanding we observe our Holy Days as they understand and teach. We separate ourselves from the Holy Days Israel was commanded to honor and claim no part in their celebrations. We are assured our churches know the truth. Accepting, without question, their teaching as biblically accurate, we are no different than the 1st Century Jews and we continue the deception.

To rightly honor the Holy Days God has hallowed, we must learn how and why Israel celebrated. As the Bible was written by Hebrews and we serve a Hebrew Lord with Hebrew disciples, we must understand our Holy Days fulfill Israel's Holy Days. Throughout the Apostolic Age, Jesus' disciples never celebrated New Holy Days; they celebrated God's ordained Holy Days as revealed in the Torah.

While we are called to follow the first-century church and understand their beliefs, we must remember this church was first predominately a Hebrew congregation. Grafted into a Hebrew family, we must learn of the root of their faith, Jesus, their Messiah, who made them what God called them to be. Only then can we know what God calls us to be. Our Holy Days and Israel's Holy Days are 'Echad', bound as One. Their Miqra Qodesh were summoned assemblies, appointed times, rehearsals of all we are called to celebrate. (Leviticus 23:4, Colossians 2:16-17)

To truly celebrate our Holy Days, we must recall Israel's Egyptian slavery, their forty years in the wilderness and their entry into their Promised Land. Understanding how they celebrate Passover, Shavuot and Tabernacles, their Pilgrimage Feasts, we discover our Lord has truly come in fulfillment of all their celebrations. These three feasts and seven Holy Festivals taught them, and teach us of Jesus and his Bride.

Learning of and understanding their celebrations, we can learn how we are to celebrate as we take our place in our Holy Land.

Only with careful study can we learn how and when we are to celebrate and what God would have us know and teach. The times and seasons Israel and the early church knew as the times and reasons for their Holy Days speak the truth God would have us know. Unless we are careful, we will deny the truth to those we teach, giving reason for others to deny what God would have them know. Teaching error, the truth is not in us and we continue the deception.

What are our Holy Days; when and how are we to celebrate? We cannot understand our salvation, revealed in these Holy Days, until we learn of Israel's salvation revealed in their Miqra Kodesh. Paul taught the church in Rome: *"First for the Jew, then for the Gentile."* Romans 1:16 We cannot receive our salvation if Israel has not received theirs.

To understand and proclaim our salvation, we must understand theirs. We must dilligently study God's Word to learn all that our Lord did for Israel and through them, has done for us. On seeing His LORD's promise fulfilled, seeing Yeshua brought before the Temple, the Righteous Simeon proclaimed Yeshua would be a light for revelation to the Gentiles, for Israel's glory. God's salvation, Yeshua YHWH, for both Jews and Gentiles, was offered through the birth, death, resurrection, ascension and return of God's Only Begotten Son.

To God be the Glory!

What are our Holy Days? What has God called us to celebrate as we honor the life of our Lord? When was he born; when did he die; when did he rise victorious? When did he promise he would return to his people, redeeming them? What was the judgment God would bring upon those who refused to turn from their disobedience? To understand all that God has done, we must study God's Holy Days as taught in the Torah and see how they connect with the Holy Days we celebrate. Only then can we know what our Holy Days teach and how we are to celebrate all God has done to bring us, both Jews and Gentiles, into Covenant with Him.

For two thousand years, the Church has taught deception. Using the pagan cultures of ancient Rome, they determined Jesus' birth would be celebrated on December 25th, Rome's celebration of 'Saturnalia'. By AD 325, forsaking their Hebrew heritage and the Holy Days Israel celebrated, Rome determined Jesus' Passion would be separated from Israel's celebration of Passover. Turning from Hebrew Scripture's message to the people of Israel and God's Promise to his own, the church taught delay in fulfillment of all God promised his faithful remnant, Jews and Gentiles. They assure us we must wait until Jesus returns to Jerusalem, setting up his Physical Kingdom. Only then can we celebrate and honor the Holy Days Rome proclaims.

What are the Holy Days God calls us to celebrate? How are we to honor and celebrate our Lord's Holy Days? How are we are to celebrate and honor our Lord's Life and Ministry?

We must learn the truth of Jesus' physical ministry to his people, Jews and Gentiles, and his Spiritual ministry to the faithful remnant and discover the truth of God's Holy Days, our Lord's birth, ministry, death, resurrection ascension and return in His Father's Glory. We must acknowledge and rejoice in God's Holy Days, his judgment and his blessings, and celebrate our entry into the New Heaven and Earth, the New Jerusalem. Abiding in our Lord's Presence, we must honor God's Miqra Qodesh, His Holy Convocations, His Appointed Feasts, His Holy Days. ***Only then can we teach!***

Chapter 1

THE BIRTH OF CHRIST

Our celebration of Christmas is a holiday most misunderstood concerning the time it should be celebrated and its place in history. Differing opinions of what happened, when it happened, if it happened, lead to the confusion. As this holiday celebrates the start of our Lord's life, we must begin our investigation with Jesus' birth and sort through all we know, or believe we know, to uncover what truly happened and what it meant. Only then can we celebrate the wonder, power and glory of our Lord's birth; only then can we teach.

What does Scripture reveal of those who witnessed this glorious Day of the Lord? Matthew and Luke tell us God gave us His Son, born of a virgin. Wrapped in swaddling cloths, he was laid in a manger. Shepherds, receiving word from an angel, found him lying in a manger in Bethlehem, as Isaiah 7:14 9:6-7 and Micah 5:2 had prophesied. (Luke 2:7-16) Sometime after his birth, guided by a star, wisemen from the East came to worship this child who would be King. (Matthew 2:1-11)

When we celebrate this Holy Day, do we understand and truly believe; did it happen as it is written? Have we learned the truth or is it just a delightful story to teach us a message? Only if we learn from those who first wrote these words, can we learn what they understood and what we are called to celebrate. Does Scripture reveal when Jesus was born? Using Biblical and historic records, what can we learn of this glorious birth?

If we step back in time, walk the roads they walked, understand the language they spoke and the faith they cherished, what can we learn from two young people who journeyed to their homeland to become part of history? What can we learn from them; what can they teach us?

OLD AND NEW HISTORICAL RECORDS

From Jewish Historian Josephus, and coins minted by Herod's sons, many assumptions are made concerning Jesus' birth. Most scholars say Herod died in 4 BC, just before Passover. Josephus reports a lunar eclipse preceded Herod's last illness. He did not date this eclipse but from his "Antiquities", many scholars believe Herod died March 13, 4 BC. (Antiq. 17,6,4 plus footnote) With Herod's concern for the precise appearance of

'His star' and his order to kill all the male children of Bethlehem, two years and under, it appears Jesus would have been born two or three years earlier. (Matthew 2:7-8, 16)

Josephus' Antiq. 18, 1, 1 and Luke 2:2 speak of Quirinius, the governor of Syria, and the calling of a census. Historians and Biblical scholars believe these censuses were at fourteen year intervals. Acts 5:37 mentions a census in AD 6, Quirinius' 2nd census. This could place the first one in 8 BC. From these records, anytime between 8-6 BC would appear to be an acceptable year for Jesus' birth.

In AD 313, Rome's Emperor, Constantine, declared Jesus' birth would be celebrated on December 25th but shepherds would not have been in the fields in December. They came in from the fields in the late Fall before the first rains began to fall. This suggests Jesus could have been born in the Fall of 6 BC, after the 8 BC census, two years before Herod's death. Does this agree with our Bible or have we missed valuable information?

The 'Census' Ordered by Augustus

Careful study reveals Herod did not die in 4 BC, as believed and taught by most scholars, but sometime in 1 BC. If these records are valid, Jesus' birth would have been around 3 BC. At the time of Jesus' birth, Caesar Augustus issued a decree that a census should be taken of the entire Roman world. (Census, 'apographo', 'registration') History records Augustus ordered a registration in 3-2 BC but at this time Quirinius was not Syria's governor as Luke appears to record. In a Greek Lexicon however, the Greek 'hegemon', translated 'governor' in English, refers to a commander, which describes Quirinius' position.

Augustus sent Quirinius to Syria, as his 'hegemon', to command this 'apographo'. All within the empire were to sign and swear an Oath, declaring political allegiance to Augustus, preparing for honors he would receive at his silver jubilee as emperor. This included Judea where Joseph and Mary lived; all were commanded to return to their homeland to register their oath of allegiance to Augustus.

Tertullian, a Christian apologist of the late 2nd century, confirms historic record of a registration taken in Judea in 3-2 BC. This was an important time for Augustus. It was his 60th year of life, born August, 63 BC, his silver anniversary as Emperor, from 1/27 BC and the 750th anniversary of the founding of Rome in 4/753 BC. The Senate and people of Rome proclaimed Augustus 'Pater Patriae', Father of the Country. At this honor, he ordered that all in the Empire had to return to their homeland to register their oath of allegiance to him.

"A decree went out from Caesar Augustus that the whole world should be enrolled. Joseph and Mary went up to the city of David to be enrolled because they were both of the House of David." (Aramaic Manuscript, Luke 2:1-5) As descendants of David, they both were required to swear allegiance to Augustus.

Josephus records this pledge of allegiance in connection with Herod's death. Twelve months before his death, six thousand Pharisees refused to pledge their allegiance to Caesar. (Antiq. 17, 2, 4, 41-45) Orosius, a 5th century historian confirmed this registration, in connection with Jesus' birth. *"Augustus ordered a census of each province and all men be enrolled. At that time, Christ was born and was entered on the Roman census list as soon as he was born."* (Orosius Adv. pg. VI, 22.7, VII, 2, 16)

Augustus' formal reception was on 2/5/2 BC, as recorded in his "Res Gestae" # 35. As most Judeans were not Roman Citizens, Augustus may have decreed that they swear allegiance before he received the formal honors. Luke's record and Augustus' decoration as Pater Patriae appear to refer to this 'Oath of Allegiance'.

EXIGUUS' NEW CALENDAR

Before Rome's fall, the years of the calendar were counted from the founding of the Empire. In AD 526, Pope John 1 determined a new calendar needed to be set up honoring Jesus' birth. A monk, Dionysius Exiguus was given the task of dating Jesus' birth but his accounting was off by three years. He set Jesus' birth 753 years from the founding of Rome instead of its 750th anniversary, as recorded in Augustus' 'Res Gestae'. Exiguus set Jesus' birth as AD 1 instead of 3 BC.

THE DEATH OF HEROD

A major obstacle against a 4-3 BC conception and birth of Jesus is Herod's long accepted 4 BC death date. Matthew 2:6 reveals Herod died after Jesus' birth; if Herod died in 4 BC, Jesus could not have been born after that date. Josephus' "Antiquities" reveals there was a lunar eclipse on a fast day shortly before Herod's death and he died before Passover. (Antiq. 17. 6.4.165) To learn the time of Herod's death, we must find the eclipses visible in Palestine.

3/23/5 BC	Total Eclipse	9/15/5 BC	Total Eclipse
3/13/4 BC Partial Eclipse	1/9/1 BC Total Eclipse	12/29/1 BC Total Eclipse	

As much scholarship teaches that Herod died on March 13[th,] 4 BC, we must study that day in Israel's history. In 4 BC, March 13th was Adar 15, the 2nd night of Purim, a feast celebrating Israel's deliverance from Haman. From Josephus, we learn that just before Herod's death, at a fast day, two Rabbis, Judas and Matthias, were executed for inciting disciples to tear down a golden eagle Herod had placed over the Temple gate. The Sanhedrin charged them with sacrilege and sedition; that night there was a lunar eclipse.

3

Josephus recorded an eclipse before Herod's death but his eclipse could not have been the one at Purim. Josephus recorded Herod died after a fast day; Purim was a two-day Feast, not a Fast Day. The people hated Herod; these Rabbis were esteemed heroes. The Sanhedrin would never have permitted their execution at Purim, and as Haman and Herod were both of Edomite lineage, the Sanhedrin would never have let them be executed by a descendant of Haman on this festal day. We also discover all the events involved in Herod's death, funeral and memorial could not have occurred in the twenty-nine days between Purim and Passover.

Stepping away from Adar 15, 4 BC, the Megillath Taanith, the Roll of Fasts, records the rabbis' execution was on January 9th, 1 BC with a fast celebrated in their honor. A full lunar eclipse followed. Just after this eclipse, Herod's body was becoming putrified. He was taken to warm baths in Callirrhoe on the Dead Sea, twenty-five miles from Jericho, but all treatment failed. He then executed Antipater for trying to take the throne before his death. Herod died five days later. A thirty-day mourning period followed. The body was carried on a bier by military officials and family, a mile a day, from Jericho to the Herodian. A grand funeral feast and seven days of mourning by his family followed, with further mourning for patriots who had been killed.

Just before his death, Herod ordered many distinguished Judeans imprisoned, to be killed at his death, to assure there would be great mourning but his orders were not followed. Instead, a Jewish holiday, celebrated on Shabbat 2, commemorated his death. Shebat 2 was January 26th, 1 BC, seventeen days after the Rabbis' execution and the eclipse, three months before Passover. (The Christmas Star pp. 1-2)

THE REIGN OF HEROD

Earliest manuscripts of Josephus' "Antiquities" record Herod's death in 1 BC. In 1544 however, a printer incorrectly recorded Herod's death, saying Herod's son, Philip died in Tiberius' 22nd year, after ruling thirty-seven years after his father's death, instead of Tiberius' 20th year. All copies of Antiquities since 1544 record this error.

Josephus' "War of the Jews" accurately records Herod's life and reign. The War at *Actium was in his 7th year, September 2, 31 BC*, placing the start of his reign in 38 BC; *Herod died 5 days after causing Antipater to be slain, reigning since he was declared king by the Romans, thirty-seven years.*" (War 15, 5, 2 & 17, 8, 1) These historic records and "Antiquities" typesetting error confirm Herod died in 1 BC.

CENSUS OF 3 BC

Josephus says Augustus' census was shortly before the decoration he received on 2/5/2 BC, twelve months before Herod's death, connected with the Rabbis' execution, the eclipse on January 9th, and Passover, three months later. Herod died on Shebat 2, January

26th, 1 BC, shortly after this eclipse, twelve months from Augustus' decoration on 2/5/2 BC. These historical records validate each other, revealing Herod died on January 26th, 1 BC.

COINS MINTED FOR HEROD'S SONS

Another conflict concerns coins minted by Herod's sons after his death, with their reigns historically recorded as starting in 4 BC. In 4 BC, Herod's son, Archelaus was acclaimed Herod's heir and they reigned together until Herod's death.

At this same time, Herod was demoted, condemned by Augustus. No longer 'Amic Caesaris', Friend of Caesar, he simply became Augustus' subject. Because of this loss, Herod had Antipater executed for seeking the throne before his father's death. Some historians suggest Herod's reign ended, not at his death but with this disgrace and his sons incorporated Antipater's regnal years into their own reigns.

RECORD OF CLEMENT OF ALEXANDRIA, EUSEBIUS, TERTULLIAN AND ORIGIN

Many ancient church historians recorded Jesus' birth in 3-2 BC. Clement of Alexandria's 'Stomata' records Jesus' birth twenty-eight years after Antony and Cleopatra's deaths in 8/30 BC. Eusebius' 'History of the Church' records Jesus' birth in Augustus' 42nd year, from August, 43 BC, twenty-eight years after Egypt's subjugation and Antony and Cleopatra's death. Tertullian however, says Augustus' rule began forty-one years before Christ's birth. He and Origen say Augustus ruled fifteen full years after Jesus' birth. As Augustus died August, AD 14, Jesus would have been born between August 3 BC and August 2 BC. In all, eighteen Christian historians place Jesus' birth in 3 BC, connected with Augustus' oath of allegiance in 3-2 BC and Herod's death in 1 BC.

These historical records strongly validate Jesus' birth in 3-2 BC. Augustus commanded a census at this time and history validates Herod died on Shebat 2, 1 BC. Clement of Alexandria, Eusebius, Tertullian and Origen confirm this dating. If we accept the signs of history as satisfied, we must turn to the signs in the skies.

ASTROLOGICAL RECORDS

"Magi from the east came to Jerusalem and asked 'Where is the one who has been born King of the Jews?" Matthew 2:1-2a They saw his star at its rising and came to worship this King. Acknowledging the historical record, what can we learn of a star guiding these magi? Who were they; what did they see in the skies? Is our biblical record historic or just a myth to enjoy and teach our children?

We discover unusual astrological activities in 3-2 BC that validate biblical record. From August 1st, 3 BC to December 25th, 2 BC, extraordinary planetary phenomena appeared in the skies. Astrological records, available through computer science, reveal wonders that might bring the most doubting to their knees in awe. A biblical understanding of the people and their times helps us understand the signs in the skies and what it meant to those who watched the heavens. To us, it would be an extraordinary stellar event to watch and record; to these Magi, it was a portent from Heaven, revealing wonders we could not begin to imagine.

In August, 3 BC, Jupiter, 'Ha Tzaddek', the Righteous, was showing wonders that surely reached the magi searching the skies. On August 1st, Jupiter rose in the first rays of the dawn. The magi saw the star in the eastern skies. (Matthew 2:2) Before 4:00 AM, on August 13th, Jupiter conjoined with Venus, already a morning star for six months. On September 1st, Venus and Mercury came into conjunction; Venus traveled into the light of the sun, emerging in the west, heading back toward Jupiter, also moving west.

From September 11-14, Jupiter came into conjunction with Regulus, 'Ha Melech', the King; this was the first of three conjunctions between them. On December 1st, Jupiter stopped its motion through the fixed stars, starting its annual retrogression, heading back toward Regulus. The second conjunction occurred on February 17th. On May 9th, there was a third crowning conjunction. These three conjunctions announced the birth of the 'Melech Tzaddek', 'Melchezidek', the crowning of the 'King of Righteousness'. This triple conjunction was a very rare occurrence that did not occur again until AD 69-70.

For forty days, Jupiter continued moving westward. On June 17th, reuniting with Venus, they collided; only .04 degrees apart, they appeared as one giant star in the skies. On August 27th, Jupiter and Mars were in close conjunction, as were Venus and Mercury, within 2 degrees of each other, eight degrees ahead of the rising sun in the constellation of Virgo.

| Jupiter's Longitude | 142.60 degrees | Venus' Longitude | 141.67 degrees |
| Mars' Longitude | 142.67 degrees | Mercury's Longitude | 143.77 degrees |

3-2 BC stood out above any near contenders for extraordinary signs heralding Jesus' birth. There were signs in 7-6 BC which many suggest were signs proclaiming Jesus' birth, but they calculated his birth believing Herod died in 4 BC. If Herod did not die until 1 BC, these sightings were several years too early. The visions in the heavens in 3-2 BC certainly proclaimed the wonders seen on the earth below. (Birth of Christ, Revisited)

THE MAGIS' JOURNEY TO BETHLEHEM

Learning of the visions in the skies, our thoughts turn to what these visions meant to the wisemen. Who were they; what were they searching for; what did those visions mean to them? Many scholars believe the wisemen were from the courts of the Parthian kings, a priestly caste similar to the Levites. (Herodotus 1,101, Pliny, National History v. 29) They provided the Medes, Persians and Babylonians with divine information about daily affairs. Their Dynasty was similar to the Houses of Parliament. The lower house members were Sophoi, the Wise Ones. The upper house members were Magoi, the Great Ones. The Magoi were not astrologers, but politicians, and it is believed there were many more than the three seen in our nativities. The Persian Empire penetrated deep into Roman territory; this delegation, led by cavalry units, consistently won out against Rome.

Missler, in "Who Were these Magi", believes these wisemen were Jewish Rabbis, Priests of the House of Levi, descendants of the remnant who remained in Babylon after Cyrus came to power. In Hebrew, Chakamin means wisemen, but Matthew calls them magos. A title given Daniel was 'Rab-mag', 'Chief of the Magi'. The Greek 'magos', translated from the Hebrew Rab-mag, in English is translated 'Priests, Wisemen or Rabbis'.

Herod and all Jerusalem were troubled. Standing at Jerusalem's gates, these Magi spoke of a newborn king, a contender to his throne; they came to worship this king and had a massive army to back them up.

Persia was in the unique position of having informed magos with Babylonian astrological knowledge and Jewish Messianic expectations. Familiar with Daniel's prophesies, they held him in great honor and high regard. He was Rab-mag, Chief of the Magicians, Master of the Magoi, a prophet of God. Daniel surely entrusted his Messianic visions to Hebrew priests who, over the years, passed their knowledge on to these magi.

In the fullness of time, his visions were confirmed by the sighting of this star. This would explain why they were looking for astrological confirmations calling for a Jewish King to be born in those days. It also explains their gifts. Gold, signifying his Kingship, frankincense, his Priesthood, and myrrh, the sacrifice he would make, confirmed Daniel's prophesy of the coming of this King. (Daniel 9:24-27)

God's promise to Israel of the appearing of his Anointed One would have included these Rabbis. While they lacked the faith to return to Jerusalem and rebuild the city and Temple, they were still God's people and by God's mercy were included in fulfillment of his promise to His Faithful Remnant. Humble shepherds were told of this glorious birth. Now these Rabbis were given the sign that God was fulfilling the words of his holy Prophets. They would journey to Jerusalem to confirm what Daniel had taught them so many years before. On their return they surely declared to all Persia glorious fulfillment of Daniel's prophesies.

Daniel 9:26 prophesied the Messiah's sacrifice. The anointed one would be cut off and have nothing. This would occur 483 Babylonian years of 360 days after a specific decree, 477 years to us. This decree was issued by Artaxerxes in his 20th year, 445-444 BC. 477 minus 444 would place the cutting off, the crucifixion, in AD 33. With this knowledge, these Rabbis knew the Messiah's birth would be at this time in their lives. The reason for their journey was the vision of 'His Star'. They had seen his star in the east and came to worship him. These magi understood and were ready to search out this child who would be King. Heaven was bursting with signs in the constellation of Leo, the sign of Judah, and Virgo, the Virgin, associated with Jupiter, the King Planet and Regulus, the King Star. All this astrological data, supported by Matthew, reveals what we were taught as children is not legend or myth but a verifiable reality.

It has long been recognized that the magi arrived in Bethlehem sometime after Jesus' birth. He was circumcised the 8th day and presented at the temple forty days after his birth. After the presentation, the family returned to Galilee, settling in Nazareth. They did not go to Egypt right after his birth but for some reason they returned to Bethlehem. They may have been in Jerusalem for religious celebrations, had family in Bethlehem to help care for the child or, understanding their child was the Messiah, believed he should grow up near Jerusalem, in reach of God's Almighty Arms. Whatever the reason, they were living in Bethlehem.

It is believed the magis' journey would have taken six to eight weeks, depending on the weather conditions and the terrain. With all the visions in the skies, we could suggest their journey started shortly after the massing of the four planets. Jupiter was journeying westward; the magi followed the star that went before them. Ten weeks later, Jupiter was shining directly over the house where the child was.

This is an important detail, suggesting something marked the very house where Jesus lived. The star rested over where the child was. Seeing the star, they rejoiced with great joy. This glorious vision proclaimed fulfillment of Daniel's words. Going into the house, they saw the child and fell before him in worship.

Planets cannot mark a single building, resting over where the child was. How did these men know which house they needed to find? Jupiter would not have revealed it to them. While Jupiter led them to Jerusalem, did another 'star' guide them to the child? Is there an explanation for this verse? An answer may lie in knowledge of the Shekinah Glory Cloud. God consistently revealed himself in the Shekinah Glory; Israel was guided to Canaan by the Pillar of Cloud and Fire. The glory of this Light was revealed to Moses in the 'Burning Bush'. We might discover its first appearance in Genesis 1:3. God declared 'Let there be light', and there was light, 'God's Shekinah Glory'.

This glorious light could qualify as a star. Daniel 7:13 spoke of the Clouds of Heaven and their connection to the Messiah. "With the clouds of heaven, there came one like a son of man." Keeping watch over their sheep, shepherds saw the LORD's Shekinah Glory. The Glory of the Lord, the Kavod YHWH, shown all around them before the angel announced their Messiah's birth. (Luke 2:9) Now, these magi have arrived in Bethlehem, just before sunrise and have seen the Shekinah Glory shining directly over the house where their Messiah was. Falling before him, they rejoiced with exceedingly great joy. This star confirmed everything Daniel revealed concerning their Messiah's presence.

On the magis' arrival, Jesus was living in a house, not the stable our nativity scenes consistently portray. Jesus was no longer an infant; he was a child. (Matthew 2:10-11)

After honoring the birth of this king, they presented gifts then returned by a different route, warned in a dream to avoid Herod. Joseph also had a dream of an angel's warning. He was to flee with Mary and Jesus and go to Egypt because Herod planned to kill the child. Hearing the angel's warning, fulfilling Hosea 11:1, Joseph fled to Egypt with Jesus and Mary. Out of Egypt, God called his son. The precious gifts the magi gave surely assisted in their flight to safety.

In fulfillment of Jeremiah 31:15, Herod murdered all the male children in Bethlehem, two years old and younger. This can be understood from the astrological phenomena of the previous two years. In addition, as will be seen later, Jesus was about fifteen months old at the magis' visitation. If the slaying of the innocents was fifteen months after Jesus' birth and we add nine months of pregnancy, the total would be twenty-four months, two years, exactly as Herod determined by questioning the magi. He ascertained from them when the star appeared and used their knowledge trying to eliminate the threat to his throne.'

With these astrological records, and learning who the magi were, we wonder what this meant to those who first heard these words. The magi saw the star rising in the east; it was a morning star. Christ declared himself 'the root and offspring of David, the Bright Morning Star'. (Revelation 22:16) The New Testament writers completely understood the symbolic significance of the heavenly bodies and the ancient world held much regard to what was revealed in the stars. Jupiter rose as a morning star August 1st and was surely the first sign the magi saw in the heavens, bringing them to their knees in wonder; they had seen his star rising in the east, 'en te anatole'!

On August 12th, just before sunrise, Jupiter was a morning star. Leaving the vicinity of the sun, Jupiter, God the Father, conjoined with Venus, the Shekinah Glory. This indicated a coming birth. To the Chaldeans, the birth of kings was associated with the appearance of Jupiter. Venus was the goddess of fertility. This conjunction of Jupiter and Venus declared to these magi that Heaven was heralding the birth of a king. At the same time, the sun, the moon and Mercury were in the constellation of Leo the Lion, the sign of the tribe of Judah. The magi saw Jupiter, God the Father, Venus, the Shekinah Glory, and Mercury, John the Baptist, in symbolic communion in the constellation of Judah, shining over Palestine, virtually shouting out for attention.

After Jupiter's conjunction with Venus and Mercury, Jupiter, 'Ha Tsaddik', the Righteous, had three conjunctions with Regulus, 'Ha Melech', the Star of Kingship, Christ, the babe in the manger, in the constellation of Leo, the sign of Judah. The third conjunction with Regulus was not visible in Palestine, as the moon had already set, but the magi would have understood. Seeing the symbolism of these visions in the skies, we can see, as they did, the glory written in the heavens.

On June 13th, Jupiter reunited with Venus in the constellation of Leo. They were so close they appeared as one star, 'Echad', in complete union. Seventy-two days later, Jupiter and Mars came into close conjunction, God against the planet of war, Lucifer.

9

Venus and Mercury, the Shekinah Glory and John the Baptist, homed in on them in a massing of four planets. The moon was entering Leo; the sun was entering Virgo, the mother Mary.

Jupiter left the union, proceeding westward. The magi's journey probably commenced at this point. Coming from the east, they followed the 'star' as it moved west toward Jerusalem. Arriving in Jerusalem, the magi were told by the Temple leaders that prophesy revealed this king would be born in Bethlehem. Though the smallest of the clans of Judah, out of Bethlehem would come one who would rule all Israel; his origins were from of old, from ancient days. (Micah 5:2)

The star they saw in the east came to rest over where the child was. This celestial body has become stationary. This leads many to believe Matthew's record is legend or myth. However, science reveals the opposite is true. Jupiter becomes stationary at its times of retrogression and progression. In proper motion Jupiter moves east through the fixed stars. The Earth moves in its orbit faster than Jupiter. At first, Earth and Jupiter are on the same line of orbit however, the Earth's velocity causes Jupiter's apparent motion to slow down until Earth and Jupiter are the same. Jupiter becomes stationary within the fixed stars. Earth's greater speed causes Jupiter to retrogress; Jupiter appears to reverse its motion, moving westward in the sky. At the end, Earth and Jupiter have matched speeds; Jupiter becomes stationary, stopping its reverse motion and returns to proper motion.

Each of Jupiter's stationary positions repeats every thirteen months. It is this natural occurrence that caused His Star to stop over Bethlehem. On December 25th, 2 BC, at the magis' predawn observation, Jupiter was in the meridian position directly over Bethlehem, stationary among the stars. At this same time, the Shekinah Glory was shining directly over the house where the child was, revealing the glorious presence of the King they were seeking. The magi rejoiced exceedingly with great joy. (Birth of Christ, Recalculated)

One might see this as an extraordinary coincidence, suggesting this could be why the church chose December 25th as the date of our Lord's birth. In the early years of church history, these people were predominately Hebrew. Many believe the Hebrew Christians celebrated Christ's 'birth' at Chanukah. The start of Chanukah and December 25th were the same day until 1583 when the Gregorian calendar took effect. As Christ's birth was possibly celebrated at Chanukah, it is possible they chose this as the date of his birth.

December 25th however, was Rome's celebration of 'Natalis Solis Invicti', 'Nativity of the Unconquerable Sun'. The Roman Church saw new significance in this day and a feast was established in honor of Christ's birth. The Son of Righteousness rose with healing in his wings. (Malachi 4:2)

In AD 313, Constantine declared the Roman Empire a 'Christian' nation. With no certain knowledge of the date of Jesus' birth, he declared Christmas would be celebrated on December 25th. In 2 BC however, it was associated with magi presenting gifts to this young King. His star guided them to the child; they fell in worship before him.

We will shortly learn of the time of Jesus' conception. Israel's understanding that life began at conception helps us understand this mystery and discover all that has been hidden from those without eyes to see for all these years. We must not neglect study of God's Word and learn the truth of Christ's birth and his Presence with us, as revealed in Scripture. Only when we know this truth can we faithfully teach and celebrate Jesus' birth and learn how we are to honestly celebrate this glorious Holy Day.

BIBLICAL RECORD
THE CONCEPTION AND BIRTH OF JOHN THE BAPTIST

John the Baptist was born six months before Jesus. His mother was in her sixth month of pregnancy when Mary was told she would have a child. Zachariah's priestly service reveals when John was conceived. Knowing this, we can learn when Jesus was born. Zachariah was a priest of the order of Abijah, the 8th course of priestly service. 1 Chronicles 24:7-10 says the 1st lot fell to Jehoiarib, the 8th, to Abijah. (Antiq. 7, 14, 7)

The first priestly course was the week before Nisan 1. In the year before Jesus' birth, this would have been March 24-30, 4 BC. At Passover, Shavuot and Sukkoth, the Priests all served together. At the 8th division, Zachariah would have served from Sivan 12-18, May 19-25, 4 BC. Zachariah was struck dumb because he did not believe Gabriel's message and may not have finished his priestly service. (Leviticus 21:16-23) However, when his service ended he went home; after those days, his wife Elizabeth conceived. (Luke 1:18-24)

The laws of separation in Leviticus 12:5, 15:19, 25 required Zachariah to wait two weeks for Elizabeth's purification. After purification, Elizabeth would have conceived about Tammuz 15, June 9th. Nine months later, John would have been born at Passover, Nisan 14, March 31st, 3 BC. Gabriel told Zachariah his son would go before Christ in the spirit and power of Elijah. (Luke 1:17) Jewish tradition says Elijah would return at Passover. At Passover, a door is left open and the 'Cup of Elijah' is set out for the prophet to announce the coming of the Messiah. After John's death, Jesus identified John as the Elijah the Jews were expecting, as Isaiah and Malachi prophesied.

The names Zechariah, 'God Remembers' and Elizabeth, 'Promise', speak of God's faithfulness to his people. God Remembered His Promise. John was truly part of the glorious promise given the children of Israel.

THE CONCEPTION AND BIRTH OF JESUS LUKE 1:30-35

Six months later, Gabriel visited Mary, telling her, though she was a virgin, she would have a child. *"Do not be afraid, Mary; you have found favor with God. You will be with child and give birth to a son. You are to give him the name Jesus. He will be great and will be called the Son of the Most High. The Lord God will give him the throne of his father David; he will reign over the house of Jacob forever; his kingdom will never end."* Mary asked, "How will *this be, since I am a virgin?"* The angel said *"The Holy Spirit will come upon you; the power of the Most High will overshadow you; the holy one to be born will be called the Son of God."* What glorious message have we been given? Though a virgin, Mary would have a child. Can we truly believe? Many faithful Christians believe a virgin birth is impossible; science assures us we all carry chromosomes from our mother and father; without one set, life is impossible. Not only was it possible however, it was essential. For our Lord to go to the cross as our substitute, he needed to be untouched by the sins of our father, Adam.

JOSEPH'S DECISION

Before we decide what we believe, we must know what Joseph believed. Joseph knew he had nothing to do with the pregnancy. Mary was pledged in marriage to him but before they came together, she was found to be with child through the Holy Spirit. How did this righteous, 'Tzaddik', God-fearing man respond? He was surely outraged, confused and angry. What did he think; what did he do? Joseph would not demand justice. Praying to God, he asked "What does God's Law demand?"

The Law demanded he put Mary away and divorce her. He knew Mary could be stoned for adultery but he was compassionate. He would not embarrass her; God's justice would be tempered with love. To protect her from the people's contempt, he would put her away privately. With his decision made, he slept. In a dream, an angel told him not to be afraid to marry Mary. What was conceived in her was from the Holy Spirit, *'ek pneumatos hagiou'."* (Matthew 1:20)

Joseph was open to God's mystery. He knew he was not responsible but believed his dream. He did not rely on man's logic or the world's wisdom. Believing God, he was no longer in fear. Mary was not an adulteress; she was a virgin, innocent, righteous and pure. He did not understand how but knew the child within her was of the Holy Spirit. He would protect her and her child and provide for them both.

Joseph was humble and wise. Listening to God, he believed and put his belief into action. After waking, with the angel's voice still fresh in his mind, he took Mary as his wife. He would protect her from the people's scornful accusations. He knew the people would ridicule Mary and knew what Jesus would face. With courage and faith, he acted on God's promise.

Joseph knew God gave laws to follow, but also knew he permitted them not to enforce them sometimes. Before anyone could suggest there was anything wrong, he took Mary as his wife. The people of Nazareth were never given the chance to accuse Mary of adultery. Joseph protected Mary's name and Jesus' honor. Jesus learned from Joseph's wisdom. Seeing a woman caught in adultery, he said "I do not condemn you" before saying "sin no more." Ancient and modern 'Pharisees' only ask 'What does the law demand', not 'How can I act with compassion'. Jesus learned from his earthly father of the love and mercy of his Eternal Father.

Even as Jesus grew, the Jewish religious leaders never spoke of him as the product of illegitimate birth. With all their hatred, they never accused him or his mother. They understood and spoke of Jesus as the son of a carpenter, the son of Joseph. (Matthew 13:55, Luke 3:23) They were assured Joseph was his father.

The Torah declared *"A bastard shall not enter the assembly of the LORD; even to the 10th generation shall he not enter the assembly of the LORD."* Deuteronomy 23:2 KJV If anyone suggested Jesus was born to Mary out of wedlock, the Sanhedrin could have condemned him with the power of the Torah, preventing him from entering the Temple, destroying his credibility before those he sought to teach.

Joseph's decision came through the voice of an angel, not through Isaiah's prophecy. If he acknowledged Isaiah's words fulfilled, Mary would surely have faced scorn. Isaiah's words were not understood in his own day, much less in Jesus' generation, not even in ours. No one would have believed Mary was a virgin. She would have been labeled an adulteress, possibly even killed. Her son might never have been born. If he had lived, if anyone suggested Jesus was born of an adulteress, the Sanhedrin would have prevented him from ever entering the Temple. All had to be kept private, known only to Mary and Joseph, and perhaps Elizabeth. Joseph protected Mary by keeping their 'secret'; Mary kept all these things, pondering them in her heart. (Luke 2:19)

Fulfillment of Isaiah's prophecy had to remain a secret. The miracle of Jesus' birth would not be proclaimed until Jesus' ascension, when Matthew and Luke could finally record the truth from Mary's own voice. She could no longer remain silent. The people had seen his miracles. They heard him preach God's Kingdom; he proclaimed the promise of their people's' restoration. They endured his death and rejoiced in his resurrection. They understood and recorded the glorious mystery; Jesus was the Son of God!

THE VIRGIN BIRTH

Knowing the truth, we still ask: How can a virgin birth produce the sinless child who became our Lord, our Salvation? Adam's sins were surely in Mary. Wouldn't her sin be passed on to her son? We are assured Jesus came into the world already God, the Eternal Son. Without ceasing to be God the Son, there was added to his deity a sinless human nature; he became the Son of God. Through the incarnation, *'incarnare'*, by the virgin birth, God became Man, *'in the flesh'*. His mother was promised to Joseph, but before they came together, she was found to be with child of the Holy Spirit. The power of the Holy Spirit overshadowed her. (Luke 1:35)

Isaiah spoke of the certainty of God's promise, in God's mind, as having already happened. *"Hear now, you House of David, the LORD himself will give you a sign; The Virgin will be with child, give birth to a son and will call him Immanuel." "To us a child is born; a son is given. The government will be on his shoulders. He will be called Wonderful Counselor, Mighty God, Everlasting Father, Prince of Peace."* Isaiah 7:14, 9:6

Gabriel told Mary of wonders God prepared for his children. God never forces his will on his people. God waited for Mary's response. Her response *"Let it be according to your word"* reveals Mary accepted her Lord's will, permitting God's Shekinah Presence to overshadow her. She placed herself in her LORD's hands. The Holy Spirit was the source of Mary's pregnancy. The Holy Spirit overshadowed Mary, creating the human body of our Lord. 'Overshadow' is a Biblical image of the Shekinah Presence that descended on the tabernacle. God's Shekinah presence overshadowed Mary, producing our sinless Lord.

This miracle may be more verifiable than we might believe, and teaches the scientific basis for the virgin birth. Biology textbooks say our father's twenty-three chromosomes fertilize our mother's ovum. Before fertilization, as with all women, Mary's egg cell was purified through meiosis. Mary's sin nature's presence, in the immature reproductive cell, crossed over into polar bodies, leaving the mature ovum uncontaminated. Adam's sin nature was not in the purified ovum; Mary conceived without corruption from the male sperm. The Holy Spirit provided twenty-three perfect chromosomes to fertilize Mary's pure ovum, producing a fetus uncontaminated by Adam's sin nature. Her fetus was free of corruption from the sins of our father Adam.

Giving physical life to the newborn's soul, God's justice should have passed on Adam's sin but Jesus had no sin nature. Born in a hypostatic union, his humanity and divinity were united. God the Son has become the Son of God, fully human, fully Divine. God has become Man, yet is still God.

Contrary to scholarly study, Paul confirms Jesus' virgin birth. *"In Christ, all the fullness of the deity dwells in bodily form."* Colossians 2:9 In his humanity, he represents us. In his divinity, he represents us before God. While the 4th Gospel does not speak of Jesus' birth, John 1:14 & 3:16 say Jesus was 'the only begotten of the Father' and 'his only begotten Son'. The Greek word 'monogenes' however, means 'uniquely born.' Just as Matthew and Luke declared Jesus born of a Virgin, John declared Jesus' virgin birth. 'Uniquely born', he was not in Adam and did not possess Adam's sins. Born of a virgin, Jesus was physically and spiritually alive; the 2nd Person of the Trinity, without ceasing to be God, became Man without a sin nature. Uncontaminated by Adam's sin, the 'Word made Flesh' was Uniquely Born. He could go to the cross for our sins, as our substitute.

Gabriel told Mary of the promise given Zachariah. Elizabeth, his barren wife, was in the sixth mouth of her pregnancy. This would have been the end of Kislev. Hearing these words, after becoming Joseph's wife, Mary visited Elizabeth. We know she went to help her with her pregnancy, but surely wanted to talk about the angel's visitation; Elizabeth, the wife of a Priest, would help her understand this glorious mystery.

Greeting Mary, Elizabeth rejoiced, saying *"Why am I so favored that the mother of my Lord should come to me?"* Luke 1:43 Elizabeth's words reveal Mary was already with child. Jesus was conceived at Chanukah, the Feast of Lights. Our Lord is the *'Light of the World'!* At the Feast of Lights, the Feast of Dedication, God dedicated Mary and Jesus for a divine purpose. God's presence would dwell in an earthly temple, dedicated in service to God. With his conception at Chanukah, nine months later, Jesus would have been born in Tishri.

VIRGIN MARY, 'ALMAH' OR 'BETHULAH'

'Almah' in English is 'Virgin'. In Isaiah 7:14, 'The Almah' would be an 'oth', a supernatural 'sign' to the house of David, a promise of Divine Deliverance revealed through a miraculous birth. This sign would not be a normal birth, a child born of a man and woman, but born of The Almah. *'The Virgin shall conceive'.*

In the Tanakh, 'almah' always speaks of an unmarried virgin maiden. The Hebrew 'bethulah' does not focus exclusively on virginity. In Joel 1:8, 'bethulah', 'separated, living apart' refers to a young married woman, grieving the loss of the husband of her youth. Almah is always an unmarried bethulah, as was Rebecca, a maiden, 'bethulah', and virgin, 'almah' whom no man had known, and Miriam, an almah, guarding Moses in the bulrushes.

Fulfillment of The Almah of the House of David was revealed in the fulness of time. *Miriam, Bad Eli, Ben David*, Mary, the daughter of Heli, of the house of David, 'The Almah', an unmarried, virgin maiden of marriageable age, was betrothed to *Yosef Ben David*, Joseph of the House of David, while still a pre-teen, 12-14 years of age.

LAID IN A MANGER

Tishri is the month when Israel celebrates the High Holy Days. Joseph went to Bethlehem to be registered with Mary his wife, being great with child. *"The days were accomplished that she should be delivered; she brought forth her firstborn son, wrapped him in swaddling cloths and laid him in a manger, for there was no room in the inn."* (Luke 2:4-7 KJV) 'The days were accomplished that she should be delivered' reveals Mary was full-term. If conception occurred at Chanukah, his birth would be in Tishri just before Sukkoth.

Joseph and Mary have gone to Bethlehem because of the census. Jesus was laid in a manger because there was no room in the inn. Many suggest there was no room in the inn because of the census, but this is not likely the case. At Passover, Shavuot and Sukkoth, all Israel was commanded to return to Jerusalem to celebrate; Jews living outside Judea had to travel some distance to arrive on time. Bethlehem, 3-5 miles from Jerusalem, would have been filled with pilgrims as early as Tishri 1, two weeks early, all needing to be in Jerusalem for Sukkoth. Joseph and Mary found no room in the inn; the city was filled with pilgrims preparing for Sukkoth.

We believe Jesus was born in a stable. Luke only says Jesus was laid in a manger. Our nativities consistently show a stable with animals surrounding Jesus as he slept in their feeding trough. We can better understand these words however, if we realize at Sukkoth the people dwelt in sukkahs built in remembrance of their wilderness journey. At Sukkoth, Jerusalem was so over-crowded that sukkahs were erected on every rooftop, in alleys and every street and hill.

If Jerusalem had all these sukkahs, Bethlehem, five miles away, surely had them as well. The Hebrew for stable is 'sukkah'. The stable where Jesus was born, might have been a sukkah built by a family in Bethlehem, preparing for Sukkoth. If this is where Joseph and Mary stayed on their arrival in Bethlehem, we truly can see the grace of God in the graciousness and sacrificial hospitality of this family who gave, or shared their sukkah with this young couple needing a place to rest, preparing for a glorious birth.

The families prepared these sukkahs for the week's celebration. Everything they needed was placed in their sukkah. The manger was not a stable manger where animals ate, but the area in the sukkah where food was stored. Jesus was laid in a manger where food was kept for the week's celebration. At Sukkoth, God, through the Christ Child, would dwell with his people, *"God with us, Emanuel"*. Jesus was the *"Bread of Heaven"*. The bread of God has come down from Heaven; whoever eats of that bread will live forever. (John 6:33)

Jesus's birth was just before Sukkoth; all Israel was coming to Jerusalem to celebrate Sukkoth, God's promise to tabernacle with his people. This time, before Sukkoth, helps us determine when Jesus was born. From Chanukah to the time before Sukkoth brings us to the beginning of the month of Tishri.

When Was Jesus Born?

Knowing the year and month of Jesus' birth, can we know the day we are to celebrate? Can scripture reveal when Jesus was born? We might learn we have two records, spoken through the voices of God's holy prophets. Haggai reveals the voice of God to the Babylonian remnant who returned to Jerusalem to rebuild their temple; John reveals the voice of God to the remnant who lived to see destruction of that glorious temple.

The children of Israel had returned from Babylon but Solomon's temple was destroyed; their Holy City was in ruin. The Jews felt it impossible, but were told to rebuild. Nehemiah 6:15 says the walls were rebuilt on Elul 25. The 1st day of creation of Heaven and earth has become the 1st day of recreation of Israel's 'Heaven and Earth'. Examination of the priesthood began. Three months later, the priests took their places in the rebuilt temple. *"From this day on, from the 24th day of the 9th month, give careful thought. Is there yet any seed left in the barn? Until now, the vine, fig tree, pomegranate and olive tree have not borne fruit."* Haggai 2:18-19

Haggai speaks of this day. From that day onward, Kislev 24th, the day the foundation stone, the chief cornerstone of the LORD's temple was laid, the seed, the child, was in the barn, 'the womb'. The grape-vine, the Messiah, the fig tree, Israel, the pomegranate, embroidered on the High Priest's garment, the olive tree, Israel in its fullness, has not borne fruit, has not yet been born. From that day on God would bless Judah.

Isaiah 28:16 speaks of our foundation stone. The temple's foundation stone was pierced with seven perforations through which living water flowed. God laid in Zion a precious cornerstone, a foundation stone, 'Eben Shetthijah', a tried stone, 'Eben-bohan', a sure foundation; he that believed would not be confounded.

Haggai revealed symbolic revelation of our Lord's conception. *"The stone the builders rejected has become the capstone."* Matthew 21:42 Christ is the Cornerstone, the Foundation Stone from whom living waters flow. The Foundation Stone was laid on Kislev 24th, the Feast of Dedication.

The laying of the Foundation Stone reveals, in metaphor, Mary's conception of Jesus. Normal gestation is 271 days for boys, 280 days for girls. If Jesus was conceived at the laying of the Foundation Stone, Kislev 24th, his birth would be in Tishri. 271 days from Kislev 24, is Tishri 1, Rosh-Hashanah. Chanukah was a time of hope and miracles; Jesus, our Miracle and Foundation Stone, at his conception became our hope.

Jesus was conceived at Chanukah. Israel did not celebrate births; conception was the start of life. Jesus' 'life' began at Chanukah. At His conception, Mary received the 'Promised Seed' of Genesis 3:15. God has given us hope. The God of hope has filled us with joy and peace in believing. By the Holy Spirit we abound in Hope. (Romans 15:13) The glory of the 2nd temple would be greater than the former. In that place God would give peace. *(Haggai 2:9)* Christ would fill the Temple with His Glory, Light and Peace.

In Revelation 12:1-6, the Apostle John reveals Jesus' birth. A great portent appeared in heaven, a woman was clothed with the sun, the moon was under her feet; she was ready to give birth. Another portent was seen. A great red dragon stood before the woman, ready to devour her child as soon as he was born.

Two great portents appeared in the skies. From August 27th to September 15th, Virgo occupied a space of fifty degrees along the ecliptic. She was clothed with the sun. God was mid-bodied in Virgo. The moon was under her feet. She was in pain to give birth. "Introduction of the Jupiter—Regulus Conjunctions" reveals that between Sept. 9-12, a second portent appeared, the Draconid constellation, 'the Great Red Dragon'. This portent was revealed in a fiery meteor shower across the skies, symbolic of Lucifer's desire to 'devour her child' at his birth.

John saw the woman clothed by the sun, Jesus in Mary's womb, connected with the Draconid meteor shower, revealing Jesus' birth amidst those days. The magi understood;

it would be the only sign under which a Jewish Messiah would be born, especially if he was born of the Virgin.

The key to Jesus' birth lies in the words 'the moon was under her feet. In "The Days of Vengeance", David Chilton reveals the woman's feet were positioned directly over the moon. Virgo's feet represent the last degrees of the constellation. At Jesus' birth, this was 180-187 degrees along the ecliptic. The moon was under this seven-degree arc with the sun mid-bodied in Virgo for less than two hours, observed from Palestine on Tishri 1. It began at sunset, 6:15 P.M. and lasted until moonset, 7:49 P.M. This is the only day of the year when this could have happened. (pp. 301-303)

Jesus became our Hope at his conception at Chanukah, Kislev 24, 4 BC. At Rosh-Hashanah, Tishri 1, 3 BC, between 6:15 & 7:49 P.M., our hope was fulfilled. He became our King. What God promised through the voice of Haggai, was fulfilled through the voice of the Apostle John; Jesus was born the evening of Tishri 1. Revelation 12 reveals it was a New Moon Day.

WRAPPED IN 'SWADDLING CLOTHS'

Luke 2:8-12 speaks of shepherds in the fields, watching over their flocks. An angel of the LORD appeared; the glory of the LORD shown all around them. They were terrified. The angel told them not to be afraid. He brought good news for all people. That day, in Bethlehem, a savior was born; he was Christ, their Messiah. They were given a sign, a heavenly message. They would find the baby wrapped in swaddling cloths, lying in a manger.

This baby was a heavenly sign, revealing more than a baby swaddled to be kept warm in an animal's feeding trough. Before we can understand this awesome message, we must know what those shepherds understood. What were they told about this wondrous birth? We are taught that Jesus lying in a feeding trough in a shepherd's stable, wrapped in swaddling cloths, indicated his humble beginning and his family's poverty. We might discover however, we are missing an important custom of ancient Israel concerning royal births. These shepherds were given an oth, a glorious sign from God.

When the son of a King was born in ancient Israel, he was wrapped in swaddling cloths, after being washed in lightly salted water. Symbolic of truth and honesty, the salt was used understanding this king would speak words salted with honesty. He would be the *"Salt of the Earth"*.

The swaddling cloths did not speak of his family's poverty; they spoke of his glory. The linen bands were wrapped around the child from head to foot. Holding his body straight, they symbolized the child's growth. As an adult, this king would walk straight and tall, free from rebellious disobedience or defiance. The child was kept in these swaddling bands only a short time while his parents prayed, promising to raise him as God commanded.

Ezekiel speaks of the lack of these swaddling bands in Jerusalem's abominations. *"On the day you were born, your cord was not cut, nor were you washed with water to make you clean, rubbed with salt or wrapped in cloths, 'swaddled with bands'."* Ezekiel 16:4 At Jerusalem's 'birth', she was untrustworthy, deceitful; she did not stand upright and was not 'raised properly'.

At Jesus' birth, Mary washed this newborn king in lightly salted water and swaddled him while she and Joseph prayed for God's care over the child. Her child was of Royal lineage, God's own Son, heir of the throne of his father, David. With God's care and proper upbringing, she knew this child would go far.

SHEPHERDS IN THE FIELD AT NIGHT LUKE 2:15-20

An angel told the shepherds they would find the baby wrapped in swaddling cloths, lying in a manger. The shepherds knew they had to hurry to discover all that happened that the Lord told them. They found Joseph and Mary and the baby lying in a manger. After they saw him, they spoke of all they saw to everyone they met. The people were amazed, 'ethaumasan', at what the shepherds said. These shepherds heard wondrous news of a glorious birth; an angel gave precise directions so no mistakes could be made. The child would be swaddled only a short time; they dared not delay. Though they were lower class citizens, despised by the temple leaders, these shepherds understood. This newborn king was resting on his manger throne, wrapped in his royal garb.

They went with haste; they had to hurry to get there while the child was still swaddled. They found the baby exactly as the angel had said, in a sukkah, proclaiming God's presence with his people. Lying in the manger, he was the *'Bread of Heaven'*. Wrapped in swaddling cloths, *'He was a King'*. They rejoiced in all they saw and told everyone of this wondrous birth; those who heard were amazed about everything they were told.

THE SHEPHERDS OF ISRAEL

According to Jewish belief, seven 'Ushpizen', 'spiritual guests', Israel's faithful shepherds visited these sukkahs. Abraham, Isaac, Jacob, Joseph, Moses, Aaron and King David, all shepherds of Israel, would enter the sukkahs and share the divine light that dwelt within. These holy quests reminded their people of the temporary shelter they knew in the wilderness and the eternal shelter they would receive at this Child's coming.

Many invited these spiritual shepherds to share a meal with them. Just as these 'supernal shepherds' gathered at Israel's sukkahs, shepherds in the field came and witnessed the Shekinah Presence dwelling within this sukkah. Mary and Joseph surely invited these wandering shepherds to sit and share a meal with them, enjoying a '**Mitzvah**', a Command, offering to them as '**Avodat Hashem**', Service to the Lord, the Bread of Life.

THE CHRIST CHILD'S FIRST FAITHFUL WITNESSES

In Bethlehem and Persia we see Jesus' first faithful witnesses. Shepherds, responsible for care of sheep, proclaimed *the Great Shepherd has been born.* This child, laid in a sukkah manger, wrapped in swaddling bands, was their King. The Magi, Persian Rabbis, could not remain silent either. *Their King has been born.* They fell before him, offering treasured gifts, acknowledging him as their King, High Priest and Eternal Sacrifice. These shepherds and Magi were forever changed. They made haste to bring the Good News of this glorious birth. From Bethlehem to Babylon, humble shepherds and learned Magi proclaimed *their Messiah had been born.*

What did those 2nd hand witnesses believe? Did the people of Bethlehem go to the sukkah or go home wondering about those foolish shepherds? Did the Persian Jews praise the God of these Magi? Did they teach their children of this King or go back to their lives as if nothing had happened? Faithful Israelites surely rejoiced, proclaiming to the entire world the miracle born to them the first day of their New Year. Unless we, as faithful 2nd hand witnesses, proclaim the truth, the miracle will remain hidden from all who follow us.

Will we go to the manger to learn the truth, or just go home?

TISHRI 1—NEW YEAR'S DAY
FEAST OF TRUMPETS—ROSH-HASHANAH

If these second-hand witnesses believed, they rejoiced. Tishri 1 was New Year's Day, the day Judah's kings reckoned inauguration of their rule. On Rosh-Hashanah, God was crowned King of the Universe. What a momentous day for the appearance of the Messiah on earth. To introduce their Messiah to the world on any other day could not compare to the celebration they would know if they understood their Lord was born to them on Rosh-Hashanah.

Rabbis say it was the day Adam was created, *"the beginning of God's revelation with man."* It was also the day Noah removed the cover from the ark. Noah removed the cover from the ark in the 601st year, the 1st month, the 1st day of the month and learned the waters were dried from the earth. (Genesis 8:13-14)

The shofar sounded, proclaiming creation. God began his rule over the world on this day. The shofar declared Jesus, King at the moment of his birth. God's revelation gloriously continues. The first day of Creation was proclaimed; fruit was on the trees for Adam and Eve. The first day of earth's recreation was proclaimed in vision of the earth redeemed. Given dry land, the earth was restored after the flood.

Rosh-Hashanah is an anniversary and renewal of creation. How tremendous that God, in his magnificent, infinite wisdom, gave us a new creation in redemption of the earth after the flood, and the New Creation, Redemption of the world in the birth of his Son. This is the New Creation Israel was truly praying for.

Rosh-Hashanah declares God's glory in creation of the world, rebirth of the world after the flood and birth of the Savior of the world, our Lord, our Christ. We could not celebrate Christ's birth at any other time and have it mean more than it does at Rosh-Hashanah.

At sunset on Tishri 1, 3 BC, priests blew their shofars in Jerusalem, celebrating the New Year, honoring God as their King. Five miles away, at that very hour, in the humble city of Bethlehem the infant Jesus, the Promised Seed, was born, reconciling all mankind to God. This joyous celebration was missed by Judah's religious leaders, concerned with their duties and obligations. Humble shepherds fell in worship before their King but Jerusalem's learned leaders missed the glorious celebration God promised from the foundation of the world. Failing to proclaim the glory of Christ's conception and birth, we miss the celebration as well, denying it to all who seek God's truth. We must sing for all to hear:

"Joy to the World, the Lord is Come; Let Earth Receive her King."

CIRCUMCISION AND PRESENTATION AT THE TEMPLE

On Tishri 9, September 19th, just before Yom Kippur, according to the Law of Moses, Jesus was circumcised. After eight days, at his circumcision, he was called Jesus, Yeshua, the name given by the angel before he was conceived. We then learn of the purification. Brought up to Jerusalem on Heshvan 10, October 21st, he was presented before the LORD, as written in the Law of the LORD. Every male that opens the womb was holy to the Lord. (Luke2:21-22)

There was a man living in Jerusalem; his name was Simeon. Righteous and devout, he was awaiting the consolation of Israel. The Holy Spirit dwelt within him. The Spirit assured him he would not die before he saw the LORD's Christ. Moved by the Spirit, he entered the temple courts as Jesus' parents brought him in to do for him according to the law. Taking him in his arms, Simeon praised God for keeping his promise. Simeon saw God's salvation, his Yeshua YHWH, prepared in the sight of all people. He thanked God for keeping his word. That child would be a light for revelation to the Gentiles, for Israel's glory. That child was destined to cause the falling and rising of many in Israel and would be a sign spoken against so that the thoughts of many would be revealed. Simeon also proclaimed to Jesus' mother that a sword would pierce her soul.

Anna, a prophetess, a daughter of Phanuel, an eighty-four year old widow of the tribe of Asher also came in proclaiming redemption in the birth of this child. She thanked God and spoke of him to all who were looking for Jerusalem's redemption. (Luke 2:25-32, 36, 38)

We might wonder why Luke spoke of Zechariah and Elizabeth, John the Baptist's parents, and Simeon and Anna as all very old, devout saints. Elizabeth and Zechariah were both 'well advanced in years', and 'walked in all the commandments of the law'. Simeon and Anna, faithful Temple goers, were also elder saints. Simeon rejoiced that he lived long enough to see fulfillment of God's promises to Israel. Anna, widowed for countless years, rejoiced in Israel's redemption. They knew and cherished the hope of the Old Covenant prophets. Simeon was looking for 'Israel's consolation', Anna, for 'Israel's redemption'.

Luke was revealing that just as those beloved saints were ready to pass away, the Age of the Law and Prophets was coming to an end. These faithful children of Abraham saw no conflict between the Age of the Law and the Age of the Messiah. They held onto the promises of the Old Covenant.

"Simeon's Farewell to the World" reveals these devout Children of the Covenant were most open to the promised New Covenant Age. They did not resent that the Messiah would be a light for revelation to the Gentiles. They rejoiced that the New Age was truly, finally coming. With this child's birth, a New Age, a New Message was proclaimed to ALL Israel. With all their hearts, these faithful Old Covenant saints welcomed Jesus. He would perfectly fulfill all the Law and Prophets. He was the Perfect Climax to their faith. They rejoiced in his appearing.

With the words of these faithful Sons and Daughters of Abraham, we hear the glorious message Jesus would reveal to all God's people. Jesus would be a light to the Gentiles for the glory of the people of Israel. Their redemption, our redemption, was presented at the Temple, and already the Good News was being proclaimed, before our Lord spoke his first words.

"My eyes have seen your Salvation, your Yeshua, which you prepared in the sight of all people."

We have been given a glimpse of the glory of our Lord's birth. Shepherds and Magi were told of this wondrous birth. They came to worship this King. Praising God, they went to the people of Bethlehem and the Gentiles in Persia, proclaiming the glorious message. At the end of Matthew & Luke's messages however, a shift has been made. We have journeyed from Bethlehem and stand at the temple in Jerusalem. Herod sought to kill this King; Simeon praised God for revelation to the Gentiles and glory to Israel but in the same breath he told Mary her child would be a sign spoken against and a sword would pierce her soul.

We have moved from Bethlehem and the glory of Christ's birth. We stand in Jerusalem and learn from righteous Simeon of our Lord's Passion. With the beauty of Bethlehem still fresh in our minds, we learn, with Mary, of Gethsemane and Calvary. Jesus, her son has been born, but alas, He Must Die!

Let all know, The Shofar has Sounded.

YOUR KING HAS BEEN BORN.

Chapter 2

THE LIFE AND DEATH OF CHRIST

THE SPRING FESTIVALS

We move from the celebration of Jesus' birth to his life, death, resurrection, ascension and the appearance of the Holy Spirit to discover the Holy Days that honor his life and ministry. Understanding the historical and Biblical records, we discover Jesus was born at Rosh-Hashanah on Tishri 1, 3 BC. In his ministry, we must discover the points in his life celebrated as our Holy Days and see how they connect with Israel's Holy Days and Convocations. When was he baptized; when did his ministry start? When did he face the final hours of his life? Can Scripture help us understand the Holy Days we are called to celebrate honoring his life and ministry?

JESUS' BAPTISM AND TEMPTATIONS

John the Baptist was born at Passover, 3 BC; his ministry began in the 15th year of Tiberius Caesar's reign. At that time, Jesus was about thirty years of age. (Luke 3:1-2, 23) History records Augustus died on August 19th, AD 14. Tiberius' reign began September 17th, AD 15; his 15th year began January, AD 29.

From Levirite law, John had to be thirty before he could start his ministry. God may have called John to start his ministry at Passover, AD 28, confirming to Israel that in the 'Spirit of and Power of Elijah' he had come to prepare for the Coming of the Messiah and the Great and Terrible Day of the Lord. John may have baptized Jesus on Elul 1, AD 29, at the start of Teshuvah, with his ministry starting on Yom Kippur, Tishri 10th, October 26th, AD 29, after being tested by Satan forty days, being about thirty years of age.

Through Jesus' baptism and testing we see the start of his ministry and discover all his works fulfill God's covenant promises to Israel. God carefully established the reign of his Messiah King. From the Torah and God's prophets, the promised King was declared. Through their history, the faithful longed for the day their Messiah would come, bringing his Kingdom. Between the Testaments, the promise of their Messiah was a major part of Jewish thought and desire. The Maccabean Revolt stirred in Israel's heart the belief that their Messiah would be seen through military conquest. They believed his kingdom would bring liberty from Roman oppression.

At his baptism, Jesus began fulfilling God's plan for Israel's Messiah King. All that Israel longed for would be fulfilled but in ways they could not begin to understand. Their Messiah was anointed by John the Baptist, the 2nd Elijah. John recognized Jesus as God's 'Chosen One' and in baptism, he anointed him. As Jesus came toward him, he acknowledged him as The Lamb of God who would take away the sins of the world. John said the man who was coming after him was greater than him. He baptized speaking of what God had revealed to him and spoke of how Jesus would be revealed to Israel. John saw the Spirit come down from heaven as a dove; it remained on Jesus after his baptism. God revealed to John that the man on whom he saw the Spirit descend and remain would baptize with the Holy Spirit. (John 1:29-34)

In his baptism, Jesus identified himself with God and humanity. For our sake, Jesus was made to be sin, though he knew no sin, so we might be made the righteousness of God through him. (2 Corinthians 5:21) After his baptism, Satan tested Jesus. Knowing Jesus was God, Satan tested his humanity. Jesus did not need to be fully human, he was God's Son; if he was hungry, if his people were hungry, he could turn stones to bread. He didn't need to go to the cross, suffer the pain or take our guilt, giving his life for us. Satan offered Jesus all the kingdoms of the world, without the Cross.

Jesus relived Israel's wilderness experience. Moses fasted forty days before receiving the Law, as did Jesus before delivering the New Law. The Manna story symbolized Jesus' 1st temptation, to feed the world, not with his body but with stones turned to bread. Moses, striking the rock at Meribah, putting God to the test, symbolized Jesus' 2nd temptation, tempting God not by doing as God commanded but by throwing himself from the temple. Israel, worshiping the golden calf, symbolized Jesus' 3rd temptation. Refusing to worship Satan, Jesus would only worship God. Jesus' responses also reflect Israel's pilgrimage feasts, Passover in the wilderness, Shavuot at the Mount of the Lord and Tabernacles at the Temple.

Jesus' testing probably occurred at Teshuvah, the forty days between Elul 1 and Tishri 10, Yom Kippur. Teshuvah was a time of repentance, returning to God. Jesus' baptism and testing, following Tiberius' assumption to the throne in September, AD 29, connects with the season of Teshuvah. John the Baptist preached repentance before baptism, the message of Teshuvah. John called Israel to repent of their sins and return to God before Yom Kippur. John and Jesus' message was the message of Teshuvah: They called the people to repent and return to the LORD. (Mark 1:14-15)

JESUS' MINISTRY

Matthew 5:3-11 speaks of the Beatitudes and the start of Jesus' ministry. Following his victory over Satan, Jesus reached out to the crowds who came to hear him speak. We hear God's message and the start of Jesus' ministry, proclaiming the coming of God's Kingdom. The Beatitudes fully affirm the teachings of the Torah and the Prophets.

In his Sermon on the Mount, his faithful application of the Law of Moses and the Prophets taught how his people were blessed as they became part of his Kingdom. The faithful disciple was assured true blessedness as he lived the words of the Torah and the Prophets. The Beatitudes proclaimed and embodied God's will for the lives of his children as they sought to live in obedience to His Law within his eternal kingdom.

THE BEATITUDES

Blessed are the poor in spirit; theirs is the Kingdom of Heaven.
Blessed are those who mourn; they will be comforted.
Blessed are the meek; they will inherit the earth.
Blessed are those who hunger and thirst after righteousness; they will be satisfied.
Blessed are the merciful; they will be shown mercy.
Blessed are the pure in heart; they will see God.
Blessed are the peacemakers; they will be called sons of God.
Blessed are those who are persecuted because of righteousness; theirs is the kingdom of Heaven.
Blessed are you when people insult you, persecute you and falsely say all kinds of evil against you because of me. Rejoice, be glad because great is your reward in heaven, for in the same way they persecuted the prophets who were before you."

'The Poor in Spirit' was the humble 'child' of God. God's blessings were realized when they saw their spiritual poverty outside God's righteousness. *"This is the one I will esteem, he who is humble and contrite in spirit and trembles at my word."* Isaiah 66:2 The Poor in Spirit, the humble would share God's righteous realm.

'Those who Mourn', mourned their sins with deep regret. God would comfort them. *"I have seen his ways but will heal him; I will restore comfort to him."* Isaiah 57:18 Those who repented, would receive God's salvation.

'The Meek' possess reverent humility. Freed from a vain sense of self-sufficiency, the humble inherited the New Earth, the Promised Land, the Kingdom. *"The meek will inherit the land and enjoy great peace."* Psalm 37:11

'Those who Hunger', hungered and thirsted for righteousness, a right relationship with God. This was nothing less than salvation. *"Come, all you who are thirsty, come to the waters; you who have no money, buy and eat; buy wine and milk without money, without cost."* Isaiah 55:1 Their spiritual hunger would be satisfied; their thirst would be quenched.

'The Merciful' understood God's mercy and longed to offer mercy to others. *"The LORD is compassionate and gracious, slow to anger, abounding in love."* Psalm 103:8 God's mercy was given those who were merciful to others.

'The Pure in Heart', in thought and desire, fulfilled Psalm 24:4. *"He who has clean hands and a pure heart will receive blessings from the LORD."*

'God's Peacemakers' proclaimed the Good News. *"How beautiful on the mountains are the feet of those who bring good news, who proclaim peace, who proclaim salvation, who say to Zion 'Your God Reigns'."* Isaiah 52:7 Those who worked in concord, reconciling men to God and each other, were the children of God.

'Those Persecuted for Righteousness' would receive God's divine blessing. Jesus' faithful disciples would suffer great tribulation, as did God's prophets, but would also share a place of glory in God's kingdom. They would be blessed. *"Do not be afraid of what you are about to suffer; be faithful, even to the point of death; I will give you the crown of life."* Revelation 2:10

THE SERMON ON THE MOUNT—THE OLD & NEW COVENANTS

Jesus knew God's Law was authoritative and obeyed it fully. He told his disciples he did not come to abolish the Law or the Prophets; he came to fulfill them. Until heaven and earth passed away, not a jot or tittle would pass from the Law until all was accomplished. (Matthew 5:17) In service to God and his people, Jesus fully kept the law, fulfilling all prophesies concerning himself; he was the destined end the Law looked toward.

In Jesus' Sermon on the Mount, the people's righteousness had to exceed that of the scribes and Pharisees in the giving of alms, in prayer and fasting. The Lord's Prayer was appropriate for Israel as they anticipated the coming of God's Kingdom. The Golden Rule was the ultimate goal of Christian ethics. Whatever they wished others do for them, they were to do for others; that was the Law and the Prophets.

Throughout the centuries, the Scribes and Pharisees continued to lower the standard but the Torah commanded Israel to 'Love your enemies'. Jesus assured his people that the Sinai Covenant was in common with and equal to the New Covenant in their ethical and spiritual lives.

THE PURPOSE FOR JESUS' MINISTRY

1. To seek and save the lost Luke 19:10
2. To bring good news to the poor Luke 4:18 a
3. To free the captive, liberate the oppressed Luke 4:18b
4. To give life, everlasting life John 10:10
5. To destroy the works of Satan Matthew 12:26-29
6. To restore what was lost or stolen Luke 19:10
7. To testify to the truth John 8:31
8. To do the will of God John 4:34

Luke 4:18-19 spoke of the start of Jesus' ministry at the Synagogue in Nazareth where he proclaimed his fulfillment of Isaiah 61. He was the LORD's Messiah. Many could or would not believe. From the start of Jesus' ministry, the temple leaders sought to kill him. Jesus proclaimed his mission, *a revolution!* He would bring good news to the poor, deliver captives from slavery, give sight to the blind, grant liberty to the oppressed and restore what was lost or stolen. He proclaimed the Acceptable Year of the LORD, God's promised Jubilee.

Throughout his ministry, Jesus proclaimed his identity as God's faithful servant, Israel's Messiah King. His works spoke of his authority as God's Anointed. Giving sight to the blind, hearing to the deaf, healing lepers and the paralyzed, raising the dead, casting out demons and feeding five thousand all brought glory to God. He was God's Anointed, promised in the Law and the Prophets from the foundation of the world.

In Preparation for the Passion—The Season of Lent

Though we have no scriptural record of Jews or Jesus' faithful disciples ever observing a forty-day fast before Passover, many of the Christian faithful celebrate Lent. Converts in the early church, since AD 313, in sacrificial fasting and repentance, remember their Lord's Passion. These forty days are celebrated the same way Israel celebrates Teshuvah, the forty days before Yom Kippur.

The early Church Fathers probably misunderstood John's message of penance before baptism at Teshuvah, believing he spoke of repentance and baptism before the Lord's Passion. They called for the church to celebrate Lent. John preached repentance and baptism in preparation for Yom Kippur. Faithful Christian converts repent before their baptism, fasting, cleansing themselves, preparing for their Lord's Passion.

At Teshuvah, preparing for Yom Kippur, Joel was read, calling the people to return to the LORD in repentance. They were to return to the Lord with all their hearts, fasting, mourning their sins. Israel was to *"rend their hearts, not their garments."* God was compassionate and did not desire to bring his wrath against them. The people were to blow the trumpet in Zion, declaring a holy fast, calling a solemn assembly. Gathered together, they were to consecrate themselves before the LORD, praying that God would spare his people so they would not be an object of scorn among the nations. (Joel 2:12-17)

At Lent, faithful Christian converts also read from Joel, preparing for their Lord's Passion. Gathered together in prayer and fasting, they confess their sins preparing for their baptism, in remembrance of their Lord's Temptations and his Passion.

Jesus' Passion

John shows three Passovers in Jesus' ministry, John 2:13, 6:4 and 11:55. Passovers from AD 30-35 are shown to determine the time of the crucifixion. As Jesus died on Friday, the only two Friday Passovers were AD 30 and 33.

Friday, April 7, AD 30   Tuesday, March 27, AD 31   Monday, April 14, AD 32
Friday, April 3, AD 33   Thursday, March 22, AD 34   Monday, April 11, AD 35

If Jesus' ministry began in the Fall of AD 29, AD 30 is too early; AD 33 must be the correct year. The New Moon was March 19th; the next day, at sunset, was Nisan 1. Passover, Nisan 14, was April 3rd, AD 33.

Church historians accurately confirm the years of Jesus' life. Clement of Alexandria and Eusebius recorded Jesus' birth connected with Antony and Cleopatra's death and Augustus' reign. Jerome, translating Eusebius' 'Chronicle', says *Jesus Christ, according to the prophesies foretold of him, came to his passion in Tiberius' 18th year.* Tiberius' regnal year began January 1st, AD 15. Eighteen years later would have been January 1st, AD 33. This places Jesus' crucifixion at Passover, April 3rd, AD 33.

At his last Passover, Jesus drove the moneychangers from the temple. When the Jews asked why, he told them that if they destroyed 'this temple', in three days he would raise it up. Believing he spoke of Solomon's Temple, they said it had taken forty-six years to build the temple; could Jesus raise it up in three days? (John 2:20) Temple renovation began in Herod's 18th year, 19 BC. It was finished eighteen months later, in 17 BC. Forty-six years from 17 BC was AD 29, the start of Jesus' ministry. (Antiq. 15,11,1 & 15, 11, 6)

At Jesus' death, darkness covered the land from 12:00 PM until 3:00 PM. At 3:00, the temple curtain was torn in two. There was a great earthquake; rocks were split. Some suggest this was a solar eclipse, but solar eclipses cannot occur at the same time as lunar eclipses. As there was a lunar eclipse at Jesus' death, there must be another explanation of the darkening of the sun. Many feel the sun's darkening cannot be verifiable, but the apocryphal Gospel of Peter and the Acts of Pilate confirm darkness covered the land.

Phlegon Trallianus' 'Olympiades' also speaks of this 'darkening of the skies' and a great earthquake. *"In the 4th year of the 202nd Olympiad, AD 32-33, failure of the sun took place, greater than previously known; night came at the 6th hour, 12:00 PM; stars appeared in the sky."* He also recorded an earthquake in Bithynia overtook Nicaea, validating the earthquake at the tearing of the temple curtain. At 3:00 PM, for 3/4 of an hour, there was a total eclipse of the moon. (Evidence for God in Science)

"THE HEAVENS DECLARE THE GLORY OF GOD."

Magnificent glory was seen in the heavens at our Lord's birth. On September 11, 3 BC, the New Moon stood at Virgo's feet and stars fell from the skies. At that moment in history, we witnessed the 'birth of the New Moon' and the birth of our Lord. 'His Star' directed Gentiles to worship at his feet. At his death, the sun was taken from the skies; the land was covered in darkness. The moon rose but it was a full moon, blood red in eclipse, revealing a life fully lived and His blood sacrifice. This day is confirmed in history; only one lunar eclipse was seen in Jerusalem at Passover with Pilate in power, April 3rd, AD 33.

Added proof for the crucifixion being AD 33 comes when we learn of Sejanus. In AD 26, weary of his imperial duties, Tiberius went into semi-retirement, choosing Sejanus as his regent. Appearing loyal, he proved to be corrupt. For five years he banished, killed and imprisoned possible successors. Tiberius' sister-in-law learned of his treachery and sent word to Tiberius of Sejanus' attempts to steal the throne. A letter was sent to the Senate, demanding Sejanus' arrest. He was executed October 18th, AD 31.

Biblical and Roman history often intersect. When Tiberius went into semi-retirement, Sejanus appointed Pilate as Judea's Prefect. Sejanus was a notorious anti-Semite and Pilate followed his lead. Rome knew the Jews shunned graven images but Pilate installed images of Tiberius in the temple, proposed to have an idol placed in the Holy of Holies and seized religious offerings to pay for Roman works. He killed Jewish worshipers, mingling their blood with religious sacrifices (Luke 13:1) and posted the sign on the cross, stating that Jesus was King of the Jews, mocking them even as he gave in to their demands.

Pilate avoided anything the Jews wanted; releasing Jesus would truly have irritated them but something made him agree to their demands. Tiberius issued countermands to Sejanus' orders; his official decree was: Leave the Jews alone! Pilate lived in constant fear; Tiberius was keeping his eye on him. If Pilate let Jesus live, Tiberius would surely take his life. As Sejanus died in AD 31, Pilate's demand to have Jesus crucified must have been AD 33.

Questions, Questions, Questions

When was Jesus crucified; when was his Last Supper; when did he go to the Mount of Olives; when did Judas betray him? Was he crucified on Friday, as the Church teaches? Jesus' sign to the Pharisees says he would be in the heart of the earth three days and three nights. Good Friday to Easter Sunday does not give the three days and nights Jesus gave as a sign to the Pharisees. What are we to believe?

Three Days and Three Nights Matthew 12:39-40

Jesus told the Pharisees that their evil and adulterous generation would receive only the sign of Jonah. Jonah was three days and nights 'in the belly of the whale'. Jesus would be three days and nights 'in the heart of the earth'. Jesus' disciples believed his miracles; the Scribes and Pharisees refused to believe. They continually asked for divine evidence to prove Jesus' authority as the Messiah.

The sign of Jonah is much more than Jesus' three days in the grave. Jesus never said he would be three days and nights in the tomb. Jonah's three days in the belly of the great fish spoke of Jesus' suffering, bearing our sins, separated from God. Jesus took our sins with his suffering and death; on the 3rd day he would rise.

What did Jesus mean by being 'in the heart of the earth'? Was he speaking of physical death in the grave or was it more than that? What could be more than death in the grave? We must understand Jesus' 'three days in the heart of the earth' did not start at his physical death but on the night he was betrayed, delivered into the hands of man. God made him to be sin for us, though he knew no sin, so we might become the righteousness of God. (2 Corinthians 5:21) At his betrayal, immersed in our sin, he was separated from God.

Jesus' suffering, crucifixion, death and resurrection totaled three days and nights. As the Sacrificial Lamb, Jesus was without sin. Before his betrayal, he was without blemish. The sacrifice could not begin until His blood began to flow. His blood began to flow at his betrayal. We were redeemed through Jesus blood, a lamb without blemish. He was pierced for our transgressions; the punishment we deserved for our sins was laid on him. Through his stripes, we are healed. (1 Peter 1:19, Isaiah 53:5)

The sign Jesus gave did not speak of physical death but of his being bruised for our iniquity, given our stripes. The bruises and beatings came as he became our sin. To offer atonement, Christ had to become our sin; only then could payment begin. The promise of our redemption began Thursday night when Jesus was delivered into the hands of man. As the first drops of blood fell, Jesus faced Spiritual Death. Separated from his Father, he was in 'the belly of the whale'.

Jesus bore our sins, becoming sin. Just as God turned from Israel and her sins, He turned from Jesus and would not hear him. Israel's iniquities separated them from God; he would not hear. (Isaiah 59:2) Jesus suffered many things; he was rejected by the elders; he was slain and was raised the third day. (Luke 9:22) Jesus said the Son of man had to suffer many things and be rejected by the elders and chief priests. They would mock him and kill him. On the third day he would rise again. (Matthew 17:22, Mark 10:34)

We must understand the fullness of Christ's death. Nowhere does Scripture say Christ would rise after three days in the grave; his suffering was an essential part of the three days. If we do not understand the fullness of his suffering in Spiritual Death, separated from the Father from Thursday to his physical death on Friday, we cannot comprehend the fullness of his Resurrection and our Spiritual Resurrection found in 1 Corinthians 15:55-56 when death would be swallowed up in victory. In His resurrection and ours, we can all stand in God's Presence.

After Jesus' burial, the Pharisees gathered before Pilate telling him they remembered that while he was still alive he said after three days he would rise. They asked Pilate to secure the tomb until the third day. If it was not made secure, his disciples might come and steal the body, telling everyone he had risen from the dead. (Matthew 27:63-64) This is the only verse that suggests the three days and nights began at his death. Only the Pharisees got the timing wrong. Unfortunately, many faithful Christians continue to misunderstand.

Many believe 'in the heart of the earth' speaks of Jesus in the tomb, but much of Scripture speaks of the earth as 'the heart of man'. Jesus often used earth to describe man's heart. In the parable of the Good Seed, the earth was the heart of man; the seed was the word sown in our hearts. The faith of the mustard seed and the treasure in the field also speak of man's heart. When Jesus became sin, he was in the heart of the earth.

Speaking of Adam and Christ, Paul said, *"The first man was of the dust of the earth. The second man is from heaven."* 1 Corinthians 15:47 When Adam sinned and when Jesus became sin, their righteousness was taken; Spiritual death was the result. Adam sinned and brought death; Jesus became sin and brought us back by his blood. Jesus was delivered into the hands of men; beaten and scourged, his blood redeemed us.

"God was pleased to have all his fullness dwell in him. In Christ, all the fullness of Deity lives in bodily form." Colossians 1:19, 2:9 Before Jesus took our sins, God dwelt in him. Jesus, the image of the Invisible God, delivered himself into man's hands. Becoming sin, his blood began to flow. Separated from the Father, Jesus dwelt in spiritual death from Thursday night until Sunday morning, when he rose triumphant over Spiritual Death. In his resurrection, we are redeemed from our Spiritual Death. No longer separated from God, we are no longer dead. We have Resurrection Life. As Christ lives, we live.

Jesus compared Jonah's experience with his. In his distress, Jonah cried to the LORD; from the depths of the grave he called for help and God listened. He was hurled into the deep, the very heart of the sea. The currents swirled about him; the breakers swept over him. Jonah was banished from God's sight. (Jonah 2:2-4) Both Jonah and Jesus were separated from God.

Through all Eternity, Jesus was never separated from his Father. No wonder he sweat blood and cried, "My God, why have you forsaken me?" The 'Shema' surely came to his lips: *"Hear, O Israel, the LORD our God, the LORD is One!"* Deuteronomy 6:4 Jesus was One with God, united with God, but God had abandoned him.

The engulfing waters threatened Jonah; the deep surrounded him; weeds wrapped around his head. Jonah was already in hell, as was Jesus, immersed in man's sin. Then Jonah arrived in Sheol. Just as Jonah went to the bottom of the mountains, Jesus, in the heart of the earth, was separated from God, suffering until in death he was cast to the depths of Sheol. Jonah was cast from God's sight. Jesus, also afflicted, was cast from God. Immersed in the wickedness of man's heart, he became sin. The grave or tomb did not separate Jesus from the Father, sin already had. Psalm 139:7-8 declares, *"Where can I go from your Spirit; where can I flee from your presence? If I go to the heavens, you are there; if I make my bed in the depths, you are there."*

Neither the grave nor death can separate us from God, only sin does. Jesus sweat blood, not at his torture before Pilate or at the cross but on the night of his betrayal. With his righteousness removed, he became sin. At the Mount of Olives, he prayed that God's will would be done. As he earnestly prayed, his sweat, like great drops of blood, fell on the ground. (Luke 22:45)

31

John 2:19 gives added help understanding Jesus' death. Cleansing the temple of the moneychangers, Jesus was asked for a sign for what he had done. He told them they would destroy 'this temple', but in three days, he would raise it up. Jesus spoke of the temple of his body, the dwelling place of God. At his betrayal, made sin, his body was no longer the dwelling place of God. Jesus told the Pharisees: though the Temple of his body would be forsaken by God, in three days he would be raised up. 'The Temple' would be restored. He would stand, 'Anastasis', resurrected, at the Right Hand of the Father.

Luke spoke of two disciples going to Emmaus, speaking of how the chief priests had handed Jesus over to death, crucifying him. They said it was the 3rd day since all that took place. (Luke 24:21) They said it was three days since Jesus was delivered to be condemned, not three days since he was crucified and buried.

PASSOVER   PASCHA OR EASTER
FULFILLMENT OF SPRING HOLY DAYS

Before we can learn of the connection between Passover and Easter, we must learn the truth of the Christian celebration. The Greek word for Passover was 'Pascha', the Jewish Feast that celebrated Israel's Exodus from Egypt. At Passover, Israel passed from death and slavery in Egypt, to life and freedom in the Promised Land. For non-English Christians, this holiday is Pascha. Through Christ's death and resurrection, we celebrate our Exodus; we have passed over from slavery to sin-death, to life and freedom in Christ.

To understand Jesus' fulfillment of Pascha, we must learn how Israel observed the ancient feast. All we learn from Jesus, as he faced the last days of his life, affirms fulfillment of God's promises to Israel. To understand Jesus' last week and his crucifixion, we must learn of Israel's faith as they celebrated Passover.

John the Baptist introduced Jesus as the Lamb of God who takes away the sins of the world. We might believe the Jews understood; Isaiah prophesied the suffering of the Human Lamb. He would be oppressed and afflicted but, like a sheep before the sheerer, he would remain silent. In judgment, he was taken, cut off from the land of the living. For the transgressions of his people, he was stricken. (Isaiah 53:7-8) If they understood their Scriptures, they should have understood John spoke of Israel's deliverance through Jesus, their Messiah.

Preparing for Passover and Unleavened Bread, on Nisan 9 the lambs were brought into the city to be examined by the priesthood. The lambs were taken to the Temple. Tied in public view, they were examined for blemish; if without blemish they were given to the people on Nisan 10, to be kept for their Passover meal. Just as the Passover lambs were without blemish, Jesus was without fault. Luke 19:47 says Jesus was teaching daily in the Temple. The temple leaders tried to destroy him but there was nothing they could do; the people hung on everything he said. They tried to trap him but could not. Just as the Passover lambs were without blemish, Jesus was without fault.

On that same day, Palm Sunday, Jesus entered Jerusalem, not on a horse as a military leader but on a donkey, as a humble servant. Just as the High Priest chose the lambs for the Passover feast, God chose Jesus as our sacrificial lamb. The sacrificial lambs' entrance had been heralded; now the crowds heralded entrance of the Lamb of God. We might believe Israel understood. Waving palm branches, the people, lining the streets, sang "Baruch Haba B' Shem Adonai.' "Blessed is he that comes in the Name of the Lord." Matthew 21:9

They greeted him with palm branches, hailing him as their king, shouting *Hosanna, Save us!* However, they expected a physical savior; they wanted and expected one to save them politically from Rome's oppression. They remembered Simon Maccabeus who entered Jerusalem waving palm branches, symbols of resistance and defiance in opposition of Antiochus Epiphanes. They believed Jesus would liberate them from Roman rule, just as Simon liberated them from Greek rule. Jesus wept; they did not understand his coming. Entering Jerusalem, Jesus identified himself with the Passover sacrifice, completely fulfilling prophesy. (Zechariah 9:9)

Exodus 12:3-6 speaks of God's command for the Passover Feast. On Nisan 10, every man was to take a lamb for his family, a year old male without blemish. They were to keep it until Nisan 14 when the whole assembly was to kill it in the evening. The people were to keep their lamb until Nisan 14: it was to dwell with them and become part of the family until Passover. At the time of the sacrifice, it would be greatly cherished and mourned. God wanted them to understand the lamb they sacrificed was precious.

Exodus 12:5-7 speaks of the sacrificial lamb Israel was to offer, preparing for God's last plague. The whole congregation was to kill it in the evening. They were to take some of the blood and put it on the doorposts and lintel of their houses. The whole of Israel was to kill it. Each family had a lamb, but Exodus speaks as if there was one lamb. Just as the whole congregation killed the Passover lamb, God declared all Israel was responsible for crucifying the Lamb of God.

Moses told the people to take a bunch of hyssop, dip it in the blood and spread it on the lintel and the doorposts. (Exodus 12:21-22) The blood, purified with hyssop, was applied to the lintel, the top of the door and the doorposts, the sides of the doorway. Hyssop was applied for the cleansing of sin. David told God to purge him with hyssop so he would be clean. (Psalm 51:7) The blood would be a sign, an oth. In that sign, they would have seen, as the blood dripped from the lintel and across the doorposts, 'the figure of a cross', the sign of Jesus' blood sacrifice, the Lamb of God, shed for their purification, to cleanse them of their sin.

After sprinkling the blood on their doors, they ate the lamb roasted with unleavened bread and bitter herbs. The lamb was roasted, in contact with the fire and bitter herbs. In his sacrifice, Jesus faced the fire of God's judgment, suffering the bitterness of scourgings, the beatings and the cross, typified in the bitter herbs.

They ate in haste, their loins were girded, sandals were on their feet, staffs were in their hands. God would pass through Egypt that night and smite the firstborn in Egypt. The blood would be a sign for them. No plague would fall on them to destroy them. (Exodus 12:12-13) The Passover was eaten in haste; they trusted God's promise. They were ready to flee. Deliverance was assured; they would know liberty, freed from Egypt's slavery.

Moving to Good Friday, we must learn of Israel's customs as they celebrated that day. At the 3rd hour, 9:00 AM, on Nisan 14, the High Priest took the Passover Lamb, ascended the altar and tied it in place on the altar. The people, in silence, were to think of the sacrifice of the lamb. At that very hour, Jesus was nailed to the cross. At the evening sacrifice, at 3:00 PM, the High Priest ascended the altar, cut the lamb's throat with a knife and said, "It is Finished," the exact words Jesus said as he died that very hour: *"It is Finished."*

To learn of the connection of Passover and our Lord's Passion, we must look back at Jesus' Last Supper. Luke 22:7-13 tells us that on the Day of Unleavened Bread, the day when the lamb was to be sacrificed, Jesus told Peter and John to make preparations for them to eat the Passover. Passover was part of Unleavened Bread. This day, just before Passover, was a Day of Unleavened Bread.

The day before Passover was Preparation Day; the house was swept clean of all leaven. Jesus told his disciples to go to a man and ask where the guest room was where he could share the Passover with his disciples. Though they made preparations, the Last Supper was not the Passover, understood in the Torah. Passover was observed on Nisan 14, after the lamb was sacrificed. The meal Jesus ate with his disciples was not a literal Passover. That would not occur until Friday, at 3:00 P.M. As the crucifixion was the antitype of the Passover, Jesus' Last Supper could not be the Passover. The Lamb, Christ, himself, had not yet been sacrificed.

Jesus said he longed to eat the Passover with them before he suffered, but he would not eat it again until it was fulfilled in the kingdom of God. While the Last Supper was not a Passover meal, it spoke of the New Covenant Jesus was bringing his people. Taking the bread, he divided it saying *"This is my body given for you."* Taking the cup, he said *"This cup is the new covenant in my blood, poured out for you."* Luke 22:19-20

Jesus' words match Moses' words in Exodus 24:8. *"This is the blood of the Covenant the LORD has made with you."* Both spoke of the blood that sealed God's covenant with his people. Jesus told his disciples: *"Do this in remembrance of me."* He wanted them to remember him, even in his death. He knew they would be reunited in the Kingdom of God.

As believers in the Messiah, Pascha has special meaning for us. We are not slaves as Israel was, but are slaves to sin. At Pascha, Jesus delivered us from 'our Egypt'. The Passover lamb was a shadow of our redemption. We were purchased from slavery through Jesus' blood, poured out for our redemption. Jesus shared his Last Supper with his disciples, promising deliverance. The LORD would redeem the lives of his people. None who took refuge in him would be condemned. (Psalm 34:22)

In 1 Peter 1:18-19, Peter assured the church that it was not with perishable things, such as silver and gold, that they were redeemed but with Christ's blood, a lamb without blemish. Israel's liberation from Egypt is celebrated at Passover. Jesus' suffering, death and resurrection are revealed in all the Passover Convocations throughout this Holy Feast.

At the Passover Seder, three matzahs are brought together as the Triune God. The second matzah, Christ, is broken in half. The larger piece, covered in a white napkin, is hidden until the end of the meal. Brought from concealment, it is shared by everyone as their final morsel. The broken, hidden matzah is the 'Aphikomen', meaning *'I have come; I am coming again.'* Aphikomen is written in Hebrew in Rabbinic text but it is a Greek word. Some believe it comes from 'epikomoi', dessert, or 'epi komon', after dinner entertainment. Others say it comes from 'epikomion', festal song. Some believe its true meaning has been lost or intentionally forgotten.

In "The Hidden Afikomen", we learn that in 1925, Austrian scholar, Robert Eisler saw the aphikomen as part of rituals observed by 1st century Messianic Jews. The whole matzah represented All Israel. The broken piece was the longed-for Messiah. The hidden piece, uncovered, prefigured the Messiah's resurrection amidst his people. Broken, it was shared, symbolic of the Passover where everyone participates. Taking the aphikomen showed anticipation of his return, and gave the Seder a sense of victory and expectancy, joy at Jesus' resurrection and redemption at his return.

In 1966, Oxford Jewish Biblical Scholar, Professor David Daube believed 'aphikomen', from the Greek 'afikomenos', meant *'The Coming One'* or *'He Who Has Come.'* He believed the bread Jesus gave his disciples was an aphikomen. He believes that at the Last Supper, Jesus blessed it saying, *"This broken, hidden matzah, which has for our people symbolized the Messiah, is fulfilled in me. I, myself, am the Aphikomen, the Coming One whom you expect."* This aphikomen symbolized Christ. It was pierced, as was Jesus by the Roman Spear, and striped, as Jesus bore our stripes. It was leaven free, as was Jesus, without sin, conceived by the Holy Spirit.

Taking the cup, he said *"Drink from it, all of you. This is my blood of the Covenant, poured out for many for the forgiveness of sins."* Matthew 26:26-28 At his Last Supper, Jesus brought the New Covenant that Jeremiah and Isaiah prophesied. Jeremiah spoke of a New Covenant God would make with the house of Israel. His law would be inscribed in their minds, written on their hearts. His covenant would be for the people of Israel and would be a light for the Gentiles, to open eyes that are blind. (Jeremiah 31:31-33, Isaiah 42:6) This Passover meal, this Seder celebration, is our Holy Communion. Jesus took the 3rd cup of the Seder celebration, the Cup of Redemption and offered it as the New Covenant in his blood.

How did Israel miss fulfillment of all these symbols of their faith? The High Priest surely performed the Passover duties throughout the week. Faithful Israelites knew what each day represented. How did they miss the wonders all around them? We must ask ourselves the same questions: How can we be so blind to not see the shadow completely fulfilled as Jesus became the Pascal Lamb, sacrificing himself for our salvation?

REJECTED AND DENIED—JESUS BEFORE CAIAPHAS AND PONTIUS PILATE

To understand the truth of the last days of Jesus' life, we must learn of the power the Sanhedrin had, or wished they had, in respect to Jesus' life and death. Early in the 1st century, the Sanhedrin's judicial power was greatly reduced. Twenty-seven years before Jesus' trial, the Sanhedrin lost their power to pass the death sentence. Shortly after Herod's son Archelaus' deposition, AD 6, Judea became a province of Rome, with Caponius its 1st procurator. Procurators, passing judgment in Augustus' name, deprived the Sanhedrin of the right to exercise the 'Jus Gladii', the right of the sword, *'The Scepter',* the sovereign right to adjudicate capital offenses. Caponius had imperial authority to perform executions. All Roman provinces had to submit to this decree. (Antiq. 17.13.1-5)

To the Sanhedrin, this was especially severe. In one event, Genesis 49:10 was fulfilled. Rome's procurator ruled Judah. David's staff was removed from beneath Judah's feet. David's throne was without an heir and the Scepter was taken. Judea's sovereign right of life and death was lost. Sixty-four years before Jerusalem's destruction, Judah was without a descendant of David on the throne, with no power to pronounce capital sentences. Judah possessed neither royal nor legal power. This was a terrible blow to the Sanhedrin. Deprived of this right, covered with sackcloth and ashes, they cried:

"Woe to us. The scepter has departed Judah. The Messiah has not come."

They understood the scepter would not depart from Judah nor the ruler's staff from between his feet until Shiloh came. In grief they cried; they could not understand nor believe Shiloh had come. In disbelief, they were assured the Word of God failed. Neither the Sanhedrin in AD 6 nor Caiaphas in AD 33 could accept the truth.

In AD 6, an eight-year-old boy, Yeshua, the son of a carpenter, was living in Nazareth. In AD 33, this young boy has grown. This man, Yeshua, stood before Caiaphas, but Caiaphas refused to believe Shiloh was standing before him. They were sure God had not kept his promise. The scepter departed Judah but Shiloh had not come.

Understanding this decree, Caiaphas knew he could not pass the death sentence but was determined Jesus would die, if not by his hand then by their procurator, Pilate's hand. Matthew 26:63-68 speaks of Caiaphas' determination and his plans. After their Last Supper, Jesus and his disciples went to the Mount of Olives. At Gethsemane, Judas came and with a kiss betrayed Jesus to the Chief Priests and elders.

The chief priests did all they could to put Jesus to death. Someone claimed Jesus said he would destroy the temple and build it again in three days. Caiaphas asked him if He was the Christ, the Son of God. Jesus told him, 'Yes, it was as he said', but he assured Caiaphas that he would live to see the Son of man sitting at the right hand of God, coming on the clouds of heaven. Caiaphas cried that he spoke blasphemy. They did not need any more witnesses; he was worthy of death.

In the morning, beaten, bruised, exhausted from an endless night, Jesus was taken to the praetorium. Caiaphas tried to convince Pilate of Jesus' offenses. After hearing their accusations, Pilate told them to take him themselves and judge him by their own law. Caiaphas told him they had no right to execute anyone. This was to fulfill the words Jesus spoke in John 12:30, to show how he was to die. (John 18:31-33)

Caiaphas' understood his lack of power; the 'Jus Gladii' was taken from the Sanhedrin. They could not put Jesus to death; his death could only come through Rome's authority. Jesus would not die by Jewish Law. He would have to face Roman crucifixion.

Pilate told the Jews he found no basis for charging him but they had a custom. He could release one prisoner at Passover. He asked them if they wanted him to release the King of the Jews. Seeing this as their last chance, they cried for Barabbas to be released.

After questioning Jesus, Pilate told Caiaphas he found no fault in him. The Jews said *"We have a law; by that law he ought to die. He has made himself the Son of God."* John 19:12 Pilate was terrified. He still tried to release Jesus but the Jews threatened him saying if he let Jesus go, he was not Caesar's friend, 'Amic Caesaris'.

Pilate knew he had no choice; he would have to crucify Jesus. If he resisted, Tiberius would learn and he would surely be killed. Knowing Tiberius had killed Sejanus for his anti-Semitic actions, he knew Jesus would have to be crucified. Washing his hands before them, he declared he was innocent in the shedding of Jesus' blood. They cried that his blood would be on them and on their children. (Matthew 27:22-25)

Jesus was taken to be crucified. Stripped of his clothes, a scarlet robe was placed on his back; a crown of thorns was placed on his head. Given a reed, he was scorned by the crowd. Kneeling in mock worship, they hailed him as their king. Thrown to the ground, he was scourged, whipped across his shoulders, back and legs. After the beatings, the robe was removed and he was forced to carry the crossbar to Golgotha. The Roman legions had beaten him as harshly as they pleased, 'forty lashes, minus one'. He was close to death before he reached the cross. The crossbar on his shoulders added to the strain on his weakened body. He may even have cried: *"I offered my back to those who beat me, my cheeks to those who pulled my beard; I did not hide my face from mocking and spitting; because the Sovereign LORD helps me, I will not be disgraced. Therefore, I have set my face like flint; I know I will not be put to shame."* Isaiah 50:6-7 With the weight of the crossbar and loss of blood, suffering from shock, he fell. To keep the procession moving, a passerby, Simon of Cyrene, was forced to carry the beam.

The crucifixion began; wrought iron nails were driven into his wrists; the bar was driven into the stake. Nails were driven deep into his feet, binding him to the cross.

The titulum, a sign with the victim's 'crime' written on it, was nailed in place: "Jesus of Nazareth, King of the Jews."

He faced hours of unbearable pain and partial asphyxiation. The temple leaders felt fully justified; Torah condemned Jesus as a blasphemer. He said they would see him seated at the right hand of Power, coming on the Clouds of Heaven; only God appeared on the Clouds of Heaven. Jesus spoke blasphemy; punishment for blasphemy was stoning. Though forbidden to stone him, they surely threw stones, shouting, crying out for him to come down from the cross. If he was the Son of God, he could come down from the cross. Only then would they believe him. In anguished grief he cried, *My God, My God, why have you forsaken me?"* Matthew 27:47

Deep in his chest he endured crushing pain, taxing his lungs and heart. With each breath, life was slipping away. With all strength gone, he closed his eyes and whispered, *"It is Finished."* John 19:30 His mission was complete; with his final breath, he cried *"Father, into your hands I commend my Spirit."* Luke 23:46

At his crucifixion there is another connection to the Passover Festival. Not one bone was to be broken on the Passover lamb. Jesus was the perfect Passover Lamb, without blemish and not one bone broken. It was the Day of Preparation. To prevent the bodies from remaining on the cross on the Sabbath, the Jews asked Pilate to break their legs so they could be taken away. Because Jesus was already dead, they did not break his legs.

At his crucifixion, a sign was placed over his head: *Jesus of Nazareth, King of the Jews'.* Caiaphas was enraged. He could not permit the sign to read as such. He told Pilate not to write "King of the Jews" but that Jesus said he was the King of the Jews. This sign proclaimed Jesus was Israel's King, something they vehemently denied. Pilate would have the last word: *"What I have written, I have written."* John 19:19, 22

LET ALL KNOW, THE SHOFAR HAS SOUNDED. ATONEMENT HAS BEEN MADE!

FEAST OF UNLEAVENED BREAD

The 1st and 7th days of Unleavened Bread are High Sabbaths, the LORD's appointed feasts. The 1st and 7th days were Holy Convocations, Miqra Kodesh, sacred rehearsals. In Leviticus 23: 10-11 they were also told that when they entered the Promised Land, they were to bring to the priest a sheaf of the first grain they harvested.

At sunset on the 1st Day of Unleavened Bread, Yom Ha Rishon, The First Day, the lamb was fully prepared. This was the Feast of Freedom, the slave redeemed from Egypt. Unleavened bread was broken; representing Jesus' sinless body. Paul said *"Christ, our Passover lamb, has been sacrificed. Let us keep the festival not with the yeast of malice and wickedness but with bread without yeast, the bread of sincerity and truth."* 1 Corinthians 5:7b-8

Four cups were taken, anciently known as the Blood of the Covenant, signifying the four parts of God's Covenant:

Sanctification: the holiness God offered his faithful remnant, and offers us, cleansing us of our sin.

Deliverance: their deliverance from Egypt's slavery, and our deliverance from slavery to sin-death.

Redemption: through the blood of the Passover lamb and our redemption through Jesus' blood.

Restoration: restoration in their Promised Land, and Restoration of All Things in Christ.

At the Last Supper, Jesus offered the Cup of Redemption. Giving thanks, he said *"This is my blood of the covenant, poured out for many."* Mark 14:23

On the 7th Day of Unleavened Bread, the people recalled Israel standing at the Red Sea, feeling the first rays of hope. Behind them the Egyptians were ready to take them back or kill them. Moses told them not to be afraid. They were to stand firm and see the salvation of the LORD, the 'Yeshua YHWH'! The Egyptians they saw that day would never be seen again. (Exodus 14:13)

Israel entered the Red Sea Mikveh on dry ground; on the other side the Egyptian army drowned. Paul spoke of this deliverance and their final deliverance. He did not want them to be unaware. Their fathers were under the cloud and passed through the sea, baptized unto Moses. They ate the same supernatural food and drank from the same supernatural Rock that followed them. The Rock was Christ. (1 Corinthians 10:1-3)

This 7th Day, Yom Ha Shbi'i, speaks of assured faith in Final Restoration; Jesus would reign with those he has restored. Understanding the four Cups of the Passover Feast, Jesus told his disciples he would not drink of the 4th Cup until he drank it new in the Father's Kingdom. (Mark 14:25) They would drink it together, celebrating restoration of all things at His Coming in Glory. They would drink it in a new way, no longer in memory of his death but in celebration of complete sanctification, deliverance, redemption and restoration.

On that Great Day, they would know Complete Restoration. In God's Kingdom, they would be gathered together, feasting with their Lord, drinking the Cup of Restoration. In Christ, all would be made New. Their faith would be full. They would reign with their Lord in his Kingdom, in his Glory. Death, separation from God, would forever be defeated. Standing before God, Anastasis, they would know Resurrection Life.

On Nisan 16, Yom Ha' Reshit, at First Fruits, the people brought a sheaf of their first fruits to the priest to be waved before the LORD, a taste of the physical harvest still in the field. This offering was a vision of the Full Harvest promised through God's First Fruits offering, Christ, raised from the grave at First Fruits. He was the First Fruits of God's Spiritual Harvest to be revealed at the End of the Age, in the Fullness of Time.

FULFILLMENT OF FIRST FRUITS—THE RESURRECTION OF CHRIST

At the crucifixion, Jesus' disciples deserted him. Watching from a distance, they would not draw close. They were terrified; their master had been crucified. Their world would never be the same. All they learned from him, his words, his miracles filled every waking hour. They could not imagine life without him. Where would they go; what would they do; what would become of his promised restoration?

Sunday morning, Mary Magdelene, Joanna, Mary, the mother of James, and Solome, the mother of the sons of Zebedee went to the tomb to anoint the Lord's body with spices. Heartbroken, grieving, they would lovingly say their last goodbyes. Their only concern was the stone on the grave.

Arriving at the tomb, they saw the stone already rolled away; the tomb was empty. A man at the grave told them not to be amazed. They were seeking Jesus of Nazareth who was crucified. He was not there. He was Risen. They were to tell the disciples and Peter that he was going to Galilee; they would see him as he had promised.

Fleeing the sepulchre, amazed at all they saw, they reported briefly to Peter and those with him. (Mark 16:6-8 & added verses) These women, with more questions than they could begin to answer, ran to tell the disciples of everything they saw and heard. John and Mark even say Mary Magdalene saw her Lord and wanted his disciples to know their Lord was 'Alive'! They knew his disciples would rejoice just as they were rejoicing. These women, with hearts first broken, rejoiced. His disciples needed to know their Lord, their Master was Alive!

LET ALL KNOW, THE SHOFAR HAS SOUNDED. YOUR KING HAS RISEN. HE IS ALIVE!

We believe we understand Christ's resurrection, but many know little of its significance in the Sinai Covenant. The saints understood their Lord's sacrifice, the Lamb whose blood was shed for remission of their sins. They also understood First Fruits, when Israel made a First Fruits offering, a taste of the physical harvest still in the field. At Jesus' resurrection, the saints prayed to God to watch over the Spiritual Harvest. God promised there would be a bountiful harvest, a full harvest.

At First fruits, Israel thanked God for the physical harvest, still in the field. In fulfillment, Jesus was the grain of wheat that fell to the ground and died. Through his resurrection, much fruit would come forth. In the Sinai Covenant, Israel thanked God for the promise of a physical harvest. In Christ's resurrection, God presented his Son, His First Fruits Offering, promising a Spiritual harvest.

Paul understood the Hebraic promise of First Fruits. Christ was raised from the dead, the firstfruits of those who 'sleep'. Each was in his own turn, Christ, the firstfruits, then at his Coming those who belonged to him. (1 Corinthians 15:20, 23) God would provide a full harvest from the first fruits he promised from the foundation of the world. At the final harvest, Israel and all faithful nations would be gathered together into God's Kingdom. As an agricultural people, Israel prayed that God would provide a physical harvest from their first fruits offering. In Jesus' death, God offered a taste of the Spiritual harvest, full ingathering of Remnant Israel and faithful Gentiles.

FROM RESURRECTION TO ASCENSION

Hearing the women, the disciples still feared but truth began to grow in their hearts. He showed himself to them and gave many proofs that he was alive. He appeared to them for forty days and spoke of the Kingdom of God. He told them everything written about him in the Law of Moses and the Prophets had to be fulfilled. He opened their minds so they could understand Scripture. (Luke 24:44-45) He assured them that he had to suffer, (Isaiah 52:14, 53:3-5) rise from the dead, (Psalm 16:10, 49:15) and ascend to Heaven to the Right Hand of God, the Father. (Isaiah 52:13, Psalm 16:8-11) The LORD would establish his throne in the heavens. (Psalm 103:19) In his ascension, they would no longer know him as the man who descended to the earth in the flesh. They would know him as their Ascended, Exalted, Glorified Lord, High Priest, Savior and King.

In his absence, they were to wait for the Father's promise. The Spirit would come in the last days. As Joel prophesied, God would pour out his Spirit on all people before the Great and Terrible Day of the LORD. There would be deliverance among the survivors whom the LORD calls. (Joel 2:28, 31-32)

At the Last Supper, Jesus assured them the kingdom would be restored to Israel. (Luke 22:28) Now, before his ascension, they asked *Lord, are you at this time going to restore the Kingdom to Israel?* They finally understood! The End of the Age was that close. God's kingdom was ready to be established. The promise of the Father was to Israel. They could not know the times and seasons but were told *"You will receive power when the Holy Spirit comes on you. You will be my witnesses in Jerusalem, Judea and Samaria, to the ends of the earth."* Acts 1:6, 8 When their journey was complete, God's Kingdom would be received. They would know the LORD's Restoration! Passover's 4th Cup would soon be shared by all the Lord's faithful sons and daughters; they would know Full Restoration!

After he said all this, as they were looking on, he was lifted up. A cloud took him out of their sight. While they were looking up, two men in white robes asked them why they were standing, looking up into heaven. This Jesus, who was taken from them to heaven, would come in the same way as they saw him go into heaven, in the Shekinah Glory Cloud. (Acts 1:10-11)

This vision was given to turn their attention from the Human, earthly Jesus to their Divine, Heavenly Lord. What did this mean to them? What does it mean to us? Jesus' ascension was the connecting link between his earthly and his Heavenly missions. In his earthly mission, Jesus descended to the earth as a babe in a manger. As a man, they saw his works and heard his words. They endured his affliction and death as the Suffering Servant. They beheld his resurrection as their Savior. For his mission to be complete and their needs to be fully met however, he needed to ascend to Heaven to present his blood sacrifice before God. As our High Priest, entering the Most Holy Place, returning as he promised, atonement would be received. In full victory, he is seated at the Right Hand of God the Father, Exalted, High and Lifted Up.

FEAST OF WEEKS—SHAVUOT—PENTECOST ACTS 2:1-4

Shavuot celebrates completion of the harvest. Jacob's sons counted the 'Omer', seven sevens of weeks, forty-nine days from the 2nd day of Passover. At Shavuot, fifty days after First Fruits, everyone was to bring two loaves of bread to the temple, made with fine flour and leavening. (Leviticus 23:17) The loaves were not to be eaten until the ceremony was complete and not placed on the altar because of the leaven. Seven lambs, a young bull and two rams were offered as a burnt offering. The feast ended in a communal meal; the poor, strangers and Levites were included.

The Feast of Weeks celebrates the Coming of the Holy Spirit. Jesus rose from the dead at First Fruits; he spent forty days with his disciples then ascended to the Father to complete the work of his once for all sacrifice. They would not be alone, without comfort. Jesus would send his Spirit. They were to wait in Jerusalem until Shavuot. At that time, the Spirit would descend on those 1st century believers.

The two loaves represented Jews and Gentiles, made one in Christ. Christ would break the dividing wall of hostility, abolishing in his flesh the commandments and ordinances, creating in himself one new man, reconciling us to God in one body, through the cross, bringing hostility to an end. (Ephesians 2:14-16) There was leaven in the loaves, as the Church was yet to be glorified. At Christ's return, the Church would be glorified. Jews and Gentiles would be One in Christ.

Our Christian Holy Days are Israel's Holy Days. Redemption was celebrated at Passover, the lamb without blemish. At First Fruits, an offering was made, a taste of the full harvest. Shavuot, the Latter First Fruits, the last festival of Passover, completed the Spring Holy Days. With great expectation, the disciples prepared for Pentecost and the

Father's promise. Fifty days after First Fruits, the Holy Spirit was revealed. From heaven, tongues of fire rested on them. Filled with the Holy Spirit, they spoke in many tongues as the Spirit gave utterance.

Jesus promised the coming of the Holy Spirit and fulfilled to the letter, all he spoke. They were filled with the Holy Spirit, as Joel prophesied. In the 'last days', God poured his Spirit out on all flesh. Their sons and daughters prophesied; their young men saw visions; their old men dreamed dreams. On his menservants and maidservants, God poured out his Spirit and they prophesied, making disciples of all nations.

At Shavuot, fifty days after First Fruits, God gave his people the power of the Law. At Pentecost, fifty days after Jesus' resurrection, God gave Jesus' beloved disciples the Spirit of the Law.

The Covenant of the Law—The Letter of the Law

Fifty Days from the crossing of the Red Sea, three thousand were slain for idol worship. God gave the Ten Commandments, the Law of the LORD written on stone.

The Covenant of Grace—The Spirit of the Law

Fifty Days from the resurrection, three thousand were baptized and received life. God gave the Holy Spirit, the Law of the LORD written on the heart.

Shavuot, or Pentecost, is essential in both Covenants. In the Covenant of the Law, Israel gathered at Sinai to hear God. *"Is not my word like fire, declares the LORD, like a hammer which breaks a rock in pieces?"* Jeremiah 23:29 Talmud Shabbat 88b says "As the hammer is divided into many sparks, God's holy fire, every word that went from the Holy One split into seventy languages."

In the Covenant of Grace, the Jews gathered in the Holy Temple, awaiting the Promise of the Father. A sound came from Heaven like the rush of a mighty wind. Filled with the Holy Spirit, the apostles spoke in other tongues, as the Spirit gave them utterance, 'the seventy languages'. (Acts 2:1-4)

They did not forget their Holy Days but Jesus gave a New Covenant, promise of restoration in God's Kingdom and the Full Harvest. They were to make disciples of all nations, baptizing them in the name of the Father, the Son and the Holy Spirit, teaching them to observe all God commanded. He would be with them always, to the end of the age. They spread the word of the Lord to Jerusalem, Judea, Samaria, to the ends of the earth. They faithfully, obediently followed their Lord's command, to the letter.

Our Holy Days, in honor of the birth, death, resurrection and ascension of our Lord, and the coming of the Holy Spirit, connect to all the Spring Holy Days God has ordained. The Gospel went to the ends of the earth. Many lost their lives, persecuted by the Pharisees and Nero but God's faithful servants brought Christ to all who would hear. Churches flourished; God's family grew, knowing that Christ would come again, unite with them and offer His Restoration. They lived the truth, taught the truth and passed the truth on to all they met.

Christ was born—Luke 2:4-7
Christ died—Mark 15:34-30
Christ Arose—Matthew 28:5-7
Christ would Come Again—Revelation 22:7

Chapter 3

THE RETURN OF CHRIST

We come to a part of our Lord's life that leaves many with questions we can't begin to answer. When is our Lord's 'Second Coming' to occur; when will He return in His Glory? What are the signs we must look for; how can we know this is truly the time? Can anyone offer honest answers to all our unanswerable questions?

After AD 70, many early church fathers saw the Temple's destruction as the end of the Mosaic Age and birth of the Messianic Age. They proclaimed Christ's finished work, his Coming in His Father's Glory and creation of the New Heaven and Earth. After AD 135, separated from its Jewish Roots, the Greek church lost its spiritual compass and awaited Christ's 'physical coming' apart from fulfillment of Old Testament prophecy.

After the Bar Kochba revolt and the writings of the 'Shepherd of Hermas' in AD 150, the church was taught delay of Christ's return. Once postponement was expressed, it took on a life of its own and continues to this day. Spreading fear and disbelief, we are assured we must watch and be ready. We cannot know when our Lord will return but must be ready. From the Gospels however, our Lord gave clear signs his disciples could understand so they would be ready for what he assured them was near.

As we learned in Christ's first advent, much error is taught affecting what we celebrate. Failing to understand fulfilled prophecy, we misunderstand Christ's Return in His Father's Glory, Resurrection of the Dead and Restoration of All Things. We continue to teach falsehood, misunderstanding what Scripture teaches. Unless we know what Jesus' Return meant for his 1st century followers, we will never know what it means for us today and how we are to celebrate this Holy Day, this glorious Day of the Lord.

We must step away from what 'today's prophets' continually teach, and learn what Jesus taught his disciples to prepare them for what was coming upon their generation. We must dilligently study His Word to learn what he told them nearly two thousand years ago. Thorough study of the Olivet Discourse can help us hear what they heard, understand what they understood and believe what they believed. Only then can we understand what he promised and discover he has fulfilled his promises to the letter.

Scholars are slowly coming to understand that the Olivet Discourse speaks of the end of the Mosaic Age and birth of the Messianic Age. In the Olivet Discourse, Jesus prophesied Jerusalem's destruction. In Matthew 23, he condemned the scribes and pharisees, calling them blind hypocrites, declaring God's judgment against them. After hearing all he spoke and seeing the temple's physical glory, his disciples asked about his judgment, the signs of His Coming and the End of the Age. Everything they asked concerned what he prophesied, the destruction of Jerusalem and the End of the Age.

Jesus told them everything they needed to know to prepare them for all that would happen and what they needed to look for as signs of his coming and the close of the age. He told them their generation would not pass until all he spoke had come to pass. Heaven and earth would pass away; his words would not pass away.

THE END OF THE AGE—THE END OF WHAT AGE?

Before we can understand our Lord's words, we must learn what he meant by the 'End of the Age'. What age was he speaking of? Most believe he was speaking of our age. We are continually told we are living in the Last Days. We are facing the 'End of the World' when 'Time' will be no more. Scripture however, never speaks of the End of Time or the end of the world; it speaks only of the 'Time of the End', the 'End of the Age'. Jesus did not speak of the end of time, but the end of the delay. The time was at hand: there would be no more delay.

Careful study of the Olivet Discourse reveals the errors we have been taught for two thousand years. Jesus told his disciples what was coming upon their generation, warning them of all they would endure in the last days of the Mosaic Age. Throughout Scripture, only two ages are spoken of by prophets and sages, the Mosaic Age, their Present Age, and the Messianic Age, the age that for them was yet to come. Jesus prophesied the end of the Mosaic Age. As God's prophets revealed, God would bring in a New Age, the Messianic Age. God's Remnant, faithful Jews and Gentiles who obediently came to the God of Israel, would dwell in their Lord's Presence in God's New Age, the Age of the Messiah.

Isaiah spoke of this New Age and all that would come to those who were faithful to the New Covenant. Isaiah 65:17-19 is God's promise of this New Heaven and Earth, not a physical creation but a Spiritual Change. God would create a New Heaven and earth; the former things would not be remembered nor come to mind. God's people would rejoice in what God would create: Jerusalem, a delight, its people a joy. God would rejoice over Jerusalem and take delight in her people. The sound of weeping would no longer be heard.

In Christ's judgment, the Old Heaven and Earth, the Covenant of Death passed away. God created a New Heaven and Earth, the Covenant of Grace. God rejoices over his New Creation; his faithful followers rejoice with him, neither weeping in suffering nor crying in desperation for deliverance. The New Heavens and Earth are a delight, its people a joy. No longer separated from their Lord or His Land, they rejoice in their Lord's abiding presence.

God would create a New Heaven and Earth, an eternal, Spiritual Creation. He would create a 'Heavenly, Eternal City' where His people could dwell with Him, where His Righteousness would dwell.

HEAVEN AND EARTH PASSING AWAY
WHAT WAS TO OCCUR AT THE END OF THE AGE?

What did Jesus tell his disciples? What did they learn from the Olivet Discourse? Jesus spoke to four of his disciples, Peter, Andrew, James and John, of the apostasy of the scribes and Pharisees. They had shut God's kingdom from his people. They would not even enter themselves. Accusing them of their faithlessness, he called them blind hypocrites.

"Woe to you, teachers of the law and Pharisees, you hypocrites. You build tombs for the prophets and decorate the graves of the righteous. You say, "If we had lived in the days of our forefathers, we would not have taken part with them in shedding the blood of the prophets.' You testify against yourselves that you are descendants of those who murdered the prophets. Fill up then, the measure of the sins of your forefathers." Matthew 23:29-32

Jesus condemned the temple leaders but to his beloved children there was grief as he knew what was shortly to be revealed. He cried over Jerusalem for killing the prophets sent to them. God would have gathered his children as a hen, but they would not come to him. Their house would be left desolate. He assured them, they would not see him again until they sang *Baruch haba, b' shem Adonai. "Blessed is he who comes in the name of the Lord."* (Matthew 23:39)

He wept for Jerusalem that they might know what would bring peace. Because of their faithlessness, peace would be taken from them. He assured them the days were coming when their enemies would cast a bank about them, hemming them in on every side, because they did not know 'the time of their visitation'. (Luke 19:42-44)

As Jesus left the temple, his disciples praised its splendor. Jesus had said not a stone would be left on another; everything would be brought down. Looking down on the glorious temple, wondering what Jesus meant, they asked him when all that would be and what would be the signs of his coming and the end of the age. Their Lord told them the Temple would be brought to the ground with not one stone left on another. When would this occur? What would be the signs of its destruction? Their glorious temple, the very dwelling place of YHWH would be brought to the ground. How, when was this to be? (Matthew 24:2-3)

Their Lord told them all they needed to know so they could teach those who would follow. They were to teach the Lord's faithful followers to watch and be ready. They needed to remember Jesus' words so they could survive the tribulation that would shortly be revealed. What would they see? Jesus told them exactly what they needed to be watching for to prepare them for all that would come upon that generation.

THE SIGNS OF THE LAST DAYS MATTHEW 24:5-14

1. *Many will come in my name, saying "I am the Christ, trying to lead you astray."*
2. *There will be wars and rumors of wars; don't be alarmed; the end is not yet.*
3. *Nation will rise against nation, kingdom against kingdom.*
4. *There will be famines and earthquakes in various places; this is just the beginning.*
5. *They will deliver you to tribulation; you will be put to death, hated for my name sake.*
6. *Many will fall away and betray one another.*
7. *Many false prophets will arise, leading many astray.*
8. *Because wickedness is multiplied, most men's love will grow cold.*
9. *He who endures to the end will be saved.*
10. *The gospel of the kingdom will be preached through all the world as a testimony.*

THEN THE END WOULD COME!

Jesus told them that when they saw the desolating sacrilege, spoken by Daniel, standing in the Holy Place, they were to leave Judea, fleeing to the mountains. (Matthew 24:15-16) When they saw Jerusalem surrounded by armies, they would know its desolation was near. (Luke 21:20) If they were in the country, they were not to return to gather anything. They were to leave with only the clothes on their backs. He warned of the urgency of flight, knowing what it would mean to them and their families. If they listened to false messiahs who said they were the Christ, they would be led astray.

Their Lord warned them of Great Tribulation. A sign, divine evidence of the Son of man in heaven, would appear. All the nations of the earth, all Judea would mourn. They would see the Son of man coming in a cloud, a 'theophany', the Glory of God, the 'Kavod YHWH'. There would be a trumpet call. His elect would be gathered from one end of heaven to the other.

Jesus said that as soon as the fig tree's branch becomes tender and leaves appear, they know summer is near. In the same way, when they saw all those things, they would know he was at the very door; but that day and hour no one could know, not the angels in heaven, not even the Son. (Matthew 24:32-36)

These words leave many believing Jesus did not know when the end would come, but studying Israel's Holy Days we learn Rosh-Hashanah commenced at the New Moon. The people awaited this day with much anticipation. Since Rosh-Hashanah occurred at the New Moon, the day and hour of its start was uncertain until confirmed by two witnesses. The day was referred to as 'The Day which only the Father Knows'.

No one could know when the New Moon would occur. Rosh-Hashanah could not begin until the New Moon was confirmed by two witnesses. Many believe Jesus' words, 'No one knows the day or hour' meant in his humanity he did not know the time of his coming. However, he understood completely. He did not know 'the day or hour' but knew he would return in their generation, on the 'Day that Only the Father Knows'.

While we are told Jesus did not know the time of His Coming, his faithful remnant understood completely. They understood their Holy Days and knew what he was saying. They did not know the year of his coming, but they knew he would return in their generation, on Rosh-Hashanah. Remarkably, he would return on the same day as his First Advent. He would be the 'Sign' of God's New Creation, the 'New Heaven and Earth'.

THE PAROUSIA—THE RETURN—THE PRESENCE OF OUR LORD

Another name for Rosh-Hashanah is Zichron Teruah, 'Remembrance of the Shofar Blast'. Saadia Gaon, a Jewish scholar living in Babylon AD 882-942, gave ten reasons for sounding the Shofar:

1. The Shofar is associated with the coronation of a King.
2. The Shofar heralds the beginning of the penitence period.
3. The Torah is given amidst blasts of the Shofar.
4. Prophets compare their message to the blast of the Shofar.
5. The Shofar reminds us of the conquering armies that destroyed the temple.
6. The Shofar reminds us of the substitutionary sacrifice of the ram for Isaac.
7. The Shofar fills one with awe.
8. The Shofar is associated with Judgment Day.
9. The Shofar heralds the Messianic Age.
10. The Shofar heralds the Resurrection.

All ten connect with Jesus' life and ministry: Kingship at his birth and Parousia, forgiveness when penance is made, Christ's Law and prophetic message, his substitutionary sacrifice as the lamb at his crucifixion, the awe known in him, judgment at the End of the Age, the promise of the Messianic Age, his resurrection and our resurrection life.

One ceremony of Rosh-Hashanah is 'Tashlikh'. The people go to a body of water, tossing the contents of their pockets into the water. Micah 7:19 is recited, symbolic of their sins swallowed up in forgiveness. God would hurl, 'Tashlikh', all their sins into the depths of the sea. God would forgive their iniquities and remember their sins no more. He would make a new covenant with them, putting his law within them, writing it on their hearts. (Jeremiah 31:31-33) Tashlikh and the promise of a New Covenant declare the Messiah would cast his people's sins into the depths of the sea. Their sins would be forgiven. The New Covenant promised Israel was completely fulfilled in Christ's atonement for their sins, and ours.

Jesus Christ is the Torah, inscribed in our minds and hearts. When we understand the prophetic message Jesus gave his disciples, we begin to see what he is trying to reveal to us. In full knowledge of what would happen, Jesus prepared his disciples for what they would witness, speaking of signs they needed to watch for. At Pentecost, the Holy Spirit gave them knowledge to fully understand the time of the end would be at Rosh-Hashanah. In the Spirit's power, they would understand scripture and the laws of observance of their Holy Days. Their Lord's words and the Spirit's power prepared them for all they would endure.

The Great Tribulation does not concern something we must be prepared to face. Jesus told his disciples what they were to see before the Great and Terrible Day of the Lord? Looking to our Lord to teach us and learning from history, we can know the truth. In his Sermon on the Mount, Jesus assured his disciples he did not come to destroy the Law and the Prophets. He came to fulfill them. In truth, until heaven and earth passed away, not one jot or tittle of the law would pass until All was fulfilled!

Do we understand what these words meant to Jesus' disciples? The children of Israel believed the Law and Prophets would stand forever. Jesus assured his disciples the Law and Prophets would see fulfillment. He did not come to destroy the Law and Prophets; he came to fulfill them, all of them! The Law and Prophets would not stand forever. They would stand until all was fulfilled. In their fulfillment, the Old Heaven and Earth would pass away, the New Heaven and Earth would descend from Heaven. God's faithful remnant of Israel and Judah, and Gentiles who turned to Israel's God, would be One, dwelling with him forever.

The Old Heaven and Earth was the Mosaic Age, the Present Age for Christ and his disciples. Its passing would fulfill all the Law and Prophets. Jesus prophesied Jerusalem's destruction, the end of the Mosaic Age and birth, or creation of God's Eternal Age, God's New Heaven and Earth. At his Coming, he would fulfill all the Law and Prophets, every jot and tittle, to the letter.

Scripture reveals the Spring Festivals have all been fulfilled in Christ. We see his suffering, passion and death at Passover, his resurrection at First Fruits, the outpouring of the Holy Spirit at Shavuot. To understand fulfillment of all the Law and Prophets, we must look to the Fall Festivals and discover Jesus has fulfilled these celebrations, these Holy Days, as well. Jesus Promised, 'All Would Be Fulfilled'!

Rabbis who taught that creation of Adam and Eve was at Rosh-Hashanah in creation of the world, also teach that the Messiah will be heralded at Rosh-Hashanah by the trumpet of God which will raise the dead. The Hebrew Scriptures prophesy the Glory of their Messiah who would come bringing his Kingdom. Their people would witness his presence at Rosh-Hashanah, at the Seventh Trumpet of God.

If we continue to wait for Christ's return in his Father's Glory, we deny all he taught his disciples, the lost sheep of Israel and us, and declare him a false prophet. If all of us, if the whole world could understand he has returned in his Father's Glory, we are in his

Kingdom and abide in his Presence, this world could truly rejoice. Creation of the New Heavens and Earth would bring rejoicing to 'All God's people'.

'THE SCEPTER SHALL NOT PASS UNTIL SHILOH COMES.'

As we learned, Genesis 49:10 was fulfilled in AD 6 when Archelaus was deposed and replaced, not by a King but by Caponius, Judea's first Procurator. The Scepter, the right of the Sanhedrin to enforce Mosaic Law and adjudicate capital offenses, was taken. There was no longer a King beneath Judah's feet. Genesis 49:10's fulfillment means Shiloh has come. Unfortunately, many do not know or understand the historical record. They believe Shiloh's coming is yet to be seen.

Many believe the scepter passed from Judah shortly after Jesus' death and will not be restored until he returns as Messiah to take what rightfully belongs to him. They fail to realize Jesus already is the Messiah, the LORD's Anointed One. Others believe the scepter departed Judah at Jerusalem's destruction and Israel's worldwide dispersion and will not be reclaimed until Shiloh returns with the Scepter to gather Israel unto Himself.

Many Christians say Israel is blind to the truth of Jacob's prophecy, without seeing their own blindness. They fail to see the Scepter would not depart until Shiloh came. The scepter was taken after Shiloh's appearing. Eight years after Shiloh's birth, the Scepter was taken. We all must open our eyes; the Torah has not failed. God has been faithful to his Word. The scepter departed Judah; Shiloh has come. God's remnant is gathered unto him.

Israel could not believe in Jesus' time. Many Christians still cannot believe. The promises given Jacob's sons spoke of promises to their descendants in their Last Days. Insisting Shiloh's Coming is future contradicts all that God's prophets taught Israel, all Jesus taught his disciples, all they taught the church.

If we continue to wait for our Lord to return, bringing a physical, earthly kingdom, we live with the acceptance that 'Satan' has ruled this world for two thousand years and is still in control. Christ has deceived his followers, and deceives us. He has no power to defeat Satan or chooses to let him rule in his stead.

If Christ is yet to return, we are still in our sins, still under the Law of the Torah. If this is not our belief, we must stand and declare he has fulfilled, to the letter, all the Law and Prophets. He has Come Again, with power to defeat Satan, and has Overcome!

LET ALL KNOW, THE SHOFAR HAS SOUNDED.
SHILOH, THE MESSIAH HAS COME!

The disciples heard Jesus and believed. They went through Judea, Samaria, the Roman Empire, to the ends of the earth. Churches grew and prospered. Everywhere they went they taught of the end. They waited eagerly for the day they would see their Lord, some for the first time, and dwell in the New Heaven and Earth, the New Jerusalem, in communion with him.

To understand what Jesus taught the disciples, we must learn what became of Jerusalem and the Temple. What did Jesus' Return in his Father's Glory truly mean? What was the Great and Terrible Day of the Lord? As we learned the truth of Christ's birth, we must learn of his return in his Father's Glory. If we teach anything but what Scripture says, we teach falsehood. We deceive ourselves and the truth is not in us. What did Jesus tell his disciples; what did they understand; what did he mean?

Not one stone would be left upon another.
All would be thrown down.

Chapter 4

DESTRUCTION OF JERUSALEM—
THE END OF THE AGE

PROPHESY AND FULFILLMENT

Before we can learn what was to become of that Holy nation, we must learn of the sins that brought its destruction. Jerusalem would be brought to the ground; not one stone would be left upon another. What did this nation do that God would bring such judgment against his own nation, his own people?

Malachi prophesied God's final decree and judgment against his unholy, ungrateful nation. They have turned from their LORD in all their ways. They refused to listen or believe their LORD, their Christ. Their LORD made his case against them. His children were blind to their LORD's love, their sins and the judgment he would bring on them for their faithlessness. God warned them of all that would happen if they did not return to him in love and obedience.

Not understanding the LORD's love, they turned from him. A son was to honor his father; a servant was to respect his master. If God was their father, where was their honor? If he was their master, where was their respect? His children refused to honor him as their father or serve him as their LORD. His priests offered worthless sacrifices and questioned why their LORD did not show them favor. He would not accept their offerings. God provided the perfect sacrifice but they profaned his offering saying the LORD's table was polluted; the food was despised. They did not honor Christ, the LORD's perfect offering.

If they would not give God the glory, he would curse their blessings, rebuke their offspring and drive them from his presence. God's covenant with Levi was a covenant of life and peace. Levi stood in awe of God's name. He turned many from iniquity. Turning from their Lord, Judah caused many to stumble, corrupting the covenant of Levi. Judah profaned the LORD's sanctuary, forsaking His covenant. Turning from their LORD, they went after other gods. In their 'prostitution', God already had divorced Israel; Judah committed adultery as well. God's judgment would fall on Judah if she did not return to him. His children could not see their sins; they forgot all he did for them from their nation's birth. They could not understand the LORD's power and justice.

With all his people's sins, God would not forsake them; redemption would come if they turned to him. God would send a messenger to prepare the way. The LORD would suddenly come to his temple; the messenger of the Covenant would purify the sons of Levi until they presented right offerings to the LORD. God would be a swift witness against all those who oppressed the hirelings, the widows, orphans and sojourners, and did not fear God. (Malachi 3:1-5)

The LORD judged these sons of Levi who turned from their LORD's Law, ignoring those who longed to dwell in the LORD's Presence, in his Kingdom. Shunning the hireling, forsaking widows and orphans, refusing to cancel their debt, refusing to offer redemption of their land, they denied God's Jubilee Promises. For denying the sojourners, 'Samaritans and Gentiles' a place in God's kingdom, they would know God's judgment.

A way was offered for redemption; a messenger would prepare the way before the LORD would judge but who could endure the day of his coming? His judgment would be more than many could bear. Who could stand when he appeared? God's judgment would purify his land and his people, routing out sin and sinner. They would be purified until a righteous remnant, a Holy Priesthood, tried in fire, cleansed with fuller's soap, offered right sacrifices to him as their LORD. Cleansed, they could stand and know Resurrection Life.

Through judgment, some believed. Those who feared the LORD turned to him. A book of remembrance was written of all who feared the LORD. God would spare them as a man spares his son who serves him. God would distinguish between the righteous and the wicked, between those who served God and those who turned from him. Hearing their LORD's warning, a remnant believed and repented. They would be his special possession; they would know their LORD's restoration. Dwelling with him, they would honor their restoration as a Holy Day to God.

God warned those who would not listen. Malachi prophesied that judgment would come, burning like an oven. Arrogant evildoers would be burned up, leaving neither root nor branch. For those who feared the LORD, the sun of righteousness would rise with healing in his wings; the righteous would tread down the wicked.

Malachi gave the final warning; Elijah would come to prepare the way. He would turn the hearts of the fathers to the children, the hearts of the children to the fathers. Israel's faithful fathers would be joined to the faithful children of the Gentiles. Faithful children of the Gentiles would be united with Israel's remnant fathers. In Christ, they would be bound as One. The nation has heard their LORD. Will they repent, returning to the LORD, or face judgment, refusing to understand their LORD's love, power and authority?

THE ABOMINATION THAT CAUSES DESOLATION—'THE MAN OF SIN'

Many suggest Daniel's 'abominations of desolation' were the ensigns of the Roman armies in their siege of Jerusalem but the abominations began after Jesus' crucifixion, after his final sacrifice. After AD 33, further sacrifices were idolatries, "the wing of abominations on which the One who causes desolation would come." Desecration came because the Zealots had defiled the physical Temple. Their downfall and the destruction of Jerusalem was brought on by their own hands because of the atrocities they committed against Christ, God's Spiritual Temple. Through the power of Rome, the Hand of God purified the city and its people.

Speaking of the Abomination of Desolation, Paul told the Thessalonians of the coming of the Man of Sin. He assured them so no one would deceive them. That day would not come unless the rebellion came first and the man of sin was revealed. He would exalt himself against every so-called god and take his seat in the Temple.

Jesus' faithful remnant knew what was restraining him. The mystery of lawlessness was already at work. He who was restraining him would continue to do so until he was taken out of the way. Then the lawless one would be revealed. At the Lord's appearing, he would destroy his wickedness by his glorious coming. (2 Thessalonians 2:3-8)

The Jewish rebellion was already underway in the early AD 60's. The power of lawlessness was at work but something was holding back this Man of Sin. History reveals the Jewish High Priesthood, responsible for the cleanliness of Temple worship, opposed the Zealot-led rebellion. Their High Priest, Ananus longed to maintain peace with Rome for the good of the nation. To the Zealots, the priests were their enemies.

As the war developed, a Zealot leader emerged, John of Gischala, fulfilling 2 Thessalonians 2:1-7. Inciting the Jews against Rome, he brought the abomination Daniel prophesied. (Daniel 9:27) John became a treacherous Zealot leader. In AD 68, assisted by the Idumaeans, he murdered the High-Priest, Ananus and thousands of priests. Leaving their bodies within the Temple, unburied, he violated Torah Law. Josephus acknowledged: *"This was the work of God who preserved this John that God might bring on the destruction of Jerusalem."* (War 4. 2. 3. 104) The slaughter of Ananus brought God's judgment. *"Ananus' death was the beginning of the destruction of the city. From this very day may be dated overthrow of the wall and ruin of her affairs, where they saw their high priest and procurer of their preservation slain in the midst of their city."* (War 4.5.2.)

John presented himself as a God-sent ambassador. To gain independence, he called on the Idumaeans. To keep the Jews from submitting to Rome, he ordered Ananus' murder and the removal of the priesthood. Establishing himself as the official Zealot leader, he promised deliverance. He then broke from the Zealots, setting up monarchial power. Instead of accepting Jesus as their Messiah, King and Deliverer, the people placed their hope in this false messiah king, a man of sin and deceit. After the coming of the Lord and destruction of the Temple, John was condemned to perpetual imprisonment by the

Roman authorities. As Paul had spoken, 'he was 'slain' by the breath of Jesus mouth, destroyed at his appearing.' (2 Thessalonians 2:8)

Josephus connected the Zealots' murder of Ananus with Jerusalem's destruction because of their pollution of the city. Their devotion to the temple and their God could not justify the atrocities they committed. Believing everything they did was for their LORD, they violated all the principles of His Law. They made the Temple unfit for worship. God would leave the Temple desolate and destroy the city.

God doomed the polluted city to destruction, purging his sanctuary by fire. Nothing less could cleanse his people. Josephus spoke of the Zealots' pollution. The Idumaeans ascended to the Temple; the Zealots eagerly awaited them. Mixing with the Idumaeans, they attacked the temple guards and killed the whole multitude.

"The Zealots joined the shouts raised by the Idumaeans. Not sparing anyone, they ran through with swords those who desired they remember the kinship between them and begged them to have regard of their common Temple. There was no place for flight or hope of preservation. Driven upon each other in heaps, they were slain. The outer Temple was overflowed with blood. That day saw 8,500 dead." (War 4.5.1. 305-313)

As this massacre occurred within the Temple courts; these murders brought irrevocable pollution to the Temple. The Torah taught that human blood and corpses caused ritual uncleanness. As this blood was shed through violent murder, the Temple could never be made ritually clean. God's Presence could not dwell within its gates.

Josephus speaks of the Temple's impurity. *"Dead bodies of strangers were mingled with those of their own country, profane persons with priests. The blood of carcasses stood in lakes in the holy courts. O most wretched city, what misery so great as this did you suffer from the Romans when they came to purify you from the internal pollution! You could no longer be a place fit for God; nor could you longer survive after you had been a sepulchre for the bodies of your own people and made the Holy House a burying place in this civil war."* (War 5.1.4, 5)

The Siege of Jerusalem—The Judgment of God

Because of their atrocities, the abomination that causes desolation has come. The War of the Jews began August AD 66, in Nero's 12th year, and ended in September AD 70, forty years from the start of Jesus' ministry and 425 years from Malachi's warnings. Final resistance came in April AD 73 at Masada. A band of Zealots desperately held out until total destruction was assured. Committing mass suicide, only dead bodies were discovered. God's judgment was brought against all who refused to turn to their Lord in obedience.

In AD 66, Roman and Syrian legions invaded; open rebellion began. Nero sent Procurator, Gessius Florus to subdue the city but the Zealots killed him and five thousand men. Nero sent Vespasian with two orders: Destroy Jerusalem; Level the Temple. War raged through the entire nation. The Jews pushed their conquest beyond the Jordan, razing Cyprus to the ground. Cestius Gallus, Legate of Syria, marching into Judea, massacred all Jews he came upon. From October 15th to November 22nd AD 66, Gallus marched toward Jerusalem. On October 30th, encamped beside the temple, he prepared for battle. The Zealots drove him back, killing four thousand. By mid-November, Rome was on the verge of victory. Then, on November 22nd, without reason or cause, Gallus and his men fled. War continued three years but Jerusalem was not seized again until April AD 70.

In April AD 70, destruction of the city began in earnest, forty years to the week of Jesus' 1st Passover. A million Jews were gathered in the city. For five months, brutal war engulfed the entire land. Jerusalem was totally overcome and destroyed. The Jews destroyed themselves and were their own worst enemies. Not trusting each other, three different parties jealously destroyed each other's' food supplies and homes, bringing famine, starvation and death. Besides those who died in battle, thousands died for lack of food. Bodies, left where they fell from battles and starvation, bred pestilence and further death.

Thousands died of hunger. The merest hint of food brought violence. Family members fought each other, fathers against sons, children against parents, each grasping the last morsel that could support the life of the other. The Zealots even searched the dying, believing they were concealing food, pretending to be dead. Starving ruffians staggered through the streets like drunkards. The same homes were searched two or three times a day. Many gnawed anything they could find, belts, shoes, even leather stripped off their shields. Withered grass was devoured or sold in bundles for four drachma. They became so desperate that a woman, grieving the suffering her child would face, killed and ate her infant son. (War 6, 3, 3-4)

Josephus described the horrors the city endured. Titus ambushed anyone searching for food. Most were the poor, afraid to desert their wives and children, letting them be slain. Hiding from the Zealots, they were taken by the enemy. After fighting against Rome, they knew they could not plead for mercy. Thousands were crucified before the city walls. Every day five hundred were crucified. Soldiers, in full hatred of the Jews, crucified anyone they could catch. When there were too many to crucify, more crosses were needed; when more crosses were available, more bodies were needed. (War 5, 11, 1)

In April AD 70, Titus, with 80,000 men, pitched camp north of the city. 2,400 Jewish warriors defended the walls but each wall was conquered. Encircling the city, Titus crucified all deserters who fled to him. The Zealots felt fully justified in their assaults but only brought more destruction on themselves. Relying on the invisible Shekinah Presence, they violated all his laws, refusing to surrender.

The famine was the worst in history. Pestilence was bred from corpses lying in streets and homes. Seized by madness, Jerusalem was possessed. From April to September, the Jews held the capital but continually lost ground. People were dying everywhere. Josephus reveals 1,100,000 Jews were killed in the siege. This did not include those dying of famine.

101,000 were sold into slavery. The temple was burned August 5th, AD 70, the 9th of Ab, the same day the 1st temple was destroyed by Babylon. (Antiq. B. xx C11.8)

Jews who escaped death were deported, sold into slavery, captive to all nations, as Jesus had prophesied. *"They will fall by the edge of the sword, led captive among all nations. Jerusalem will be trodden down by the Gentiles until the times of the Gentiles are fulfilled."* Luke 21:24 All that Jesus prophesied in his Olivet Discourse was fulfilled in Jerusalem's judgment and desolation.

Jerusalem, the beloved city, was totally destroyed. All that was left were ash-covered, bloodstained ruins. The once glorious City of God was totally forsaken, unrecognizable. The most beautiful city of the east was laid ruin. Not one stone was left on another.

Let All Know, The Shofar has Sounded Your King has Returned in Judgment.

"Talmudic Evidence of the Messiah in AD 30" reveals the Jerusalem and Babylonian Talmud, the 'Tractate Yoma 67A', says the Shekinah Glory left the temple forty years before its destruction, revealed in four signs:

1. The Lot for the Lord, cast on Yom Kippur, was never drawn. The stone for Azazel came up every time.
2. The menorah's western candle would not stay lit or burn continually.
3. The doors of the temple would open by themselves.
4. The red cloth no longer turned white supernaturally.

The random lot cast on Yom Kippur determined which goat was for the LORD and which was the scapegoat. Before AD 30, the black stone was randomly drawn half the time, the white stone half the time. From AD 30-70, only the black stone was drawn. The lot for the Azazel goat came up every time. This revealed a dramatic change in the Yom Kippur ritual. The Talmud says the Shekinah Presence had departed the temple, the Holy of Holies was deserted and goats were no longer accepted as a sacrifice for sin.

The western lamp, the most important lamp of the Menorah, would not shine. For forty years the main lamp went out without reason. The priests could not prevent it. It is believed this started when Jesus said the Temple would be destroyed. The western lamp was always to be lit, but each night the lamp went out. The Light, representing contact with the Presence of God, was gone. God's light did not shine.

The temple gate opened without human assistance. With great difficulty the guards shut it. This was a solid brass gate. Twenty men were needed to shut it. Many believed God had opened the gates of happiness but learned men understood the Temple's security was dissolved of its own, for their enemy's advantage. Rabbi Yohanan Ben Zakkai cried,

"O Temple, why do you frighten us? We know you will be destroyed. It has been said 'Open your doors, O Lebanon, so that fires may devour your cedars'." Zechariah 11:1

The Red Cloth. At Yom Kippur, the priests took a piece of the red cloth they tied to the Azazel goat and bound it to the temple door. If, after the Yom Kippur sacrifice, this cloth turned white supernaturally, it signified atonement by God for another Yom Kippur; Israel could rejoice. If it remained crimson, they were full of sorrow.

The white cloth showed God approved the Day of Atonement rituals and forgave their sins. From AD 30 until the temple's destruction however, this cloth remained red; God no longer forgave their sins. The Yom Kippur sacrifice had no power to cleanse them. Israel's sins were not pardoned; they were not made white. The nation lost their Lord's attention. This was in relation to what occurred in AD 30. The beginning of these signs appears to match the year Jesus started his ministry.

Many believe these mysteries began at Jesus' crucifixion, when the temple curtain parted, but if we have correctly dated Jesus' life, he was crucified in AD 33. While it is believed these four mysteries lasted forty years, it is possible they began in AD 33, at Jesus' death, lasting thirty-seven years, not the perfect forty.

Israel endured forty years in the wilderness, but only 38.5 years were judgment for their lack of faith in God and their refusal to enter the Promised Land. After Jesus' crucifixion, Israel was given 37.5 years before their judgment. The forty years in the wilderness and the forty years from Jesus ministry to Jerusalem's destruction match, but the years of these mysteries may not have been a full forty years. For refusal to enter God's Promised Land, both faithless generations faced God's judgment.

The Talmud says the Shekinah had departed the Temple these forty years, but the Temple was not left desolate until the Roman War began in AD 66, as prophesied by God's prophets and our Lord, himself. These 'Signs of the End' could have been forewarnings of the temple's desolation but God's presence remained in the Temple until AD 66 and departed because of the abominations committed as the zealots took possession of the Temple. Before he spoke of the signs of the Last Days, Jesus cried over the city's coming desolation, as if it already was. *"Your house is forsaken, and desolate."* Matthew 23:37 Jesus spoke of the temple's desolation as a present reality to him, assured of its certainty without doubt.

'THE BITTER TEARS'—"THE LAMENTATIONS"

Jeremiah's Lamentations focus on Jerusalem's condition in 586 BC in its destruction by Babylon. This was the most disastrous event the nation had ever faced. Prophets foresaw the coming disaster but few believed it would be so irrevocable. Some understood God's judgment. In grief they cried lamentations, justifying God. Fully acquainted with grief, they cried their repentance pleading for God's mercy.

These Lamentations concerned their physical suffering as the Temple and land were totally destroyed. In bitter grief and mourning, they questioned God, their bitter suffering, their physical exile from the Land, their abuse under Babylon and disintegration of their society.

Their Spiritual suffering, far more crushing, revealed worship had been disrupted and the Temple was burned. Prophets waited for word from God but He made no reply. No one came to appointed feasts. There was no dedication to God. With all their suffering, they questioned if God still loved them. They knew God sent this misery and many believed he was his people's enemy. The faithful remnant knew this judgment was deserved but wondered if it should be so great. Remaining hopeful, they knew God's love would never fail. God would not cast off his people forever; he would bring newness if in faith they repented.

Just as Judah lamented Babylon's destruction, those suffering this 2nd desolation cried to their LORD. Few however, saw this as God's judgment. All they understood was Rome's oppressive hand in their suffering. The Zealots felt fully justified in their vengeance against their Roman oppressors.

Lamentations 1:1	"How deserted lies the city, once so full of people! How like a widow is she who once was great among the nations! She who was queen among the provinces has now become a slave."
Lamentations 1:4	"The roads to Zion mourn; no one comes to her appointed feasts. All her gateways are desolate. Her priests groan; her maidens grieve. She is in bitter anguish."
Lamentations 1:10	"The enemy laid hands on all her treasures. She saw pagan nations enter her sanctuary, those you had forbidden to enter your assembly."
Lamentations 1:11	"All her people groan as they search for bread. They barter their treasures for food to keep themselves alive. Look, O LORD, and consider for I am despised."
Lamentations 1:13	"From on high he sent fire; sent it down into my bones. He spread a net for my feet and turned me back; he made me desolate, faint all day long."
Lamentations 1:19	"I called to my allies but they betrayed me; my priests and elders perished in the city while they searched for food to keep themselves alive."
Lamentations 2:3	"In fierce anger he has cut off every horn of Israel. He has withdrawn his right hand at the approach of the enemy; he has burned in Jacob like a flaming fire that consumes everything around it."
Lamentations 2:6	"He laid waste his dwelling like a garden; he has destroyed his place of meeting. The LORD has made Zion forget her appointed feasts

and her Sabbaths; in his fierce anger he has spurned both king and priest."

Lamentations 2:20 "Should women eat their offspring, children they have cared for? Should priest and prophet be killed in the sanctuary of the LORD?"

Lamentations 3:22-24 "The LORD's compassions never fail. They are new every morning. Great is your faithfulness. The LORD is my portion therefore I will wait for him."

Lamentations 4:11 "The LORD has given full vent to his wrath, he has poured out his fierce anger; he kindled a fire in Zion that consumed her foundations."

Lamentations 4:13 "It happened because of the sins of her prophets, the iniquities of her priests who shed within her, the blood of the righteous."

Lamentations 4:16 "The LORD himself has scattered them; he no longer watches over them. The priests are shown no honor, the elders no favor."

Lamentations 4:18 "Men stalked us at every step; we could not walk in our streets, our end drew near."

"Our days were numbered for our end had come."

God's Judgment, Marriage to the Bridegroom, The Great Tribulation

The people of Jerusalem were brought to their knees; there was nowhere else to go, nothing left to do. Israel cried out to anyone who could help defend her from the siege assaulting her from within and without. They may have called on Christian Jews to help defend them but they refused. They remembered Jesus' warnings of the signs they should look for, especially the desolating sacrilege. They remembered Luke's warning. They were watching, ready to flee without looking back. (Luke 21:20)

When they saw Jerusalem surrounded by armies, they knew desolation was near. The Zealots were at the Temple gates, within the Temple itself. The Idumaean armies were coming to the Zealots' assistance. Entering the Temple, they desecrated it. Christ's saints knew they were not to remain to fight. Seeing the Zealot and Idumaean armies surrounding the Temple, they took their Lord's warnings seriously. Without looking back, they fled to the Pella wilderness. Their rejection of their heritage created a permanent rift between them and the Jews. By AD 135, history reveals they would have nothing to do with each other.

Their flight, at their Lord's command, separated them from the faith they were brought up in but also from God's wrath poured out on that perverse, sinful generation. In God's

Judgment we hear the words of the Jews speaking to Pilate as Jesus faced his crucifixion that his blood would be on them and their children.

All that Jesus spoke was witnessed by that faithless generation but also by his faithful saints who fled, secured for 1260 days, 3.5 years. As commanded by the Lord, they fled the tribulation poured out on those who desecrated the Temple, persecuted the Lord's prophets and messengers and crucified their Messiah, as Hosea 2:14-16 and Revelation 12:6 prophesied. Just as he promised, every jot and tittle was coming to pass, to the letter.

Confirming Jesus' message to flee when Jerusalem was surrounded by armies, in 'Pella Flight', we learn Epiphanes recorded: *"Their sect began after the capture of Jerusalem, when those who believed in Christ settled at that time in Pella, of the Decapolis, next to Batanaea and the land of Bashan. They moved there and stayed. When the city was about to be captured and sacked by the Romans, as they were warned beforehand by an angel to remove from the city, deemed as it was to utter destruction, they settled at Pella, across the Jordan."*

As Numbers 10:9 prophesied, their LORD remembered them; they would be saved from their enemies. Jerusalem's destruction was approaching. The New Age and New Covenant would soon be realized in all fullness. Christ's promise to his disciples, God's promise to the faithful remnant was fulfilled in that 'moment' of history. Their LORD brought judgment to the apostate; atonement would be given the faithful remnant. We come to the time of the Crowning of the King, marriage of the Bride and Bridegroom and resurrection of the dead

MARRIAGE OF THE BRIDE AND BRIDEGROOM

To learn what the Bible refers to as the marriage of the Bride and Bridegroom, we must learn of Israel's 1st century weddings. Scripture's understanding of the wedding feast speaks more than poetry or a message of Christ's love for his Church. Those words were fulfillment of ancient Jewish wedding practices and help us understand what Christ meant when he spoke of the Marriage and Wedding Feast of the Bride and Bridegroom.

Our engagement and wedding practices do not give a true understanding of ancient Israel's preparation for the marriages of their young men and women. Their engagements were not the same as we celebrate as we plan for marriage; they were much more than that. Their engagement was a betrothal, almost a marriage, but not quite.

Studying 1st century Israel's marriage festivals, we must learn what it meant when a man approached a young woman and her family, asking for her in marriage? Studying their celebrations, we can better understand and celebrate the Covenant Jesus made and what it meant when he promised he would return for His Bride.

Ephesians 5:31-32 is symbolic of the Wedding Ceremony Jesus had in mind for his Beloved Church. *"For this reason a man will leave his father and mother and be united with his wife. The two will become one flesh. This is a profound mystery; I take it to mean Christ and his church."* Christ's church has received a marriage proposal. What did this mean to his followers; what does it mean to us? He promised "We would be One Flesh." What did the early Christians and the Hebrew nation understand this to mean?

THE MARRIAGE COVENANT
'THE BRIDE'S PRICE'

To understand Jesus' covenant with his Bride, the Church, there is much we must learn of the ancient Jewish marriage contract. When a young man wanted to marry a young woman, he prepared a covenant or contract, a 'Ketubah'. He presented it to the girl and her father. This showed them he would provide for her, and described the terms under which he would propose marriage.

He had to understand the importance of the Bride's Price, how much it would cost him if he wanted to marry her. The price was paid to her father. The Bride's price was quite high, as it cost the father much to bring his daughter up to marrying age. The man, agreeing to pay the bride's price, showed his love for the girl and how valuable she was to him. He would go to her home, present his offer of a price to the girl and her father and offer the Ketubah.

Jesus came to his bride's home to present his marriage Covenant, offering his body in forgiveness of his bride's sins. Jesus willingly, lovingly paid the Bride's Price. As in ancient ceremonies, the price was quite high. At the Last Supper Jesus promised he would pay the Bride's Price.

"This is my body, given for you."

THE WEDDING CUP

If the price was acceptable, a glass of wine was poured. The man would give her the glass. If she drank from the cup, she accepted the proposal. They would be betrothed, a legally binding contract but not a complete marriage. The betrothal might last one or two years. During this time, they prepared for the marriage but during the betrothal they were separated and could not see each other.

At the Last Supper, Jesus poured wine for his disciples, revealing the next step in the marriage contract. He took the cup and offered it, telling them to drink of it, all of them. It was the blood of the New Ketubah, poured out for many for the forgiveness of sin. (Matthew 26:28-29) The disciples drank from the cup, each accepting the Ketubah, his Covenant.

Separation of the Bridegroom and Bride.

After the betrothal, the bride and bridegroom were separated until the bridegroom completely prepared the wedding chamber. After the cup, Christ and his bride, the Church, were separated while they each prepared for the wedding day. Christ was separated from his bride at his death. In his ascension, he went away to prepare a place for her while she prepared herself for his return when they would be united as One.

Gifts for the Bride

After the cup, the Bridegroom gave the Bride special gifts to show her how he looked forward to the marriage. The gifts helped her remember his love while she awaited his return. Christ's gifts to his Bride were the gifts of the Holy Spirit. Christ's bride was assured the Spirit of the LORD would rest on her, the spirit of wisdom and understanding, counsel and might, knowledge and the fear of the LORD. (Isaiah 11:2-3) In 1 John 4:13, John declared they could know they lived in him, and he in them because he gave them his Spirit.

After Jesus' ascension, the Holy Spirit dwelt with the bride, giving her wisdom, knowledge, counsel and power, assuring her of her Lord's return, reminding her of his abiding love while he was away.

The Mikveh

The Hebrew betrothal continued with the Mikveh, a cleansing bath. This is the same word as is found in 'Baptism'. The waters of the Mikveh were symbolic of the purifying waters of rebirth. Immersed in the Mikveh, the bride was rendered ritually pure. In this cleansing, she prepared for her bridegroom's return. In the Mikveh, she would be as close to her bridegroom as it was possible to get.

Jesus provided his bride with the Mikveh, Baptism of the Holy Spirit. The disciples were not to leave Jerusalem; they were to wait for the Father's promise. (Acts 1:4) In baptism, they would be cleansed, reborn in the purifying waters of God's Holy Spirit. Immersed, cleansed in the Mikveh, baptized in the Holy Spirit, they would be as close to the bridegroom as it was possible to get.

"I go to prepare a place for you."

In his absence, the bridegroom prepared a chamber to bring his bride to for the honeymoon. His father gave the specifications for the wedding chamber. He could not go for his bride until his father approved of the wedding chamber. When asked about the time of the wedding, he would say, *"It is not for me know; only my father knows."*

Jesus told his disciples he had to go away to prepare a place for them. He promised he would come back and take them to himself, that where he was, they would be also. (John 14:1-3) As in Israel's ceremonies, the bridegroom's father gave the specifications for the wedding chamber. God determined when the chamber was ready. Only God, the Bridegroom's Father, knew when the wedding would occur. Jesus told his disciples exactly what the bridegroom told his friends: "Only My Father Knows."

THE BRIDE IS CONSECRATED.

While the man prepared the bridal chamber, his bride was consecrated, set apart. If she went outside, she covered her face with a veil, showing she was betrothed, 'bought with a price'. She prepared herself for the wedding, making sure she was beautiful and everything was ready for when her bridegroom returned. In Hebrew tradition, the bridegroom often returned late at night. His bride would have her lamps and all her belongings ready. Her sisters and friends, her bridesmaids, waiting for the bridegroom's return, were ready to celebrate.

While he was away, Jesus' bride was consecrated, set apart, waiting for her Lord's return. Preparing for his return, she made herself beautiful. She 'wore a veil' showing she was betrothed and had been bought with a price, the blood of Christ, which covered her sins as a veil covers the face.

THE BRIDEGROOM RETURNS FOR HIS BRIDE.

When the father determined the chamber was ready, he told the bridegroom to get his bride. Drawing close, he would blow the shofar and shout, telling her to gather all she needed. He and a friend would go into her home and snatch her away. This date was known by all who prepared for the wedding ceremony.

The bride and bridesmaids knew when the bridegroom would arrive. The Parable of the wise and foolish virgins reveals this. The kingdom of heaven was compared to ten virgins who took their lamps to meet the bridegroom. Five were wise; five were foolish. The foolish took no extra oil for their lamps; the wise took flasks of oil with their lamps. The bridegroom was delayed and they slumbered. At midnight, the cry went out that the Bridegroom was coming. They rose and trimmed their lamps. The foolish asked the wise for some oil but the wise told them there would not be enough. They needed go to the dealers to buy some for themselves. While they were away, the Bridegroom came; those who were ready went with him and the door was shut. (Matthew 25:1-10)

All ten virgins had their lamps filled, waiting for the bridegroom's arrival. Jesus painted a picture of the bride and bridesmaids anticipating the bridegroom's planned arrival. The bridegroom in ancient Israel arrived one half hour before midnight in a grand procession to take his bride to the wedding chamber. When the shout was made that he was on the way, they would trim their lamps and go out to meet him.

The Bride was not surprised by that day. Her Lord told her he would return on the Day that Only the Father Knows. They were not in darkness, so that day would surprise them. (1 Thessalonians 5:1-11) She knew 'the Day and Hour'. At her home, their lamps were ready to light the procession once he arrived. They were celebrating; his coming was repeatedly reported by God's holy prophets, but after hours of waiting, they slept. Hearing the shout that he was on the way, they gathered to greet him. Needing oil to refill their lamps, the foolish virgins had to run to get more. In their absence, they missed his arrival.

Jesus did not return without warning. His coming was repeatedly announced by faithful messengers. The prophets, the Gospel writers and the letters to the churches all prepared the bride for the Day and Hour he would return. Paul assured his people they did not need to worry about times and dates. They knew the day of the Lord would come as a thief in the night. Paul's 'brethren' were not in darkness, so that day would surprise them as a thief. They were not 'sleeping'; they were alert and watching. (1 Thessalonians 5:1-6) The bride was not in darkness; she knew the day and hour.

At his return there was a grand procession. As He approached, his bride sang out, *"Baruch haba!"* *"Blessed is he who comes."* Idiomatic wedding talk, they shouted, welcoming him who was coming for his bride, fulfilling Jesus' words as he cried over Jerusalem that they would not see him again until they said, *"Baruch haba, b'shem Adonai!"* *"Blessed is he who comes in the name of the Lord!"* (Matthew 23:39)

At his return, the 'dead in Christ', the saints of the Old Covenant, ascended in resurrection life to meet their Lord 'In the Air'. Gathered with his faithful living saints, they were joined as his faithful Beloved Bride. The Old Covenant Saints, the redeemed of Israel and Judah and the redeemed Gentiles, welcomed him and rejoiced in the return of the beloved Bridegroom. Together they sang:

"Baruch Haba, B' Shem Adonai!"
"Blessed is He who comes in the Name of the Lord!"

Our Bridegroom has returned for his Bride. Paul assured the Thessalonians their Lord would come from heaven with a shout, the voice of the archangel and the trumpet of God. The dead in Christ would rise first. Those who were alive would be caught up together with them in the clouds, the Shekinah Glory, to meet the Lord 'in the air', in the Spirit Realm. They would be with the Lord, forever. (1 Thessalonians 4:16-7)

God determined the wedding chamber was ready. The Father told the Bridegroom to get his Bride. With his shout, at the sound of the shofar, the dead in Christ and all living saints were ready. Christ, with the hosts of heaven, gathered the bride and bridesmaids. With their Bridegroom they were brought to the wedding chamber.

LET ALL KNOW, THE SHOFAR HAS SOUNDED.
THE BRIDEGROOM HAS RETURNED FOR HIS BRIDE.

WITHIN THE BRIDAL CHAMBER

In Israel's ancient weddings, the bridegroom and bride celebrated for seven days in the wedding chamber. The bridegroom took his bride to the wedding chamber while a friend waited outside the door. When the marriage was consummated, the bridegroom told his friend through the door. He would tell the guests. They would celebrate for seven days until the Bride and Bridegroom emerged from the wedding chamber.

The seven days in the bridal chamber are misunderstood by many of us. Pre-tribulation dispensational thought says Jesus raptures his bride, the Church, to heaven for the seven years of tribulation. After these seven years, the Bridegroom returns with his bride to bring Israel into the fold so they can become his Bride. Nowhere in Scripture are we told of two brides, Christian saints and the people of Israel.

In "We shall meet Him in the Air", Don Preston assures us the Wedding occurred on the earth. The Bride, faithful remnant Israel, was not taken to heaven for the wedding; she celebrated with her Lord, secured beneath her Lord's canopy. The faithful Gentile saints, acknowledging the Lord's restoration of remnant Israel, rejoiced in the marriage. At the consummation of the wedding, they joyfully anticipated the Wedding Feast. (pp. 161-4)

In "Prophecy Fulfilled", he also shows that in ancient Jewish marriages, if the bride had never been married, the wedding would be seven days; if she was widowed or divorced, it would only be three days, the three years of Great Tribulation, AD 66-70. Though God had divorced faithless Israel, He promised to marry faithful Israel. God would allure her and bring her into the wilderness and speak tenderly to her. They would call him 'My Husband'.

God would make a covenant that day with the beasts of the fields, the birds of the air and the creeping things on the ground. God would abolish the bow, the sword and war from the land. They would lie down in safety. God would betroth his faithful bride to him forever in justice and righteousness. In the Pella wilderness no harm would come upon the Bride. The 'wild beasts' would be held away; war would not come nigh; they would abide under their Lord's Huppah in his Shekinah Presence. (Hosea 2:14, 16-20)

The wedding could not start until judgment was ready to fall on the land and was celebrated on earth. Biblical understanding of the 'wedding canopy' or 'huppah' does not refer to heaven, but Christ's covering of his bride, his shelter and protection. 'Huppah', in Isaiah 4:2-5, refers to God's eternal Temple covering, the Shekinah Presence, Christ, Himself. On that great day, the Branch of the LORD would be glorious; the fruit of the land would be the glory of the survivors of Israel. All who were left in Zion and remained in the New Jerusalem would be holy. The Lord would wash away the filth of the daughters of Zion and cleanse the bloodstains of Jerusalem by judgment and burning.

On that Holy Day, the LORD would create over Mt. Zion a cloud by day, smoke and flaming fire by night. Over all there would be a canopy, the Shekinah Presence.

In the Great Tribulation, the Bridegroom kept his bride secure under his huppah. In His Shekinah Presence, she was secluded from the wrath poured on the desolate. Jesus warned his bride that when she saw Jerusalem surrounded by armies, she would know its desolation had come near. (Luke 21:20) His Bride understood; at the 7th Trumpet and the shout of her Lord, she fled to the wedding chamber, the mountains of Pella. Covered by Christ's Presence, she was secure. Sheltered in Pella, the faithful Gentiles, the bride's faithful bridesmaids, rejoiced in their coming vindication. Acknowledging their Lord's judgment against their persecutors, they awaited the glorious Wedding Feast.

MARRIAGE SUPPER AND WEDDING FEAST

The wedding feast could not start until God's judgment was complete. We learn of the timing of God's judgment and the Wedding Feast in Revelation 19:1-11. God judged the great harlot who had corrupted the earth with her fornication and avenged on her the blood of his servants. They all cried 'Hallelujah; the Lord God Almighty reigns'! They rejoiced, giving him the glory. The marriage of the Lamb has come; the Bride had made herself ready for her beloved Bridegroom.

Judgment of the Great Whore was complete. A divorce decree was issued for faithless Israel who had become a harlot. A new covenant, a new Ketubah has been given. The virgin, chaste bride, faithful Israel and Judah have been joined in marriage to her beloved Bridegroom. His people rejoiced. The glorious marriage feast has come. The saints rejoiced in destruction of Mystery Babylon. They celebrated, anticipating the glorious Marriage Feast. The bride made herself ready; she rejoiced in her marriage to the Lamb.

Isaiah prophesied this Great Day. 'The moon would be confounded, the sun ashamed'. The LORD of hosts would reign on Mt. Zion. He would manifest his glory. He made the city a heap, the fortified city, a ruin. The palace of aliens is a city no more, never to be rebuilt.

On that mountain, the LORD of hosts made a feast of fat things, full of marrow, wine on the lees, well refined. He destroyed on that mountain the covering cast on all peoples, the veil spread over all the nations. He has swallowed up death forever! The LORD God has wiped away all tears from their faces. The reproach of his people has been taken away from all the earth. (Isaiah 25:2, 6-8)

Christ's bride in Revelation 19 is the faithful remnant of Israel and Judah but our Lord proclaims his glorious bride is the redeemed of All Nations, faithful Israel, Judah and Gentiles, as revealed by Paul in Ephesians 5:31-32. At his return in glory, God's New Covenant brought all faithful nations together as his Virgin Bride. In Christ, all his people are joined together in Him as His Bride.

The marriage feast started after three years in the bridal chamber. Vast multitudes celebrated with great merrymaking. After 'three days', the three years of tribulation, Christ and his Bride celebrated the Marriage Supper. The wedding was consummated through the destruction and desolation of Jerusalem. The feast started after the wedding, lasting seven days, as in Genesis 29:21-27 & Judges 14:10-18. The wedding feast of the Lamb was revealed in a great feast. The veil of disbelief was taken from all nations. Spiritual death, separation from God, was forever destroyed. All tears were wiped away. Reproach of his faithful people was taken away.

CHRIST'S MISSION, FULFILLED IN THE FALL FESTIVALS

Christ's life and ministry, from his conception to his glorious Parousia, fulfill all the Jewish feasts, the Spring and Fall Festivals. The marriage feast is the culmination of the High Holy Days of the Fall Festivals. Rosh-Hashanah, Yom Kippur and Sukkoth proclaim completion and consummation of our Lord's mission to his bride. Faithful Israel and the Gentile nations are One with the Bridegroom.

The 7th trumpet brought God's judgment. At his judgment, the Bridegroom returned for his Bride. At Yom Kippur, at the sounding of the Great Trumpet, atonement was brought to all who had turned in obedience to the God of Israel. Sukkoth, the Feast of Tabernacles, brought the New Jerusalem down from heaven as a bride adorned for her husband. The seven days of Sukkoth were the seven days of the wedding feast. Christ's Church rejoiced in the Bride and Bridegroom's glorious Wedding Feast.

The celebration continues as new saints proclaim the Bridegroom's faithfulness. The celebration continues today. We have received our invitation; we are all welcome to join the celebration.

'It was granted her to be clothed with fine white linen,
bright and pure,
For the fine linen is the righteous deeds of the saints.' Revelation 19:8

The Wedding Feast
Of the Bridegroom and his Bride
The Hatan and the Kallah
Come, for all things are ready!
The Lamb and the Bride of Christ
Cordially invite you to a Glorious Wedding Feast.

The Bride will be adorned in finest white linen.
There will be Music, Harpists, Flutists, Trumpets,
Cymbals and much Singing.

The Flowers will be provided by The Lamb's Eternal Father.
Following the Wedding Ceremony, There will be a Great Feast.
You are all Cordially Invited to Attend.

Dress in Your Finest.
Come, Prepared to Celebrate with the Groom and His Beautiful Bride.
Come, For All is Ready.
We are Most Anxious for You to Attend.
With all My Love,
Christ Jesus, the Lamb

Did you receive your invitation? Will you be attending?
R.S.V.P.

We see complete fulfillment of the Wedding of Christ and his Bride. We rejoice in the betrothal of our Lord with his Beloved Church and understand why he had to go away to prepare a place for his Bride. He has returned for his faithful Bride and held her secure in the Bridal Chamber in the Pella wilderness. (Revelation 12:6) God, his Father determined the chamber was ready to receive the Bride. All was secure; she would be protected from God's wrath against the faithless of his Covenant.

These feasts, Rosh-Hashanah, Yom Kippur and Sukkoth, the glorious marriage, the sanctification of the remnant who in obedience turned to the Lord, and the Wedding Feast were celebrated by the faithful saints of the New Covenant Church, the first-fruits of the believers, just as Christ was their first-fruit. We are called to follow in witness to all who come after us. These faithful witnesses, Christ's Bride and Bridesmaids proclaimed, and we must proclaim, all are welcome to the Wedding Feast.

The feast will continue to be celebrated as each new generation comes to the knowledge of the love of their Bridegroom. These early Christians were the seed from which the New Covenant Church was born. This Church, from that tiny seed, grew to become the largest tree, just as Jesus taught in his Parable of the Mustard Seed. These Christians, with their Savior, were the seed that was planted. In their Lord's vineyard, in His glorious Shekinah Presence, that seed flourished and grew. It will continue to grow until:

"The Earth will be filled with the Presence and the Glory of God,
As the Waters Cover the Seas."

Departure for Home

After the wedding festivities and celebrations in ancient Israel, the bridegroom left his father's home and the wedding chamber with his bride. He took her to the new home he had prepared for her; they started their lives together, united as husband and wife.

We see the shadow of the entire Jewish wedding ceremony, this glorious Holy Day, this Holy Celebration, completely fulfilled in Revelation 21:1-3. Following the Wedding Feast, the Bride was brought to their glorious home, the New Heaven and Earth, the New Jerusalem. John shows us a New Heaven and Earth; the first heaven and earth had passed away, the sea was no more. The Holy City, the New Jerusalem, descended from Heaven, prepared as a Bride adorned for her husband. A voice from the throne declared:

Behold the Dwelling Place of God is with Man.
He will dwell with them. They will be his people. God, Himself, will be with them.

The sea was no more. There was no longer a separation between Heaven and Earth, no longer a separation between Jews and Gentiles. The bride of Christ, the faithful redeemed remnant of All Israel and the faithful Gentiles were united with their Bridegroom. The Sea no longer separated them; it no longer separates us from each other and from God. United with Christ, they were One; we are One in Him. We can rejoice, knowing:

Christ is in us; We are in Christ.
In Christ, we are One Flesh, Echad!

Chapter 5

CELEBRATING THE HIGH HOLY DAYS

ROSH-HASHANAH—YOM KIPPUR—SUKKOTH
CHRIST AND THE CELEBRATION OF THE FALL FESTIVALS

The Spring Holy Days show us God has brought salvation to his children. These Holy Days of the Jewish year were celebrated through Jesus' entire life and ministry in witness to the promises God gave his people. His ministry through 3-years of service to God culminated in his death at Passover as the Pascal Lamb, his resurrection at First-Fruits, his ascension and the outpouring of the Holy Spirit at Shavuot.

This is not the end of the story. Turning to the Fall Festivals, we discover much our faith has over-looked. Learning what Israel celebrates in these Fall Festivals helps us see what we are called to celebrate as we acknowledge all our Lord has done to bring his people sanctification, deliverance, redemption and restoration.

From the end of the Spring Festivals to the start of the Fall Festivals, four months have passed, symbolic of the forty years Israel wandered in the wilderness until they were gathered with the LORD in His Promised Land. After Shavuot and the birth of the Church, we approach the Fall Festivals, Rosh-Hashanah, Yom Kippur and Sukkot, God's High Holy Days. We are called to rejoice in the regathering of faithful Israel into covenant with the Lord, Marriage of the Bride to the Bridegroom, Atonement of the remnant and Restoration of All Things.

We must be careful as we continue to study God's Holy Convocations and Appointed Feasts. Too many are taught falsehoods, confusing the faithful, denying the truth to those who most need to hear it. Too much of the Church believes that at the sound of the Trumpet, faithful Christians will be raptured to heaven. The world will face unfathomable tribulation brought on by Antichrist and his legions. After seven years, Christ will visibly return, destroy the faithless nations and reign with his saints in his earthly kingdom.

Careful study reveals the Fall Holy Days speak of the '2nd half' of Jesus' ministry. For 3 ½ years, from April AD 66 to September AD 70, we see completion of our Lord's ministry to Israel, in the Fullness of Time. In the Sabbatical Month of Tishri, at Rosh-Hashanah, judgment was brought on those who had forsaken the LORD's Covenant. At Yom Kippur, atonement was given the faithful remnant, tried in the fire. At Sukkoth, the New Jerusalem descended from Heaven. God's faithful servants were delivered and restored.

Throughout the High Holy Days, we learn of the last days of the Mosaic Covenant and the First Days of God's Heavenly, Eternal Covenant. As Jesus' earthly mission lasted 3 ½ years, these 3 ½ years complete his Heavenly mission. In Christ's Kingdom, faithful Israel, Judah and Gentiles are One.

THE SEASON OF TESHUVAH

To start their Fall Festivals there is the season of Teshuvah, celebrated for forty days, from Elul 1 through Tishri 10, Yom Kippur, mid-August to October. Elul is interpreted as an acronym, "Aleph-Lamed—Vav-Lamed" representing The Song of Solomon 6:3 *Ani L'Dodi V'Dodi Li "I am my Beloved's. My Beloved is mine."* 'My Beloved' was God; 'I' was the Jewish people.

Teshuvah, in Hebrew, means 'return or repent'. Israel was to approach the throne of God in a season of soul-searching and repentance. In God's command to return to him, Teshuvah draws both Jews and Christians closer to God and his Torah, his Christ, than at any other time in the year. In the month of Elul, Israel was to repent, returning to God, their Beloved. Returning to him, God promised he would return to them in love.

Teshuvah is actually a process of returning to the way God intended everything should be from the beginning. In creation, God gave us perfection, harmony with his creation, each other and him. In our repentance God corrects the defect of sin, restoring us to our original character. In God's hands, our turning to him in repentance restores the beauty, perfection and peace of his creation, as it was 'In the Beginning.' Offering Teshuvah, God promises, 'All Things' can be made new.

Thirty days into the celebration, on Tishri 1, are the final ten days of the celebration. The days between Rosh-Hashanah and Yom Kippur are the Days of Awe. The Sabbath falling within these ten days is 'Shabbat Shuvah', Sabbath of Return or 'Shabbat Teshuvah', Sabbath of Repentance. On Shabbat Shuvah, the 1st Sabbath of the New Year, everyone strives to live out the prayers and promises made on Rosh-Hashanah. They commit themselves to Torah study, prayer and repentance, to receive forgiveness of sins committed on other Sabbaths.

Many Rabbis suggest that the closer one comes to God, the more he sees how far he still is from Him. This helps them face their shortcomings in service to God. At Shabbat Shuvah, with each step forward they must repent of past shortcomings when they were further removed from God. During Shabbat Teshuvah services, the 'Song of Moses', Deuteronomy 32, is read, prophesying Israel's turning from God's command and the punishment she would endure because of her straying.

At Shabbat Shuvah, Israel is called to return to their LORD. Hosea 14:2-10 is chanted in the Sabbath service, calling them to return to the LORD so their iniquity would be taken away and the LORD would accept that which was good.

As they faced their LORD's judgment, Joel 2:11-16 called the people to return to God. The day of the LORD would be terrible; none could endure it. The LORD called them to return to him with all their heart, fasting, weeping and mourning. If they returned to the LORD, he would be merciful. They were to blow the trumpet in Zion, sanctifying a fast, calling a solemn assembly. All were to be gathered together. The whole community was to come to the LORD in repentance.

Teshuvah, returning to the LORD, was exactly what John the Baptist preached, calling Israel to return to the LORD in repentance. In John's ministry, he preached Teshuvah, baptism of repentance for the forgiveness of sins. His message of repentance and return was to prepare Israel for the day their Lord would return to them. John called the people to repentance, crying for them to bear fruit that befit repentance. Even then, the axe was laid to the root of the trees; every tree that did not bear good fruit would be cut down, thrown into the fire. (Luke 3:8-9) John's words were God's command; all were to offer Teshuvah, returning in repentance before the Lord, preparing for his return. During the forty days that Jesus dwelt in the wilderness, tempted by Satan, John preached repentance. At Teshuvah, John was calling God's people to repent, returning to the Lord, serving him in holiness.

Hebrew scholars say we do teshuvah when we seek and grant forgiveness, refusing to continue in our transgressions against others and against God. Much time was needed, as much spiritual and physical effort was required. The month of Elul and the first ten days of Tishri gave time before Yom Kippur for God's people to repent and return to God, and time to ask forgiveness of others who they had offended.

Yom Kippur only atoned for sins committed against God. In transgressions against others, Yom Kippur did not atone until the offended was appeased. (Mishnah Yoma 8:9) Repentance for transgressions against others included restoration of what was taken but that was only the start of the process. The person who had been wronged had to be appeased, approached repeatedly until he forgave. If he did not forgive, the repentant returned with three friends, seeking forgiveness. The process was repeated if the victim was still not appeased. After repeated attempts, if he did not forgive, he was left alone. The person who refused to grant forgiveness was the sinner. In Teshuvah, God considered those who did not ask forgiveness and those who did not offer forgiveness both sinners.

John the Baptist prepared Israel for the High Holy Days. During those forty days, he called the people to observe Teshuvah. In repentance, they were to ask forgiveness for offenses committed against their neighbors and against God, returning to Him in obedience.

Every day of Elul except the day before Rosh-Hashanah, the shofar was blown, calling Israel to repent. On that last day, the shofar remained silent, revealing Rosh-Hashanah was concealed. Rosh-Hashanah is 'Yom Ha' Keseh', the Hidden Day. 'Keseh' comes from the Hebrew verb 'Kacah', meaning conceal, cover or hide. The significance of Rosh-Hashanah, when their LORD would return in judgment, was concealed but knowledge of ancient

Hebrew idiom reveals Christ would return on Yom Ha' Keseh, this Hidden, Concealed Day.

Psalm 27 was recited after each morning and evening liturgy, in self-evaluation. *"The LORD is my light and salvation, whom shall I fear? The LORD is the stronghold of my life, of whom shall I be afraid? One thing I ask of the LORD; this is what I seek, that I may dwell in the house of the LORD all the days of my life, to gaze upon the beauty of the LORD, to seek him in his temple. He will keep me safe in his dwelling. He will hide me in the shelter of his tabernacle and set me high on a rock."* Psalm 27:1, 4-5

The Midrash, the Oral Torah, says "The LORD is my Light" speaks of Rosh-Hashanah; "My Salvation" speaks of Yom Kippur; "He will hide me in the shelter of his Tabernacle" speaks of the Feast of Tabernacles. The message to the children of the LORD was clear; they were to offer Teshuvah before Rosh-Hashanah. As Rosh-Hashanah was concealed as the Day of Judgment, they were not to wait until Rosh-Hashanah. They were to live lives of repentance. If they waited until Rosh-Hashanah, they would have to endure the Days of Awe.

At Teshuvah, as faithful servants of our Messiah, we must examine our lives and see how we have departed from God's will. Dwelling in God's presence, God draws us ever closer to him. Living repentant lives, we must thank him for his forgiveness and his presence with us and proclaim fulfillment of our Lord's promises.

Understanding Teshuvah, we see the Children of Israel knew their need for repentance. At the same time they were to return to their LORD, their LORD, their Messiah was ready to return to them, to draw his faithful remnant to himself. They could dwell with him for all eternity. The season of Teshuvah, returning to the LORD, prepared them for their LORD's Return. He promised he would Return to them.

LET ALL KNOW, THE SHOFAR HAS SOUNDED.
YOU ARE CALLED TO PENITENCE; RETURN TO YOUR GOD.
"REPENT; THE KINGDOM OF HEAVEN IS AT HAND."

ROSH-HASHANAH—'YOM TERUAH'—THE AWAKENING SHOFAR BLAST

'Yom Teruah', the Day of the Awakening Blast, was the time of repentance. The Jewish months began with the blowing of the Shofar. At their appointed feasts, at the beginning of their months, they were to blow the trumpets over their burnt offerings and peace offerings, as remembrances before God. (Numbers 10:10)

The festive year was seven months long; Tishri was the last month of the festival trumpets. The last trumpet was sounded on this New Moon Day, the 'Final Trumpet's

Day'. On the 1st day of the 7th month, they observed a day of solemn rest, proclaimed with trumpet blasts, a Holy Convocation. (Leviticus 23:24, Numbers 29:1)

Yom Teruah proclaims rule of the Messiah King and the counting of the years of kingly rule. The final ceremony in the coronation was the Trumpet Blast. John spoke of the Day of Trumpets and the sounding of the Last Trumpet. When the 7th angel blew his trumpet, loud voices in heaven cried out that the kingdoms of the world had become the Kingdom of our LORD and of His Christ. He would reign forever. The twenty-four elders fell in worship to God. He had taken great power and began his reign. (Revelation 11:15-17)

'ZICHRON TERUAH'—MEMORIAL AT THE BLOWING OF THE SHOFAR

The Day of Trumpets was 'Zichron Teruah', a Memorial Day. At the beginning of their year, Israel understood the dead would be joined with their descendants, ushering in God's Kingdom on Earth. Paul referred to the Last Trumpet, resurrection of the dead and Jesus' 2nd Advent, all connected with this glorious day. He told his people a mystery. They would not all sleep but would all be changed. In the twinkling of the eye, at the last trumpet, the dead would be raised imperishable; the living would be changed. (1 Corinthians 15:51-52)

The Lord descended from heaven with a cry of command, the archangel's call and the trumpet of God. The dead in Christ rose first; those who were alive were caught up with them in the Shekinah Glory Cloud, to meet the Lord 'in the air', in the 'Spiritual realm'. They would forever be with the Lord. (1 Thessalonians 4:16-17)

In Numbers 10:1-2, the LORD told Moses to make two silver trumpets to call the congregation and direct their movements. On that Great Day, the shofar called the faithful remnant to gather, separating themselves from the judgment that was ready to fall on that faithless generation. Their LORD drew them to him, sheltering them in His Presence. Psalm 27:5 also speaks of this Great Day. In the time of 'Jacob's trouble', God would hide them in his pavilion; he would set them on a rock. The faithful remnant understood at the time of 'Jacob's trouble', the Rock, Christ, would cover them, protecting them from the time of trouble.

Learning of Israel's celebration of Rosh-Hashanah, the Last Trumpet Day, we discover the shofar has sounded. All were to wake from their sleep. Paul called his people to wake and rise from the dead. Christ would shine on them. They were not to grieve the Holy Spirit, in whom they were sealed for the day of redemption. They were to put away all bitterness, wrath and anger; they were to be kind to each other, forgiving each other, just as God, in Christ, forgave them. (Ephesians 5:14. 4:30-31)

Sealing to the day of redemption guides us to Yom Kippur. God gave Israel and his church this festival to prepare them for Jesus' judgment coming at Rosh-Hashanah. With this judgment, God's remnant was promised redemption; they were sealed to the closing of the gates on Yom Kippur. God would grant mercy to all who repented, and justice to those who did not repent. It was Yom-Teruah, the Sounding of the Shofar, Zichron Teruah, the Remembrance Blast, Yom Ha' Din, the Day of Judgment. The Shofar announced resurrection of the dead and judgment against the unrepentant. The faithful were sanctified; the faithless faced God's justice.

Rosh Hashanah—'Yom Ha' Keseh'—The Day of Concealment

Rosh-Hashanah is also known as 'Yom Ha' Keseh', The Day of Concealment. Isaiah 57:1 speaks of this day. The righteous perished; no one took it to heart. No one considered that the righteous were taken from the evil. In Hebrew, 'perishes' is translated 'vanishes'. The righteous vanished, they were concealed but no one took it to heart; no one understood. God's mercy to the faithful remnant was hidden from the unrepentant. Though no one considered the righteous were taken from the evil, the repentant were fully aware of their guilt and the mercy and forgiveness God granted. The unrepentant did not acknowledge their crime, the accusations brought against them, the trial they had to face nor the outcome of that trial. In their blindness, this was concealed. They could not see, would not see and refused to see.

Yom Ha' keseh, this Concealed, Hidden Day was the Day that Only the Father Knows. As it was a New Moon Day, a 'Rosh Chodesh', its Appearance, its Coming, was hidden, concealed from all but God. Man could not know; angels could not know; even the Son could not know its coming. As the Son was man, he could not know when the New Moon would be seen. He could not know the Day or Hour of his Coming, but he knew his Coming would be on Yom Ha' Keseh, this hidden, Concealed Day. Yom Ha' Keseh could not be celebrated until it was confirmed by two faithful witnesses. On the last two days of Elul, the Sanhedrin's High Court, the 'Beit Din', called witnesses to record their sighting of the New Moon Crescent. When the Sanhedrin received confirmation of the New Moon Crescent by two faithful witnesses, they sanctified the New Moon and the celebration could begin. The Day that only The Father Knows could not be celebrated until the Sanhedrin confirmed the New Moon Crescent acknowledged as appearing.

Rosh-Hashanah—'Yom Ha' Din'—Day of Judgment

Yom Ha' Din, the Day of Judgment, has come to the children of God. The books of Life and Death have been opened. The righteous dead were resurrected, 'anastasis'. They could stand before God in his Presence and his Glory. The wicked faced God's wrath. Sealed in the book of death, they were separated from the faithful and from God. The intermediate, the average individuals had until Yom Kippur until their fate was sealed. Their fate was written in neither the book of life nor the book of death. They had to endure the Great Tribulation, the Days of Awe until Yom Kippur when their fate would be sealed.

Through the 3-years of Great Tribulation, they were tried as silver is refined, cleansed as with fuller's soap. After the Great Tribulation, if they turned to the Lord in repentance they would receive life. United with their Lord, they could stand at the Wedding Feast and rejoice in God's Eternal Kingdom, the New Jerusalem. The disobedient, who refused to repent, would be separated from their Lord and His Kingdom. Their names would be forever sealed in the Book of Death.

'KIDDUSHIN' TO 'NISSU' IN'—THE WEDDING OF THE BRIDEGROOM

The Marriage of the Bride has come. The Bride's Kiddushin, her betrothal, has reached its completion. She has come to the Nissu' in, the day of her Nuptials. The shofar has sounded; the Bride has been snatched away by her beloved. Taken from the world, the Mosaic Covenant Age of death, she fled with her Bridegroom to the Wedding Chamber, his pavilion where she was sheltered in His Shekinah Presence.

This Wedding Day, this Nissu' in, was 'Yom Ha' keseh', the Hidden, Concealed Day. As we learned in the preparation for the wedding, the Bridegroom could not go for his bride until God the Father determined the chamber was ready for the Bride. Only the Father knew!

Understanding God's omnipotent wisdom, we see his careful planning through the forty years preparing for the Day of Judgment. We also acknowledge Christ's diligent preparations for the Wedding Chamber where the Bride would abide with the Bridegroom. The Father was assured everything was ready.

The Bridegroom perfectly prepared the Bridal Chamber; the wilderness shelter was ready to receive his beloved Bride. The Father proclaimed Yom Ha' keseh had come; the Bridegroom could go for his Bride to bring her to the safety of the Wedding Chamber; they would be united as one. The woman fled to the wilderness mountains of Pella, the place prepared for her, to be nourished for 1,260 days. (Revelation 12:6)

Through all the years of destruction and desolation throughout Jerusalem, the bride was covered in the arms of her Beloved. In her Lord's Presence, crossing the Jordan, she fled the abomination and knew security with and in her Lord. (Hosea 2:14-16, Revelation 12:6, 14) His 'huppah' covered her; his abiding presence secured her. She knew the fullness of her Lord's love; the nation's desolation would not come nigh.

The Bride lived in the abiding presence of her Bridegroom through the tribulation and desolation. His Shekinah Presence stood over her, assuring her she was safe. She celebrated with her Lord, awaiting the glorious Wedding Feast. The faithful remnant, who turned in repentance to their Lord, would celebrate as well, rejoicing in the marriage of the Bride to her Bridegroom. They celebrated in Pella, awaiting the day the Bride would come out of the Wedding Chamber to celebrate the Marriage Feast.

HA' MELECH—THE KING ON HIS THRONE

A term associated with Rosh-Hashanah is Ha' Melech, the King. The shofar blown on Rosh-Hashanah was the Last Trumpet. At the sound of the shofar, the Lord descended from heaven. The dead in Christ rose first; those who were alive were caught up with them in the Shekinah Glory Cloud. There was a glorious coronation; the Messiah was crowned Ha' Melech, King of All the Earth.

Daniel 7:9-14 spoke of this coronation. Thrones were set in place. The Ancient of Days took his seat. The court sat in judgment; the books were opened. With the clouds of heaven, there came one like a son of man. He was presented before the Ancient of Days and was given dominion, glory and kingdom. All peoples, nations and languages served him. His dominion is everlasting; it will never pass away or be destroyed.

John saw the same vision. In heaven, he saw an open door. A voice like a trumpet told him 'Come up hither; I will show you what must take place after this.' A throne stood in heaven with one seated on the throne. (Revelation 4:1-2) Daniel and John proclaimed the coronation of Christ the King, the Ha' Melech, and the start of his reign as King of kings and Lord of lords, the King of the Kingdom of Heaven. As we sang at his birth, we must proclaim:

"He Has Come to Make His Blessings Known, far as the Curse is found!"

LET ALL KNOW, THE SHOFAR HAS SOUNDED.
OUR LORD HAS TAKEN HIS THRONE. OUR KING WILL REIGN FOREVER!

THE DAYS OF AWE

Between Rosh-Hashanah and Yom Kippur are the Days of Awe, the Days of Repentance. Time was short; they were to repent, cleansing themselves of their sins. Isaiah 1:18 speaks of their sinfulness and God's command for repentance. *"Let us reason together, says the LORD. Though your sins are like scarlet, they shall be as white as snow."* The ten Days of Awe were a time for serious introspection to consider the sins they had committed the previous year and to repent before Yom Kippur.

Synagogue tables and vestments are draped in white. Worshipers wear white gowns to remember the depth of their sin and how they long to be made white as snow. Everyone sees their sins, the color of scarlet, the outcome of impurities that had to be removed. They were surrounded by pure white, reminding them of their sins' blackness. Their sin reddened them with shame but they were assured they could be washed clean.

A theme of the Days of Awe was their belief that God had Books he wrote their names in. On Rosh-Hashanah, God wrote the names of those who would live and those who would die. They believed acts of repentance, prayer and good deeds, acts of charity could change these decrees. They strived to repent, cleansing themselves. They asked God to forgive them and grant them atonement.

Restoration came at Yom Kippur. Regeneration, started at Rosh-Hashanah, was complete. Through the Days of Awe, everyone's wish was to have his name inscribed in the Book of Life. At the final service of Yom Kippur, their wish was that their names would be sealed in the Book of Life. Once the seal was made, it was binding, not subject to change.

Two Rabbinic Schools spoke of the Books of Life and Death. The House of Hillel believed three books were opened, one for the thoroughly wicked, one for the thoroughly righteous, one for the intermediate. The thoroughly wicked were immediately inscribed in the Book of Death, the thoroughly righteous, in the Book of Life. The Intermediate were held off until Yom Kippur. If they repented and returned to their LORD, they were inscribed in the Book of Life. The House of Shammai believed there were only two books. The thoroughly righteous were immediately inscribed in the Book of Life, the thoroughly wicked, in the Book of Death. This leaves us with a question. If Shammai was correct, the intermediate had no deliverance, no forgiveness.

However, the Tanakh assures us that: *"There is no one who does good."* Psalm 14:1b
"Cursed is the man who does not uphold the words of the law by carrying them out." Deuteronomy 27:26
"The LORD is our righteousness. Jeremiah 23:6

These verses reveal the seriousness of our sins and our inability to achieve our own righteousness. Only our Lord's righteousness can save us from our sins. Our self-righteousness can do nothing to grant atonement. Israel knew they needed to turn to God in repentance. John the Baptist confirmed this. Those who repented would be cleansed, spared the wrath that would befall their nation and people.

To the New Covenant Church, these Days of Awe were the shadow of the Great Tribulation. The righteous were written in the Book of Life, the wicked, in the Book of Death. Forsaking the Lord, they would face God's judgment. The righteous, secured in Pella, dwelt in their Lord's Presence. The intermediate faced great tribulation. For their names to be inscribed in the Book of Life, they had to face the awesome wrath of God. They would be tried as silver is refined, cleansed, as with fuller's soap.

Fulfillment of these Days of Awe came in the tribulation Israel faced. Atonement would be received by those who repented. That faithless generation would face God's judgment; the faithful remnant would be forgiven. The remnant could rejoice and we rejoice knowing their names and ours have been inscribed and sealed in God's Book of Life. God's decree was binding; in Christ, they were forever cleansed. They have their Yom Kippur, their Day of Atonement.

"THOUGH THEIR SINS WERE AS SCARLET,
IN CHRIST, THEY WERE AS WHITE AS SNOW."
(ISAIAH 1:18)

Jesus spoke of the power of those Days of Awe and all that would happen after the tribulation. Immediately after the tribulation, the sun would be darkened; the moon would not give its light. The stars would fall from the skies; the powers of the heavens would be shaken. At that time, the son of man would appear in the skies. He would send his angels with a loud trumpet call. They would gather his elect from one end of heaven to the other. (Matthew 24:29-31)

The sun was darkened. The moon did not give its light. As at his birth and death, at his return, the Heavens declared God's Glory, completion of our Lord's mission to his people. We can't begin to imagine what our Lord was telling his disciples, but they understood. They had heard those words many times. Scripture foretold the destruction of nations, including Jerusalem's condemnation. With Jesus' warnings, their prophets' words surely rang in their ears. (Joel 2:1, 3:10-11, Ezekiel 20:45-48, Zephaniah 1:14-18, Micah 1:2-5, Jeremiah 6:1-8)

Josephus spoke of glorious signs in the heavens. *"Before sunset on Iyar 21,* six days before Shavuot, seventy six days before the 9th of Ab, *chariots and troops of soldiers in armor were seen running among the clouds, surrounding cities. At Pentecost, as the priests were going by night into the inner temple court to perform their sacred ministrations, they felt a quaking and heard a great noise; after that they heard a sound of a great multitude saying "Let us remove hence."* (Wars 6, 5, 3, 297-300)

If we were there we might have heard the LORD's angels with God's Shofar, calling his elect from the four winds. We might have heard the shout of victory of the faithful of Israel who heeded the Word of God spoken through Malachi. John spoke of this mighty army in the heavens. With the Rider on the White Horse, armies of heaven followed on white horses. Out of his mouth a sharp sword came to strike the nations. He would rule them with an iron scepter, treading the winepress of the wrath of God. On his robe and thigh his name would be written: 'King of kings and Lord of lords'. (Revelation 19:15-16)

Redemption, restoration and resurrection of the remnant, tried in the fire, has come. They were united with their Lord, with the apostles on their thrones, judging the house of Israel. (Matthew 19:28, Luke 22:30) God's judgment was brought against the apostate of the Old Covenant who had forsaken his Law, murdered his prophets, scourged his messengers and crucified his Son, prophesied by Malachi, (Malachi 4:1-5) John the Baptist, (Matthew 3:1-12) and our Lord, Himself. (Matthew 24:4-22)

God fulfilled all that was spoken by his beloved prophets who warned his Covenant people of the wrath that would fall on the unrepentant. God's judgment came down on his once Holy Nation; the city was laid in ruin, the Temple was destroyed. Not one stone was left on another. We see the End of the Age and can fully understand Matthew 24:22.

"If those days had not been cut short, no one would survive.
For the sake of the elect, those days were shortened."

In God's grace and mercy, the days were shortened for the elect's sake. Tried in the fire, cleansed with fuller's soap, God's Elect would turn to their Lord in repentance. But for the grace of God, the entire nation would have perished, had God not shortened the days. God's eye was ever on the Elect. Who God's Elect were, we cannot know but God knew and preserved those he knew would come to repentance and turn to him in obedience. In God's merciful knowledge, through his divine mercy, they would repent and know his redemption, *'geullah'*, restoration, *'apokatastassis'*, and resurrection, *'anastasis'*.

Timothy James, reviewing "Rethinking Realized Eschatology," speaks of the faithful remnant who lived through those last days. He assures us that after AD 70, we no longer live in the Last Days; we live in a New Day that brings glory to God. Judaism's Old Age passed away in AD 70. We dwell in an Eternal Age where we are assured of *"Ages in which God might show the immeasurable riches of his grace expressed in his kindness to us in Christ Jesus."* Ephesians 2:7

In our Lord's judgment we see a New Beginning, creation of the New Heaven and Earth. Following these Days of Awe is atonement and redemption. We see fulfillment of the Fall Festivals, the High Holy Days of the Sabbatical month of Tishri, the three annual feasts of the religious year, consummation of God's eternal plan for salvation of both Jews and Gentiles. Destruction of Jerusalem, God's judgment, was only the start.

Paul knew the Days of Judgment, Atonement and Tabernacles would soon come. He spoke a mystery. They would not all sleep but would all be changed in the twinkling of the eye, at the last trumpet. The dead would be raised imperishable; the mortal would put on immortality. Death would be swallowed up in victory. *(1 Corinthians 15: 51-55)* Paul was assured a glorious Day was coming. The Lord would come in the Father's Glory. All God promised Israel and the world would be fulfilled, to the letter.

Christ returned to his children, redeeming them. With spiritual eyes, these 1st-century saints saw his return. In the Glory of God, the faithful remnant rose in resurrection life to be with their Lord: Adam, the first man, Eve, his helpmate, their descendants through the ages, Abel, Seth, Noah, Shem, Abraham, Isaac, Jacob, Sarah, Rebecca, Leah and Rachel, Moses, Aaron and Miriam, Joshua and Caleb, Hannah, Esther, Naomi and Ruth, Samuel and Nathan, David and Solomon, the faithful kings who served the Lord, the prophets, Elijah, Elisha, Isaiah, Jeremiah, Ezekiel, Daniel, Malachi. All God's faithful remnant witnessed God's glory. Beside them were the New Covenant Saints, martyrs who gave their lives in love and service to their Lord: Stephen, the first to face martyrdom, James, the first disciple to die, refusing to deny his Lord, John the Baptist, the 2nd Elijah,

James, Jesus' brother, Peter and Paul, who died at the hands of Nero, and the countless saints who believed their Lord's promises.

These, and the living saints, firm in their faith in God, stood before him in Resurrection Life. Christ's atonement was received. Christ has destroyed sin and the power of Satan. He is no more. God has judged his children. Their sins, our sins have been forgiven. Death has been destroyed, swallowed up in victory. These saints stood, 'Anastasis', before Christ and heard the most glorious words they could imagine.

"Come, you who are blessed by My Father; take your inheritance, the kingdom prepared for you." Matthew 25:34

YOM KIPPUR—THE DAY OF ATONEMENT

After enduring the Great Tribulation, seeing their beloved Holy City destroyed, they saw their Lord return with power and glory. At the 'Great Shofar' the celebration began. Our Lord summoned his faithful remnant. His angels gathered his elect from the four winds, from one end of Heaven to the other. In Jerusalem's fall, the end of their world, we see fulfillment of all our Lord's prophecies. Our LORD's wrath has come down on the nation that forsook him. As Jesus told Caiaphas, they saw his coming in the Clouds of Heaven.

We hear the glorious message. *"Behold, he is coming with the clouds. Every eye will see him, everyone who pierced him. All the tribes of the earth will wail on account of him."* Revelation 1:7 They witnessed this Great Day of the LORD, His coming in Heaven's Clouds. All the earth, All Israel, all who pierced him, mourned that day.

At Yom Kippur, the Great Shofar has sounded. Moses was given the Lord's command for observing Yom Kippur. Aaron was God's 'Kohan Gadol', his High Priest. Through many cleansings, vestment changes and sacrificial blood of animals, the High Priest, chosen by and for God, purified himself, his family, the Temple and the nation. *"This will be a lasting ordinance for you. Every year on the 10th day of the 7th month, you must deny yourselves and do no work; you will be cleansed from all your sins. It is a Sabbath of rest; you must deny yourselves."* Leviticus 16:29-31

Before destruction of the Temple at Yom Kippur the High Priest walked to a young bull, offering for himself and his family the 1st of three confessional prayers. Outside the Temple, worshipers fell to the ground praising God, praying:

'BARUCH SHEM KEVOD MALCHUTO LE'OLAM VA'ED'.
'BLESSED BE THE NAME, THE GLORY OF HIS KINGDOM FOREVER'.

The High Priest began the day with a mikveh, immersing himself in water, just as Jesus was baptized by John the Baptist. The High Priest laid aside his ornate priestly garb for simple white linen, symbolizing sinless purity. Jesus laid aside his divine privilege, making himself of no reputation to expiate his people's' sins. The High Priest made a special sacrifice for his own sins so he would be seen by God as a sinless mediator. Jesus was sinless by his own nature. The High Priest's sprinkling of the blood of the bull on the 'Kapporet', the Ark covering, represented presentation of the sacrifice before God, opening a way to approach the LORD, YHWH. The sacrifice covered, 'Kippur', the people's sins, making God approachable. When Jesus died, the 'parokhet', the veil before the Holy of Holies, was torn in two, indicating the start of the New Covenant and an intimate relationship with God. No longer separated from God, we can stand in his presence.

The High Priest entered the Holy of Holies every year with a new sacrifice; Jesus' sacrifice as our High Priest was 'Once for All'. The High Priest entered a physical Holy of Holies made with hands; Jesus entered the heavenly Holy of Holies, God's Throne. The scapegoat carried away the people's' sins; Jesus, our High Priest, has carried away our sins. Once the expiatory sacrifices were done, the High Priest put on his Priestly robes; when Jesus accomplished his atonement before God, he again took on his Divine Glory. When the High Priest returned from the Holy of Holies, the people rejoiced in their atonement for that year; when Christ, our High Priest, returned from God's Throne with his people's' atonement, his people rejoiced in eternal atonement.

With the temple destroyed, the faithful remnant knew the celebration that should have been. It was Yom Kippur, a Sabbath of Sabbaths. They could not serve God as Torah demanded; the High Priest was gone; the temple was destroyed but before their eyes they saw wonders they could not begin to imagine. Moses and Abraham, all the faithful remnant stood before their LORD. They did not need the Temple, the High Priest or thescapegoat to atone for their sins. Their LORD, their Eternal High Priest, offered them atonement, cleansing them of all their sins. On their knees they cried: "Baruch Shem Kevod Malchuto Le' olam Va' ed", "Blessed is the Name, the Glory of His Kingdom Forever!"

This was their Yom Kippur, their Day of Atonement. Gloriously, it was ours as well!

At the Great Shofar, the saints saw realization of God's Ultimate Jubilee. Salvation was proclaimed and received. Good News was preached to the poor; prisons were opened; captives were freed. Those bound in Sheol were liberated; their debt was paid. In covenant with their Lord, they were sanctuaried in Him. The blind could see; the oppressed received liberty. The year of the LORD's favor was proclaimed.

SUKKOTH—THE FEAST OF TABERNACLES

Sukkoth, the Feast of Tabernacles, the Feast of Ingathering was celebrated from Tishri 15-21, commemorating Israel's wilderness journey when they dwelt in tents. For those seven days, Israel dwelt in sukkahs, remembering God's providence for all their needs in their wilderness journey. They also prayed for the harvest at the end of the year.

The Feast of Tabernacles sees spiritual fulfillment in the fullness of Christ in his Church. He is our shelter and refuge. Resurrected, we stand in His Presence, cleansed and forgiven. From the Psalms and prophets we see the refuge he offers. *'Who may ascend the Hill of the LORD; who may stand in His Holy Place? He who has clean hands and a pure heart.'* Psalm 24:3-4a *"In the day of trouble he will keep me safe in his dwelling' He will hide me in the shelter of his tabernacle and set me high upon a rock."* Psalm 27:5 *"The dwelling place of God is with men; he will live with them."* Revelation 21:3 *"The survivors from all the nations that have attacked Jerusalem will go up year after year to worship the King, the Lord Almighty, to celebrate the Feast of Tabernacles. If any of the peoples of the earth do not go up to Jerusalem to worship the King, the Lord Almighty, they will have no rain."* Zechariah 14:16-17

Sukkoth reveals joy in the harvest God has gathered in. The saints thanked God for ingathering the full harvest and rejoiced in Jesus' glorious appearing. From Mark 13:27, we hear the promise: *"He will send his angels and gather his elect from the four winds, from the ends of the earth to the ends of the heavens."*

We might believe nothing could compare to the joy these faithful saints knew at their atonement and redemption. However, there was a glorious conclusion to their celebration. The New Jerusalem, the Holy City was brought down from Heaven as a Bride adorned for her Husband. The glorious Wedding Feast, long promised, long awaited, had finally come.

The Torah says Moses ascended Mt Sinai to the LORD for forty days and nights to receive the 2nd set of tablets. On Yom Kippur, he carried them to the people, a sign of God's forgiveness for the sin of the golden calf and his promise of his eternal Covenant. Moses relayed God's instructions for building the mishkan, the Dwelling Place of God. Establishing the relationship between God and Israel, Exodus 25:8 says *"Have them make me a sanctuary; I will dwell among them."* The Tabernacle was built by God, for God, so he could dwell with his people. John 1:1, 14 proclaims, *"In the beginning was the Word; the Word was with God; the Word was God. The Word became flesh and made his dwelling among us: we have seen his glory, the Glory of the One and Only"*, the Father's Uniquely Born Son. The Word was made flesh; God dwelt with them. The children of Israel however, had the Temple. From the time of Moses to the early years of the 1st century, they understood God dwelt within the Temple and was only fully present there.

The Christians knew Jesus would dwell in his people, his Eternal Temple. In Christ, God would tabernacle with his people, in His People.

HOSHANA RABBAH

Hoshana Rabbah, 'the Great Salvation' speaks of this Seventh Day. The final day of Sukkoth is 'The Great Hoshanah', final sealing of judgment, a mini-Yom Kippur. The heavenly decrees made on Rosh-Hashanah and sealed on Yom Kippur were sent out to be fulfilled. Judgment was delivered. This somber day of reflection is a day of joyous celebration. In the first six days of Sukkoth, the people shake the lulav, palm branches, and sing praise psalms. At the Hoshanah, a hymn is sung: Save us please! The Torah is taken from the ark and placed on its table. Seven Hashanahs are recited with the ardent plea: *Save us please!* Circling the table seven times, they strike the willows on the ground five times until all the leaves fall off, symbolic of their casting away of sins that might influence God's decision to seal their names in the Book of Life.

Jesus taught the blessing of water on Hoshana Rabbah. If anyone thirsted, they were to come to him to drink. All who believed in him, as Scripture says, (Ezekiel 47:12), rivers of living water would flow out of their hearts. (John 7:37-38) From Christ, God's Sanctuary, his Dwelling Place, Living Water flows into our hearts. Quenching our thirst, it gives us life. Christ, the Living Water flowing from our hearts, is poured out, cleansing, healing and giving life.

The trees in the Kingdom on each bank of the River are fed by Living Water. Our leaves do not wither; our fruit will not fail. We bear fruit every month because of the Living Water that flows from the Temple, from Christ, to all who believe. In God's Kingdom, we are to offer the Water of Life to all who thirst.

Rain was the symbol of the gift of life, the Living Water Jesus offered. At Sukkoth, we are dependent on God for His Living Water. In the sukkah, Israel was exposed to the skies and God's rain. In God's kingdom, if we do not humble ourselves, dependent on him for all we need, God's rain will not fall. Reliance on our Lord's sacrifice and atonement is essential; without it, God's life-giving water will not fall.

At Yom Kippur, Moses brought the sign that God had forgiven Israel. In Christ's return, God has forgiven us of the sins we have committed against him. His covenant is eternal. Hoshana Rabbah is completion of God's judgment. The joy of the festival reaches its climax in devotion. On Yom Kippur our fate was sealed, but the writ containing God's Supreme Court decision was not stamped until Hoshana Rabbah.

Until that Last Day, God's judgment was incomplete.
After that Last Day, that Great Day, God's deliverance was made manifest to the whole world. Israel's prayer, **Save us please,** and ours have been answered. In Christ, we have God's Salvation.

As we have already learned, Jesus' connection to God's Holy Days passes from Chanukah to Rosh-Hashanah, his 1st Advent, to Passover, First-Fruits and Shavuot, the Spring Festivals, celebrated in his Earthly mission, his life, death, resurrection, ascension and the outpouring of the Holy Spirit. We move to the Fall Festivals, his 2nd Advent, and see completion of Christ's Heavenly mission to his people, his Church.

We celebrate the Holy Days honoring fulfillment of all the Law and Prophets. Christ, the Bridegroom has returned for his Bride, the Church; he has granted his people, Jews and Gentiles, his atonement. In his Kingdom, in his Glory, we tabernacle with him for all eternity.

There is an additional connection with the Holy Days of God, Christ's ministry and the Destruction of Jerusalem. Pentecost, the Birth of the Church and Messianic Age, was fifty days after Christ's Resurrection as God's First Fruit. The Feast of Tabernacles, the Fullness of the Church and the Bringing in of the Full Harvest, was fifty days after the 9th of Ab, the destruction of the Temple and the End of the Mosaic Age.

Astronomy and Josephus give the date of the burning of the Temple. The 9th of Ab was August 5th, AD 70. Fifty days later was Hoshana Rabbah, Tishri 21, October 13th, AD 70. If these calculations are accurate, our Lord's prophesy is fulfilled to the letter. Before us is Jesus' promise to his disciples. Some would live to see his glorious return. Jesus told His Disciples:

"I TELL YOU THE TRUTH. THERE ARE SOME STANDING HERE WHO WILL NOT TASTE DEATH, BEFORE THEY SEE THE KINGDOM OF GOD." LUKE 9:27

Chapter 6

The Life of Christ Fulfillment of God's Holy Days

Chanukah	Jesus' Conception (Kislev 24, 4 BC)	12/13 4 BC
Passover	John the Baptist's Birth (Nisan 14, 3 BC)	c. 4/26 3 BC
Rosh-Hashanah	Jesus' Birth (Tishri 1, 3 BC)	9/11 3 BC
Circumcision & Presentation	Tishri 9 & Heshvan 10	9/19 & 10/21 3 BC
Visitation of Magi	Kislev 28, 2 BC The 5th day of Chanukah	12/25/2 BC
Start of John the Baptist's Ministry	(Nisan 14)	c 4/ AD 29
Teshuvah	40 Days of Temptation Teshuvah	9/17-10/2 AD 29
Yom Kippur	Start of Jesus' Ministry (Tishri 10, AD 29)	10/26 AD 29
Entry of Passover Lamb	Palm Sunday Nisan 9	3/29 AD 33
Passover	Jesus' Crucifixion and burial (Nisan 14)	4/3 AD 33
First-Fruits	Resurrection (Nisan 16)	4/5 AD 33
Feast of Weeks	Ascension (Iyyar 26)	5/15 AD 33
Shavuot	Outpouring of Holy Spirit (Sivan 6)	5/25 AD 33
Rosh-Hashanah	Day of Judgment, Christ's 2nd Advent	9/23 AD 66
Shabbat Shuvah	Sabbath of Return Tishri 6	9/28 AD 66
9th of Ab	Temple Destroyed Ab 9	8/5 AD 70
Yom Kippur	Day of Atonement Ultimate Jubilee	10/2 AD 70
Sukkoth	Feast of Tabernacles (Tishri 15-21)	10/7 AD 70 to Present.
Shemini Atzeret	8th Day of Assembly (Tishri 22)	10/14 AD 70
Simchat Torah	Rejoicing in Christ (Tishri 23)	For all Eternity.

Our New Celebrations

Understanding the celebrations that honor our Lord's life and ministry, we must look to the Hebrew Feasts, shadows of our Christian Holy Days that have been fulfilled in Christ and seek to understand the convocations, the Miqra Qodesh we are called to celebrate.

In Christ's birth, we must acknowledge Chanukah as our Holy Day. Jesus Christ is *the Light of the World.* At his conception, he left the light of his glory in Heaven to be our Light to draw us into his Kingdom. God's light shines in him; we must be his light, shining in our world's darkness. At Chanukah, the Festival of Dedication of the Temple, Jesus, the Son of God was dedicated as God's Anointed Messiah, *the Dwelling Place of God.* We are called to dedicate ourselves, our Lord's Spiritual Temple, in service and dedication to him.

Rosh-Hashanah is also our Holy Day. Our Lord was born in a Sukkah, laid in a manger where food was stored. In preparation for Tabernacles, our Lord has dwelt with us from his birth. Christ, the *Bread of Heaven,* has given us eternal life. God gave us His Son on Rosh-Hashanah, the 1st Day of His New Year. In Adam, all have died; in Christ, all are made alive. Adam, the first man, became a living being; Christ, the Last Adam, became a life-giving Spirit. (1 Corinthians 15:22, 45) Adam, the 1st man, created on Tishri 1, brought sin-death, separation from God. Christ, the 2nd Adam, born on Tishri 1, brought us redemption from sin-death. At his 1st Advent, a Savior was born to save us from the sins we have committed since time first began.

In Christ's Passion, we celebrate our Passover. At Palm Sunday and Pascha, this is our true celebration. God has passed over us, delivering us from slavery to sin. He provided His Lamb, a sacrifice for the sins we have brought upon ourselves. We also celebrate First-Fruits and Shavuot. God provided the first-fruit, Christ. His Resurrection has provided us with Resurrection Life. His resurrection was the first-fruit of the harvest of all mankind. We are to welcome all whom God draws to Himself. At Shavuot, Pentecost, our Lord gave us His Spirit, our comforter, our instructor. Through his Spirit, God inscribed His Law on our hearts. The Spirit of the Torah, the Spirit of Christ is inscribed on our hearts. The power of the Spirit dwells in us. We are to bring knowledge of God to all whom he calls, to all with ears to hear.

At His 1st Advent, we celebrate Rosh-Hashanah and our Lord's birth. At his 2nd Advent, at Rosh-Hashanah we are called to celebrate anew. He Has Come Again in all His Glory. We celebrate our Lord's Return, His Parousia, His Abiding Presence with us and in us. We are brought into His New Creation, the New Heaven and Earth, the New Jerusalem. He first came as a child in a sukkah, a temporary dwelling place, in humility. He returned in the Glory of God, reigning in his people, his permanent dwelling place, His New Israel, His Holy City. We have New Life in Him.

We must remember and celebrate Yom Kippur, the Day of Atonement. At Yom Kippur, the High Priest offered sacrifices to cover Israel's sins. Two goats were offered. One was slain; its blood was sprinkled on the Mercy Seat. The sins of the people were laid on the 2nd goat. Taken out of the city, it was the scapegoat, carrying Israel's sins. Yom Kippur was given Israel to prepare them for the Lord, himself a Priest after the order of Melchizedek. The LORD swore and would not change his mind; Christ was a priest forever, after the order of Melchizedek." (Psalm 110:4)

God could only be approached as he demanded. Sin had to be removed as a condition of God's acceptance. Because of our sin, a mediator, a redeemer had to go before God to intervene. To stand before God, our High Priest had to be without sin. Through his sacrifice, Christ has put away our sins, to be remembered no more. The command to do no work on this Sabbath of Sabbaths, declared there was no work we could do to bring atonement. Our atonement could only come through the work of God's High Priest.

Our High Priest covered our sins with his blood, sacrificing himself for our atonement. Just as the High Priest entered the Holy of Holies to present the blood sacrifice before God, to secure atonement for his people, Jesus has entered Heaven, appearing before God on our behalf. Christ did not enter a sanctuary made with hands but into Heaven to appear before God on our behalf. (Hebrews 9:24) He entered, once for all, into the Holy Place not with the blood of goats or calves but with his own blood, securing an eternal redemption. (Hebrews 9:12) Just as the High Priest came out of the Holy of Holies with Israel's atonement, Christ, our High Priest has returned from Heaven with our atonement.

Christ, our High Priest has returned from Heaven.
He has given us our atonement.

We also celebrate the Feast of Tabernacles, the Feast of Ingathering. In Christ, God is tabernacled with us. In his Eternal Kingdom, the full harvest has been brought in. We reign with and in Christ. In his presence, we have the Water of Life and never thirst. We have the Bread of Heaven and never hunger. Tabernacled with him in his glory, we are his Beloved Bride. In Christ, we are One.

With all we have learned, with all our celebrating and rejoicing, we discover

The Celebration, the Festivals are not over!

We must rejoice and proclaim that Christ has fulfilled the Spring Festivals, Passover, First-Fruits and Shavuot. He has also fulfilled the Fall Festivals. We proclaim His Return and Righteous Judgment at Rosh-Hashanah, His Atonement at Yom Kippur and his Presence with us in his New Jerusalem at Sukkoth. We are in his eternal kingdom. We are his Eternal Kingdom. We dwell with him, in him. He dwells in us. However, there are two additional festivals most know little or nothing about which add a magnificent finale to the Holy Days we are called to honor.

These festivals start the day after Hoshana Rabbah. The first is 'Shemini Atzeret', the Great Day, the 8th Day of Assembly, followed by 'Simchat Torah', Rejoicing in the Torah.

SHEMINI ATZERET—THE EIGHTH DAY

In Numbers 29:3, Israel was told: *"On the 8th day, hold an assembly, do no regular work."* Rabbis interpret this to mean that those in Jerusalem for Sukkoth are asked by God to tarry with him an additional day.

Shemini Atzeret reminds us of Shavuot. Fifty days after the seven days of Passover, Israel's liberation was complete. Shemini Atzeret is the conclusion of the seven days of Sukkoth, completing our liberation. The number seven reveals completion, as the week ends on the 7th day. Shemini Atzeret speaks of the 8th Day, a New Beginning, creation of the New Heaven and Earth. (Isaiah 66:22)

> *"As the New Heavens and Earth that God made will remain forever,*
> *so will Israel's descendants and her name remain."*

Shemini Atzeret, the 8th Day, celebrates God's Eternal Day. On this Great Day, the Bride abides with her Lord in the New Heaven and Earth. God's New Israel, Sons and Daughters of Abraham dwell with him.

So will her descendants and her name remain.

At Shemini Atzeret, the Torah decrees an 8th Day. Leaving the Sukkah, Israel dwells with their Lord an additional day. In this 8th day, God calls us to share an intimate union, bonding with our Beloved. Shemini Atzeret is a reprise of Sukkoth. We remain tabernacled with our LORD without the ritualistic symbols. We dwell in true, pure joy, united with Christ and all who abide in Him. We are Echad; we are One with our Lord, bound together with him like the cords of a rope.

The shadow in God's Covenant with Israel is fulfilled in His Eternal Covenant. This 8th Day is God's Eternal Day. Through Christ, life is affirmed and enriched. God's bond with us is strengthened. We are called to reach out and draw others into this intimate bond with our Lord. This 8th Day is more than a New Beginning, creation of the New Heaven and Earth. It is Completion of the Old and Creation of the New, an Eternal, Glorious Beginning, a New Creation, the 8th Day.

Shemini Atzeret is the completion of time

and the beginning of time, at the same time.

Completion of Earth's Physical, Temporal Time,

Creation of Heaven's Spiritual, Eternal Time.

We have more than the Promise of God's Redemption;

We abide in its fullness.

God calls us to remain with Him an Extra Day.

Shemini (Eighth Day) Atzeret (Assembly, Gathering) A Time Beyond Time.

We gather with our Lord to the completion of His Time,
the Completion of His Eternity.

For the seven days of Sukkoth, seventy bulls were sacrificed as offerings for the seventy nations of the earth. On Shemini Atzeret, only one bull was offered, for Israel Alone. In fulfillment, the one offering was also for Israel alone, the Israel of God, Jews and Gentiles, bound as One in Christ.

As Sukkoth celebrated the Wedding Feast, we see the celebration has drawn to a close; the guests have all gone home. Turning to his Bride, the Bridegroom says *"Everyone has gone. Come, let us celebrate together; sit with me. Let us have a small meal together, just You and I."* Christ's Bride, Christ's Church, All Israel tarries with her Lord. In blessed communion, they share a meal, never to be separated, 'Bound as One'.

Shemini Atzeret also reveals perfection of our rejoicing. We cannot rejoice perfectly in temporary buildings, the sukkahs used at Sukkoth. Moving into our permanent home, our rejoicing is perfect, complete. After Sukkoth, the Israelites took down their sukkahs, returning to their homes. In the same way, the temporary booths we live in, our human bodies, have been replaced with God's permanent home, Christ, our Spiritual body. At Shemini Atzeret, we proclaim this 8th Day. God's Torah, Christ, affirms and enriches our lives.

We dwell with him, in him, in his Eternal Kingdom.
We have Christ, our Spiritual Body.
Our Rejoicing, our Resurrection is Perfect and Complete!

Simchat Torah - Rejoicing in the Torah

Our most joyous celebration is Simchat Torah. In Hebrew, 'Torah', means 'instruction'. The Torah teaches the way God wants us to live. On Hoshana Rabbah, Jesus went to the Mount of Olives. The next morning he went to the temple. Standing amongst them, he taught. This was Shemini Atzeret. In ancient Israel this was also Simchat Torah. The author of the Torah was questioned about the Torah in celebration of Simchat Torah.

At Simchat Torah, the weekly Torah readings are completed. After Deuteronomy, they return to Genesis, reminding them the Torah is a circle and never ends. At the end of Deuteronomy, Moses has died in the wilderness. The Spirit-filled Joshua, Yeshua will lead this remnant into the Promised Land. Just as Joshua prepared Israel to enter the Promised Land, the Spirit-filled Jesus, Yeshua prepared his faithful remnant to enter their Promised Land, the New Jerusalem, and as in the 1st verses of Genesis, the New Eden, God's Paradise.

At the last readings of Deuteronomy, they offer a blessing on the Torah, 'Hatan Torah', Bridegroom of the Torah. Returning to Genesis, a second blessing is given, 'Hatan Bereshit', Bridegroom of Genesis. Additional blessings are given the 'Kallah' the Bride of the Torah, the Bride of Genesis, acknowledging that love and commitment to the Torah is compared to a marriage. Christ and his Bride are totally committed to each other.

Completion of the Torah brings joyous processions around the synagogue. Everyone carries the Torah, celebrating in exuberant dancing. The Torah is not opened; they dance with it wrapped in its mantle. There was no further study of the Torah, only singing and dancing. Intellect alone did not hold them to the Torah.

There are two ways to rejoice in the Torah. We understand its intellectual meaning, what it means to our minds. The other is beyond our finite knowledge. Receiving the Torah, Israel declared, *"We will do and we will listen."* As they would do and listen, we must follow God's law, not through our finite understanding but through our Spirits, to its internal core. We must mirror its infinity.

On Simchat Torah, we celebrate with joy, knowing the Torah, Christ and his Faithful Bride are One. We circle with the Torah Scrolls, with Christ wrapped in our arms. Linked with God, married to Christ, we dance with Christ who fills everything. We, the Bride, rejoice in Christ, the Bridegroom who fills us.

On Simchat Torah we must reach out to God
and connect with the Torah that is one with Him.

Israel stepped beyond their finite knowledge of the Law and embraced the Torah, dancing with the scroll in their arms. All Israel shared equally in the celebrations. No difference existed between one Jew and another. The communion linking them made them join hands and dance together without any barriers between them. On Simchat Torah, even the Torah wanted to dance. Since it had no feet, they carried it in the celebrations.

> *We are to be so completely surrendered to the Torah*
> *that we are lifted beyond ourselves and become the feet of the Torah.*

Celebrating Simchat Torah, we see fulfillment in Christ, our Torah. Rejoicing in the Torah, Israel offered a blessing, a 'Hatan Torah'. Christ is the Torah, the Bridegroom of his Church. We, Christ's Church, are the 'Kallah', the Bride of Christ. We are to be as committed to Christ as a bride is committed to her bridegroom.

The life of Christ has more than an intellectual dimension. Just as Israel committed themselves to do God's will, not based on their finite understanding of the law, we must commit ourselves, not based on our finite understanding of Christ. Our faith must have an infinite dimension, beyond finite understanding. In his love, God gave us an understanding of his will and law. We celebrate, dancing, rejoicing in his Torah, in Christ.

> *We are to reach out to God, connecting with our Torah, with Christ, who is One with God.*
> *He has taken us into his arms in love.*
> *We are to take him into our arms and dance.*
> *We are to be so completely surrendered to Christ that we are lifted beyond ourselves,*
> *and become the feet of Christ.*

No one has shown more understanding of the Torah than Christ, himself. Only Christ was worthy to read the scrolls. (Revelation 7) As the Bridegroom of the Torah, he has fulfilled all the Law and Prophets. (Matthew 5:17) As the Groom of Genesis, Christ has made all things that were made. (John1:1, 3) He is the Groom of prophecy and has come for his bride. (Matthew 25:6, 10, Revelation 21:9-10)

Just as the children of Israel knew they were to dance together, whether learned men or common folk, we must welcome all to the dance. Whether Christian or Jew, slave or free, male or female, all are welcome to the dance. We must remember the Torah had no feet. We are to be the feet of our Torah, the feet of Christ. We must bring our rejoicing to all who want to dance.

> *Taking him into our arms, He will surely dance with us.*

Understanding the celebration of Sukkoth which brought us into God's kingdom, we see the fullness of Simchat Torah. God judged his people according to the lives they lived. Understanding the magnificence of this celebration, we might be brought to tears when we see how we have failed to keep the truths of God's Torah, the truth of Christ, and fail to believe he has fulfilled, to the letter, all he promised. Jesus is fulfillment of the Torah in its completeness. We would weep but God would tell us:

"Do not grieve; the joy of the LORD is your strength." Nehemiah 8:10

WE ARE NOT TO WEEP.   WE ARE TO REJOICE AND DANCE!

We are no longer celebrating the dress rehearsal of this festival. We celebrate Simchat Torah in its glorious fullness. We must rejoice. Christ dwells within us. We rejoice with Him, in Him. He has written his Law on our hearts and we must dance. He will teach us and all the earth the ways of the Torah, if we will but listen.

OUR HOLIDAYS OR GOD'S HOLY DAYS.

God's Holy Days, his holy convocations, his Miqra Kodesh are glorious. We are called to separate ourselves from this world and the holidays we celebrate and come together as a family under His Messiah to celebrate our LORD's Holy Days. We must realize the Holy Days God calls us to celebrate call into remembrance all he has done for his creation, his Hebrew family and those grafted into his family.

We are to celebrate the Holy Days that honor Christ's Life, his earthly mission and his Eternal, Heavenly mission. We must remember all they teach us about Christ and his Covenant. Throughout his life, Christ fulfilled all the Miqra Kodesh, the Holy Days God ordained. We are to joyfully acknowledge his celebrations, understanding Christ has fulfilled, to the letter, all the Law and Prophets.

All has been Fulfilled! We are to Celebrate Forever!

We must joyously proclaim the Trumpet has sounded. The dead have been raised incorruptible; we have been changed. Jesus, the Christ has offered his atonement, his salvation. The Feast of Tabernacles, Shemini Atzeret and Simchat Torah, the last of God's High Holy Days, have come. It is a time when we, as Jesus said, thirst for the Word. We can come and be fed. We must be mindful of each other, working together for God. God's blessings and protection are on us as we feast with him. We must proclaim unity and true peace are possible in our world if we acknowledge *He Has Come Again!* Sukkoth is the feast where we must learn to live in harmony with all God's children.

"The Kingdoms of the World have become the Kingdom of our LORD and of his Christ.
He will reign Forever and Ever. Hallelujah!" Revelation 11:15
We are to Joyfully Dance.
Our Lord, our King will Surely Dance With Us.

Chapter 7

REMEMBER THE SABBATH.
—KEEP IT HOLY.

Studying Israel' Holy Days, we come to the Sabbath which poses many questions few can answer. Should we honor the Sabbath on Saturday, the 7th day, or Sunday? Are we still obliged to honor the Sabbath or is it no longer commanded? Has the Sabbath been fulfilled, as were all God's Holy Days? If the Sabbath is fulfilled, does God call us to observe it as a memorial? If so, how is it to be observed? What does the Sabbath teach? To find answers, we must study the Sabbath in the Torah. *"The heavens and the earth were finished; God finished the work he did on the 7th day. He rested that day from all his work; he blessed the 7th day and hallowed it because he rested from all the work he did in Creation. God commanded Israel to remember the Sabbath and keep it holy."* The LORD blessed the Sabbath and hallowed it; God commanded Israel to hallow the 7th day.

The Sabbath was given to remind Israel of the glory of God's Creation. God rested on the Sabbath; they were to rest from their labors. From Hebrew law, any labor, however minor, was forbidden on the Sabbath. Building a fire, even tossing a stick in the fire was forbidden. How are we called to remember the Sabbath Day, to keep it Holy?

We need to return to creation of the Sabbath. What does it mean that God rested? We certainly realize God did not need rest after his glorious creation; he did not even have to work hard to create the universe. With the word of his mouth there was light. The Everlasting God does not grow weary and does not need rest. He did not rest because he was tired but because he was finished with his creation.

In six days, God maintained dominion over creation, actively changing it. From chaos, he created order, from darkness, light. From barrenness and emptiness, he created life, abundant life. On the Sabbath he rested, no longer maintaining dominion over his creation. He finished his work, declared everything perfect and rested. Honoring the Sabbath, Israel was to surrender her dominion over the world and rest.

Hebrew scholars tell us that for six days we labor as slaves. All week we lack freedom, bound to the physical world, slaves to the demands of our labor. By our labor, we show dominion and control over the world. On the Sabbath, we take a day of rest, step back and realize we are freed from this slavery. We can exist in harmony with the world, no longer trying to control it. As God completed his labor on the Sabbath, we are not to interfere with God's creation. We and the earth can rest, secure in God's hands.

The Sabbath is more than a day of rest. It is symbolic of God's completed creation. On the Sabbath, the process of creation stopped. God finished his work and rested, however Genesis 2:2 says 'on the 7th day God finished all his work and rested from his work on the 7th day'. If he rested on the 7th day, he finished his work on the 6th day. Hebrew teaching suggests that on the Sabbath, God created Rest. God added tranquility, harmony and peace to the world. The world was no longer in the process of change and could rest in God's peace. The world was created; it now became holy and blessed. On the 7th day, the Sabbath became the day of eternity. The world was without fault, eternal.

The Hebrew for Sabbath is 'Shabbos', related to Sheaves, 'to dwell'. On the Sabbath, God made the world his dwelling place. Instead of changing the world, he brought it into harmony with himself, giving his creation his peace. In the Sabbath, we dwell in God's eternity, in harmony, at peace with God.

Before sin entered God's creation, all was Sabbath. Creation was at rest; all was at peace. In this first glimpse of eternity, we could see the face of God. We could walk, talk and dwell with him in his presence. A Sabbath greeting for many Hebrews is 'Shabbat Shalom', 'Sabbath Peace'. Celebrating Sabbath, Israel is searching for the Sabbath Peace known in the first days of creation. All was at rest. All was Shabbat Shalom. They long to recapture that Sabbath Peace with others, with all creation and with their Creator.

'WHEN ALL WILL BE SABBATH'

As with all the Hebrew Holy Days, the Sabbath is a Shadow of the Holy Days God calls us to celebrate. *"There are six days when you may work; the 7th day is a Sabbath of rest, a day of sacred assembly,* a holy convocation", a 'miqra qodesh'. Leviticus 23:3 This appointed time, this 7th Day served as a dress rehearsal for future, spiritual fulfillment. In fulfillment, God's people can rejoice in their LORD's Shabbat Shalom, their LORD's Sabbath Peace.

The great hope of the Jewish people is the Messianic Age, a time of universal harmony. They believe man will learn to live in peace with his fellow man and nature. This will mark an end of war, injustice and exploitation. In the Talmud, the Messianic age is 'Yom She Kulo', 'Shabbos Day'. All will be Sabbath; all will be Rest. "Everyone will sit under his vine and fig tree; no one will make them afraid. The Lord of hosts has spoken." (Micah 4:4) On this great day they will know their LORD's Sabbath Peace.

They believe the coming of their Messiah will herald a great revolution for mankind, ultimate triumph of man over evil. The Sabbath of the Torah was a shadow of this revolution. However, our revolutions usually fail; the new regime is as corrupt as the former. We believe we know what must be destroyed but have no idea how to make it better. No matter how we long to bring this revolution, we will fail. We cannot restore peace to the world. Through Adam, we drove God's peace from the land. No matter how honorable our intentions, we cannot bring it back by ourselves. We cannot live in peace with God or nature, not even our fellow man.

God created a perfect world. Through sin we destroyed it, bringing it to ruin. We cannot restore God's perfection. Our attempt to recreate his perfection is exactly what Sabbath forbids. We are not able do this and must not try. Even with our best intentions, we cannot bring an end to war, injustice or exploitation. Our Sabbath Peace can only come through him who created the world in perfection.

The Sabbath Peace we search for is with us. The ancient Hebrews and many Christians today still expect this Sabbath Peace, God's Messianic Age to be a future revolution. We must be ready for the day when war will cease, justice and peace will prevail and all will be Sabbath.

Hebrew teaching calls Shabbos an eternal sign. Rabbi Kaplin, in "Sabbath Rest, Sabbath Day of Eternity" suggests a door will open a crack, revealing a spark of eternity. From the future world a breeze will blow. War and discord will cease. There will be harmony between Man and God. All Will Be Sabbath. God's Sabbath is an eternal sign but we must realize God's Sabbath Rest is ours today, not something we must endlessly await.

The Shadow of the Sabbath was one day in seven; the True Sabbath involves a complete change of thought. The Sabbath was a lesson for Israel, a shadow of things to come. In Christ, the shadow was taken away. On the Sabbath, Israel set her mind and heart solely on the Sabbath which was her delight. This is the Shadow of Christ. In Christ, we step away from our works. Purged of our sins, our hearts are solely on Christ, our Sabbath Rest.

Throughout his ministry, Jesus worked on the Sabbath but his work was compassion and service to his Father. At his death, he completed his physical work. Instead of continual animal sacrifices, he became the Lamb of God, offered once for the sins of the world. In place of literal circumcision, is circumcision of the heart, in the spirit not the letter. Instead of a Sabbath every week, he gave God's Sabbath Rest. Offering himself on the cross, ascending to Heaven and returning with Atonement, he has completed his spiritual work, fulfilling God's intention of the Sabbath. The shadow is no longer needed. In his presence, we can enjoy His Sabbath Rest.

Paul affirms the demands of the weekly Sabbath ended at the cross. Dead in our sins, God made us alive in Christ. He forgave our sins and cancelled the written code that was against us and was opposed to us. He took it away, nailing it to the cross. (Colossians 2:13-17) Hebrews 4:9-10 speaks of God's Sabbath Rest. There remained a Sabbath rest for the people of God; all who entered God's rest ceased from their labor as God did. This Sabbath Rest was longed for by faithful 1st century saints but is available today. Ceasing in our labors to make ourselves right with God, we celebrate God's Sabbath Rest. Our Lord has offered his Sabbath Rest. We rest in him.

WE CAN DEPEND SOLELY ON THE COMPLETED WORK OF OUR LORD, OUR CHRIST.

God's Shabbat Shalom, His Sabbath Peace, is revealed in his Heavenly Kingdom. In Christ, God's people are blessed and holy. The Sabbath has become the Day of Eternity. God, in Christ, has completed his Creation. He has made the world his Dwelling Place. God, in Christ, walks with us, dwells in us. We see the very face of God.

He has given his New Creation his Sabbath Peace. There is harmony between God and the world. Looking into the window of eternity, we can feel the very Presence of God. No longer changing the world, he has given the world his Shabbat Shalom. God has judged the world, redeemed the world and given the world his Sabbath Peace. In his presence, in his glory, we dwell in our Lord's Sabbath Rest and know his Sabbath Peace.

In Eden, Adam and Eve dwelled in God's Presence. In Christ, this earth is the Very Dwelling Place of God. In recognition of Christ's Finished Work, we abide in His Sabbath Peace. In Christ, we have our Sabbath Rest!

At Creation,	In the Shadow,	In Fulfillment,
All was Sabbath Rest.	All will be Sabbath Rest.	All Is Sabbath Rest.

"ALL is Shabbat Shalom!"

THE SABBATICAL YEAR—THE YEAR OF JUBILEE

We must not neglect two Holy Days overlooked by most Christians and Jews, the Shemita, the Sabbatical, and the Yovel, the Jubilee Years. Leviticus 25:1-4 speaks of the Sabbatical Year. When Israel came into the land God had given them, the land was to keep a Sabbath to the LORD. They were to sow their fields, prune their vineyards and gather their fruit for six years. In the 7th year, there was to be a Sabbath of Solemn Rest for the land, a Sabbath to the LORD.

Leviticus 25:8-12 speaks of the Jubilee. They were to count seven weeks of years, seven times seven years, forty-nine years. On the 10th day of the 7th month, the Day of Atonement, they were to hallow the 50th year with a loud trumpet call, proclaiming liberty throughout the land. It was to be a Jubilee for them. They were all to return to their own property and family.

In this 50th year, Israel was to celebrate an additional Sabbath, neither sowing, reaping nor gathering grapes. It was to be a Sabbath rest to the land. All Israel was to return to their property. If any Israelite had sold his land or bought another's land, it was to be returned to its original owner. The Jubilee commanded redemption of ancestral property. A poor Israelite was not to be forever enslaved because of debt. If a brother had to sell his ancestral property to pay his debt, it remained in the buyer's hands only until the Jubilee.

If a brother went into further debt, he could sell himself to another Israelite, not as a slave but as a hired servant, but only until the Jubilee when he could return to his father's possessions. God's Jubilee year promised that no Israelite would be permanently enslaved or forever lose his inheritance.

Israel was commanded to follow all God's decrees, including the Jubilee. They were to follow God's decrees, carefully obeying his laws so they could live safely in the land. The land would yield its fruit; God would bless their obedience. There would be no lack of grain while the land lay fallow. God would supply all they needed. God would send such a blessing in the 6th year that the land would have enough to last three years. When they planted in the 8th year, they would still be eating from the old crop and continue to eat of it until the time of the harvest of the 9th year. (Leviticus 25:21-22)

The land was God's possession. It was not to be sold permanently. Israel did not own the land; they were merely tenants. Throughout the land they held as a possession, they were to provide redemption of the land. (Leviticus 25:24) The children of Israel were not to have two masters. The servants of the LORD were not to be servants of Man. The Jubilee assured them they would be freed from slavery to man.

The Torah commanded these Holy Days be honored and celebrated regularly. Every seven years they were to celebrate the Sabbatical year; every fifty years, they were to celebrate the Jubilee. However, Scripture reveals they did not truly celebrate the Sabbatical and never honored the Jubilee.

God gave Israel the Jubilee to function as we understand bankruptcy law, only its provisions were far more sweeping. The family inheritance could be sold only until the Jubilee. Every family of every tribe was assured their land would always belong to them, as long as they honored God's laws, including observance of the Sabbatical and Jubilee Years. Bondage, in servitude to others, would not be a permanent situation. The Jubilee would set them free from slavery and service to others, giving them liberty to serve God. All debt would be cancelled. The nation could enjoy freedom from bondage to others. They and their land could rest in their LORD.

Jeremiah grieved the land's desolation because of Israel's refusal to honor God's Jubilee. Denying the power and glory of the Jubilee, Israel saw destruction of the land God loved. Promised the richness of the Jubilee, Jeremiah wept over its poverty. Longing to celebrate the Year of Jubilee, he endured servitude and desolation. Remembering God's promise of the covenant of the Jubilee, he witnessed the contract of its devastation. Awaiting the promise of the Gospel of the Jubilee, he grieved the document of its destruction.

Jeremiah lived in a time of war, adversity and affliction. Babylon besieged their cities, driving toward Jerusalem. Fields were set afire; the harvest was destroyed. For denying the liberty of the Jubilee, they endured seventy years of slavery, desolation for the people, the temple, the state and the nation.

Israel failed to honor the Sabbatical and Jubilee from the very beginning. The word of the LORD came to Jeremiah: *"I made a covenant with your forefathers when I brought them out of Egypt. Every seventh year each of you must free any fellow Hebrew who has sold himself to you. This is what the LORD says: You have not obeyed me. You have not proclaimed freedom for your fellow countrymen. I proclaim 'freedom for you, freedom to fall by the sword, plague and famine'. I will make you abhorrent to all the kingdoms of the earth. I will hand them over to their enemies who seek their lives."* Jeremiah 34:13-14, 17

Moses prophesied this desolation. The land would rest, enjoying its Sabbaths all the time of its desolation. While they were in their enemy's land, the land would enjoy its Sabbaths, having the rest it did not have during the Sabbaths when they lived there. (Leviticus 26:34-35) Babylon's power was punishment for the seventy Jubilees Israel refused to honor, from entry into the Promised Land to the destruction of the 1st Temple, four hundred ninety years. The land would rest, desolate, seventy years.

Daniel's seventy weeks of years speaks of God's Ultimate Jubilee. *"Seventy sevens are decreed for your people and your holy city to finish transgression, put an end to sin, atone for wickedness, bring in everlasting righteousness, seal up vision and prophecy and anoint the most holy."* Daniel 9:24 The shadow of God's Jubilee was fulfilled in God's Ultimate Jubilee. God's vision to finish the transgression, put an end to sin, bring atonement for iniquity, bring everlasting righteousness, seal vision and prophesy, and anoint the Most Holy is fulfilled in the completed ministry of our Messiah from his birth to his Parousia, his Abiding Presence in us.

From Israel's Jubilee we see man in physical debt to his brothers. In God's promised Jubilee, we see Adam and his race, slaves to sin and death through human weakness. In the shadow is sale of ancestral property; in the body, forfeiture of earth's blessings, justly deserved because of sin. In the shadow, Israel was to be delivered from debt to his brother, his family's inheritance restored. In fulfillment, our debts have all been paid; our sins are forgiven. In Christ, we have our Lord's Restoration.

God never wanted his children to continue as slaves to imperfection and ignorance, our heritage lost forever through spiritual death, separation from him. God designed from the foundation of the world, the bringing in of his Ultimate Jubilee, revealed in his Son and his Messianic Kingdom.

God's prophets associated the Jubilee with the coming of the Messiah, a King like unto David. Coming into power, other nations' kings declared a Jubilee, cancelling debts. God's prophets were assured their Messiah would do the same. Isaiah prophesied God's Jubilee. *"The Spirit of the Sovereign LORD is on me because the LORD has anointed me to preach good news to the poor. He has sent me to bind up the brokenhearted, proclaim freedom for the captives and release from darkness the prisoners, to proclaim the year of the LORD's favor and the day of vengeance of our God, to comfort all who mourn and provide for those who grieve in Zion, to bestow on them a crown of beauty instead of ashes, the oil of gladness instead of mourning, a garment of praise instead of a spirit of despair. They will be called oaks of righteousness, a planting of the LORD for the display of his splendor."* Isaiah 61:1-3

'The Year of the LORD's Favor' comes from the Hebrew verb 'ratsah' when a debt is paid or the LORD accepts payment. In the Year of the LORD's Favor, God declared judgment and offered forgiveness. All debt was paid. The brokenhearted were comforted; captives were liberated: prisoners were set free. All the promises given Israel when God commanded the Jubilee are fulfilled.

In Luke 4:18-19, Jesus spoke of these promises in the Nazareth Synagogue. When finished, he said Isaiah's words were fulfilled in their hearing. The Gospel of the Jubilee was proclaimed. Christ declared Isaiah's words fulfilled in him. Luke gives glorious vision of the Messianic King right after his anointing by God through his baptism.

GOD'S JUBILEE IN THE LIFE AND MINISTRY OF OUR LORD

Good Tidings to the Afflicted—In Christ, we are spiritually freed from all that afflicts us. Cleansed of sin and shame, we are freed from all that keeps us from our LORD's love.

Binding the Brokenhearted—In celebration of God's Jubilee, all that was lost has been restored. We dwell on Mt Zion with our Lord and all who have gone before us. In Christ's Jubilee, we have restoration.

Liberty to the Captive—In Christ's Glorious Jubilee, we who were captive to sin are set free. Our debts are forgiven, cancelled, remembered no more. At physical death, we are no longer captive in Hades, in Sheol; we dwell in the presence of our LORD; we are delivered from separation from God.

Prisons are opened—We are freed from the prisons than bind us. The Covenant of the Law that held Israel captive no longer holds us. We have gladness instead of mourning. God's Covenant of Grace gives us liberty. His blessings, originally our portion in the beginning, are ours for all eternity.

Comfort to all who mourn—All who mourn their sins and seek forgiveness, returning to God in repentance, are comforted. God's salvation is poured out on his faithful remnant as He is glorified.

Luke's words show the start of God's Ultimate Jubilee; Jesus was just beginning his ministry when he spoke these words but the promise was declared. He would fulfill the words of Isaiah's prophesy, all the promises God made of his Jubilee. Jesus was fulfilling Isaiah's words as he stood in the Synagogue but many would not listen or believe. Because of their lack of faith, they could not be participants in God's Glorious Jubilee. If in faith they returned to their LORD, his Jubilee promises would be theirs. They would know remission of their sins. As prisoners of sin, they would be set free; their debts would be paid, remembered no more. They would know their LORD's Ultimate Jubilee and rejoice in His presence.

The Epistle to the Hebrews speaks Jeremiah's words. The days were coming when God would establish a new covenant with the house of Israel and Judah, not like the covenant made with their fathers, when they were taken out of Egypt. The LORD would put his laws in their minds and write them on their hearts. He would be their God, they would be his people. (Hebrews 8:8-10)

Isaiah's prophecy of God's Jubilee was revealed before the infant church as Jesus started his ministry but would not be completely fulfilled until his Coming in Glory. God's New Covenant, promised from the days of their Babylonian Captivity, as spoken by Jeremiah, would be seen in all fullness in God's Ultimate Jubilee. God's Jubilee continues. God's faithful remnant, faithful Israel, will forever know their LORD's salvation. Our debt has been paid; our sins have been forgiven. We dwell on Mt. Zion, His New Jerusalem. He is our God; we are his people. The Land is the LORD's. Secure in his fold, we abide in His Presence.

The times of the Messiah's Kingdom and Eternal Jubilee are seen as The Times of Restitution, laid in Jesus' death, who died a willing sacrifice, the just for the unjust. The times of restitution continued with the return of Christ. Our High Priest offered his blood for our atonement in the Holy Presence of God. In AD 70, on the 10th day of the 7th month, Yom Kippur, his kingdom was established. God restored to the willing and obedient what was lost in Eden. We dwell in sanctuary with our Lord Forever!

Knowing the glory of God's Ultimate Jubilee, we can see its connection with Atonement. At Yom Kippur, Christ, God's High Priest, made atonement for his faithful remnant. Our sins have been forgiven. Our debt has been paid. We dwell with God's faithful remnant and with our Lord. Our inheritance has been restored. We dwell in our Lord's Holy Land, Mt. Zion, the New Heaven and Earth, the New Jerusalem.

At Pentecost, Peter cried to the people of Jerusalem to repent and turn from their sins, that times of refreshing might come from the Lord and he might send Christ who was appointed for them, whom heaven received until the establishment of all God spoke through his Holy Prophets. (Acts 3:19-21)

We must rejoice; God's prophets have spoken. The times of refreshing have come. Heaven has received him, appointed for us. In his return, he has fulfilled all his prophets proclaimed. In the presence of our Lord, we have God's restoration. Redeemed from sin-death, our debts have been paid. We dwell in the Land promised Abraham, a land not made with hands, but eternal, Heavenly. In God's Jubilee, His Heavenly Land is ours, never be taken from us. We are secure in the presence of our Lord as we proclaim his Glorious Jubilee. The Messiah reigns with and in his children. We are in Christ; Christ is within us.

The reign of sin and death has been forever defeated. We are restored. We have our Jubilee and abide in Christ, God's Dwelling Place, His Holy Land. As Paul declared to the church in Rome, the creature would be delivered from the bondage of corruption into the glorious liberty of sons and daughters of God. (Romans 8:2)

We are liberated from our bondage and slavery to the curse of sin; we dwell in the holiness of God. We must truly rejoice and proclaim God's Glorious Jubilee! The Church must share God's Jubilee with the world. God's Ultimate Jubilee is not a physical earthly celebration, but eternal, Spiritual, celebrated as we acknowledge all God has done to bring us into his kingdom, into His Holy Land.

As Israel's priests were to blow the silver trumpet, the Great Shofar, announcing the Year of Jubilee, we, God's Royal Priesthood, must proclaim God's restitution. God, in his love and mercy, has given us his New Covenant. We must worship and praise his name. We must proclaim the glorious truth.

"The Year of Jubilee Is Come!"

Charles Wesley 1750   Lewis Edson 1782

Blow ye the trumpet, blow the gladly solemn sound
Let all the nations know, to earth's remotest bound.

Extol the Lamb of God, the all atoning Lamb
Redemption through his blood, to all the world proclaim.

Jesus, our Great High Priest, has full atonement made
Ye weary spirits rest; ye mournful souls be glad.

Ye who were sold for naught, whose heritage was lost
May have it back unbought, A gift at Jesus' cost.

Ye bankrupt debtors, know the sov'reign grace of Heav'n
Though sums immense you owe, a free discharge is giv'n.

The seventh trumpet, hear the news of heavenly grace
Salvation now is here, seek ye the Savior's face.

Chorus: The Year of Jubilee is come;
        Return, ye ransomed sinners home;
        Return, ye ransomed sinners home.

Let All Know, The Shofar has Sounded.

The Year of Jubilee Has Come!

Chapter 8

THE KINGDOM OF GOD—THE KINGDOM OF HEAVEN

The Kingdom of Heaven was Jesus' central theme and primary message throughout his preaching. He hardly spoke of anything else. From the start of his ministry, he preached that the Kingdom of God was at hand. John the Baptist declared the Kingdom's presence to those he baptized. "Repent, the kingdom of heaven is near." After John's arrest, Jesus proclaimed the same message. Leading his disciples in their ministry, he told them to preach, saying 'The time is fulfilled; the kingdom of heaven is near you.' Whenever they entered a town, if the people did not receive them, they were to go into its streets telling them that even the dust on their feet would be wiped off against them. However, they were to be sure the kingdom of God was near. (Luke 10:11)

To understand the Kingdom of God and how we are to celebrate our place in His Kingdom, we must learn of the Kingdom as known to Israel. In the wilderness, God reigned on Sinai; he dwelt amongst them in the Tabernacle as they journeyed to the Promised Land. For forty years, as they wandered in the wilderness, God ruled as their King. At the time of the Judges God ruled amidst his people. After settling in Israel, God's Shekinah Presence dwelt within the Temple, in the Holy of Holies.

Before the coming of the kingdom, God gave the nation human symbols of his authority. Judges brought his word and delivered them from their enemies; priests offered sacrifices, making intercession for the people. At the time of the kings, the king ruled while Prophets spoke the Word of the LORD.

At the time of Christ, the Temple leaders understood their kingdom consisted of these symbols of worship but they failed to understand it was only a shadow of God's Kingdom. In their longing for God's Heavenly Kingdom, they expected a continuation of what they knew from history. God would be their King but his kingdom would be a physical kingdom, centered in Jerusalem with a physical Temple. They would be in control; all people would bow to them in awe.

The Epistle to the Hebrews assures us we have not come to a mountain that can be touched, that burns with fire. (Hebrews 12:18) God's Kingdom would not be a repetition of the kingdom they knew, a kingdom they could see and touch but its fulfillment and so much more than they could imagine. God's kingdom would be heavenly, eternal, ever-growing. He also wanted his disciples to understand God's Kingdom had come!

The Epistle to the Hebrews declared we have come to Mt. Zion, the Heavenly Jerusalem, the city of the Living God, to thousands of angels in joyful assembly. (Hebrews 20:22) The disciples understood this glorious message. They were coming to the heavenly Jerusalem where God reigns, where they would reign with him. The Kingdom Israel understood was an earthly kingdom; the Kingdom of Heaven is a Spiritual kingdom, 'on the earth', not 'of the earth'. In faith and obedience, the whole world could dwell with their King in his glory.

The kingdom of Israel was a shadow of God's Kingdom. The Kingdom of God is within us. It did not come with signs to be observed; it is in the midst of us. (Luke 17:20-21) God's Kingdom is Spiritual, Eternal, Heavenly, more abiding than any kingdom of the earth.

In "The Christ Has Come", Earnest Hampden-Cook says we should not be surprised that God's Kingdom came without observation. Our Lord came to judge the Jewish nation and receive his faithful remnant. Only those who were personally interested in his return expected its occurrence. No one recorded a physical kingdom change. No outside observers spoke of, or experienced the presence of this kingdom or the glorious reunion of Creator and creation. There was no physical temple the world could see or enter. All this was seen only by those called to enter, those with Spiritual Eyes, who acknowledged the glorious presence of their Lord in their midst.

The Kingdom of God fulfilled the shadow, proclaimed six hundred fifty years after the destruction of the 1st temple. Jesus preached the Good News; His Kingdom has come. The anointed offices of the kingdom are filled by Christ. He is our High Priest, Judge, Prophet and King. As High Priest, he offered the ultimate sacrifice, laying down his life for his servants. Entering the Holy of Holies, he presented his blood before God, obtaining our atonement. As Judge, he judged the disobedient and offered mercy to the faithful. As Prophet, he foreknew all that would come. As King, he rules in righteousness. His faithful servants are his Royal Priesthood.

His Temple is not built with stones that can be destroyed. It is built of Living Stones, those called by Christ, who responded in faith and obedience to him. These faithful 'living stones' willingly laid down their lives for the Kingdom and endured to the end. His temple is made up of those living stones, resurrected believers who belonged to him at his coming. His holy temple stands today, built of those living stones. It continues to grow as new stones are added. With each new stone, his kingdom grows. With each new believer, God's Temple grows.

God's Kingdom is a Heavenly Kingdom, but more real and abiding than all the earthly kingdoms of the world. It is a spiritual kingdom. Those born of the Spirit enter by faith in Jesus, the Christ, the Uniquely Born Son of the Father. The Kingdom of God is a present reality. Wherever God is reigning, His Kingdom is present for all to enter.

Jesus declared his Kingdom was at hand and referred to himself as the King. Reigning in the lives of his disciples, he was their King. For us to follow him, we must make him our King. If there is no kingdom now, then our Lord is not King. Matthew declared that not everyone who called Jesus Lord would enter the Kingdom of Heaven. Only those who did the Father's will could enter the Kingdom. (Matthew 7:21)

Matthew was not speaking of Heaven, the 'Abode of God', within the skies, but the Kingdom now, the Kingdom of God's Love and Peace. He who does the will of the Father can enter its gates. If we fall short, turning from our Father's will, we will be outside the gates of the Kingdom, outside his presence, outside of his Covenant peace.

THE KINGDOM OF GOD HAS COME.

Many are deceived concerning the Kingdom of God. We are told God's Kingdom is still to be revealed. Jesus accused the Scribes and Pharisees of shutting the Kingdom of God against men. We might discover we have wise, learned scholars, ministers and elders following in the footsteps of these Scribes and Pharisees. Our Lord might deliver to them, and to us, the same message he delivered to the scribes and Pharisees as he cleansed the Temple.

"Woe to you Pastors, elders, scholars; you are blind hypocrites. For two thousand years you have shut my Kingdom from the sheep of my flock. Your preaching and teaching mislead and delude my people. You even deceive yourselves. You shut and barricade the door of my Kingdom by postponing it. My children cannot enter its gates. You do not enter nor allow those who would enter to go in. Your laws force them to worship and pay homage to you and your beliefs. You bind heavy burdens on them, burdens they cannot bear, laying them on their shoulders." ('Paraphrase' of Matthew 23:13-14)

Are we to believe all our learned scholars and preachers or what our Lord tells us. To see the glory of God's eternal kingdom, we must turn to his Word. Luke says *"The law and prophets were until John, since then the kingdom of God is preached and every man pressed into it."* Luke 16:16 KJV John began his ministry near the end of the Mosaic Age. After John, something above and beyond the Law and Prophets had come. Luke speaks of the presence, or the start of the Kingdom of God which was visible and available after the time of John's witness.

The kingdom of God does not mean food and drink, the dietary commands of the Torah, but righteousness, peace and joy in the Spirit. (Romans 14:17) His kingdom is not physical, visible, temporal, but spiritual, invisible, eternal. God's righteousness, joy and peace abound in the presence of the Spirit. The kingdom would not come with signs that could be observed. The Kingdom of God was in the midst of them. (Luke 17:20-21)

The kingdom was available to those who first read his words, yet to be revealed in its fullness but in their midst. Jesus told Pilate his kingdom was not of this world, not a visible kingdom. If Christ's kingdom was of this earth, his servants would have fought the Jews to prevent Jesus' arrest. (John 18:36) The Kingdom of God was already in their midst in the 1st century. Now it is here in all fullness.

When was the kingdom first revealed? In Acts we learn that at Pentecost, at the outpouring of the Holy Spirit, the Infant Kingdom was born in the fire of the Holy Spirit. John the Baptist foretold this, saying that he baptized with water but one more powerful then he would baptize with the Holy Spirit and with fire. (Luke 3:16) The power and glory of God's kingdom was being revealed right before their eyes.

God's kingdom was already revealed to the disciples but not yet seen in its fullness. Luke 1:31-33 speaks of Gabriel's message to Mary in the birth of her son. She would be with child and give birth to a son; she was to call him Jesus; he would be great, the Son of the Most High. The Lord God would give him the throne of his father David; he would reign over the house of Jacob forever. God's kingdom would be eternal. God's kingdom was already there for the disciples and early church but not fully revealed until AD 70. It is in existence today and if we plant the seeds, it will thrive and grow for all eternity.

Scholars try to convince us we are an 'In Between' generation. They say the Kingdom is already amidst us but not revealed in its fullness. If we accept their words, we truly miss the glory of God's Kingdom. Jesus' priority was for his people to seek his Kingdom. Anyone who points us toward a future kingdom takes us away from this priority. If we are waiting for his kingdom to come or expect a visible, earthly kingdom, we are stepping away from our obligation to lead all whom he calls, to bring them to God's Spiritual Kingdom where they can abide with Him in his Glory.

As we journey through life, we find souls struggling with the same problems we face. They hear the same messages we hear and long to find someone who can honestly answer all the questions they ask. What can we say that will satisfy them? Searching scripture, Acts 1:3-6 appears to claim God's Kingdom is future. Jesus presented himself alive after his passion for forty days, speaking of the Kingdom of God. While with them, he told them not to leave Jerusalem but to wait for the Father's promise. John baptized with water; they would be baptized with the Holy Spirit. When they came together, they asked if he would at that time restore the kingdom to Israel. He assured them it was not for them to know the times or the seasons which the Father fixed by his authority.

These verses lead many to believe the disciples expected a physical kingdom and we must wait until the time our Lord has fixed by his authority. Bible commentaries use this verse to teach a future kingdom but Jesus did not correct his disciples' understanding of the restoration of the kingdom to Israel. For forty days, he gave them knowledge to understand. His Kingdom would not be a physical kingdom. It was Spiritual and it was ready to be revealed. At Pentecost, in the fire of the Holy Spirit, Israel's restoration would begin.

Jesus gave them their mission. With power from the Holy Spirit, they were to witness in Jerusalem, Judea and Samaria to the ends of the earth. They were to preach the Good News of the Kingdom. When they reached the ends of the earth, the whole of the Empire,

God's Kingdom would be established in all fullness. Spreading the Good News, they witnessed to all the earth so all Israel would know restoration. The faithful remnant, the Israel of God, Jews and Gentiles, faithful Sons and Daughters of Abraham, not by blood but by covenant promise, would inherit the Kingdom of God. They would be God's People. He would be their God. They would rejoice in him. Rejoicing in His Presence, they would celebrate this Holy Day, their Presence in God's New Kingdom.

'PARABLES' OF THE KINGDOM OF HEAVEN

Following John the Baptist's death, Jesus' ministry entered a new phase. He preached repentance, assuring his people that the kingdom of God was at hand. He spoke of the coming of the Kingdom. Repentance was essential for entry into his kingdom. Speaking parables, he declared the glory of the Kingdom and how his people could become part of his Kingdom.

'The Good Seed in Good Soil' (Matthew 13:3-8)
A sower planted seed, some fell on the path where birds came and devoured them. Others fell on rocky ground. Without soil, they sprung up but when the sun rose they were scorched. They withered and died. Others fell among thorns where they were choked. Other seed fell on good soil; they brought for much grain, some a hundred fold, some sixty, some thirty.

'The Mustard Seed' (Matthew 13:31-32)
The kingdom of Heaven is like a grain of mustard seed planted in a field. Though the smallest of seeds, it will become the largest of the garden plants, becoming a great tree. Birds can perch in its branches.

'The Net and Fishes' (Matthew 13:47-50)
The kingdom of Heaven is like a fisherman's net. Let down in the water it caught all kinds of fish. When full, the fishermen pulled it to shore, collecting the good fish in baskets but throwing the bad away. That is how it would be at the end of the age. Angels would separate the wicked from the righteous. The wicked would be thrown into the fiery furnace where they would weep and gnash their teeth.

'The Good Seed and the Weeds' (Matthew 13:24-30)
A man sowed good seen in his field. While his workmen slept, his enemy came sowing weeds among the wheat. When the wheat sprouted the weeds appeared. The servants came to their master and asked him, 'Didn't you plant good seed; where did the weeds come from?' He told them, 'An enemy did this.' His servants asked him if he wanted them to pull up the weeds. He told them, 'No, if you pull up the weeds, you may root up the wheat as well. Let them grow together until the harvest. I will tell the harvesters to first gather the weeds, tie them in bundles and burn them. Then they can gather the wheat and bring it into the barn.'

'Hidden Treasure and the Pearl of Great Price' (Matthew 13:44-45)

The Kingdom of Heaven is like a treasure that was hidden in a field. When a man found it, he sold everything he had and bought the field. The kingdom of heaven is like a merchant searching for fine pearls. Discovering a pearl of great price, he sold everything he had and bought that pearl.

'The Wicked Tenants' (Matthew 21:33-41)

A landowner planted a vineyard, put a wall around it, dug a winepress and built a watchtower. He rented his vineyard to farmers and went on a journey. When harvest had come, he sent his servants to collect the fruit from the tenants. They seized his servants, beat one, killed another and stoned a third. He sent other servants but they did the same. Finally he sent his son, believing they would respect his son. When they saw his son, they said 'This is the heir; kill him so we can take the inheritance from him.' They took him and killed him. When the owner of the vineyard comes, what will he do to those tenants? He will bring them to an end and rent the vineyard to other tenants who will give him his share of the crop at the time of harvest.

'Landowners and Laborers' (Matthew 20:1-15)

The kingdom of heaven is like a landowner who went to hire men to work in his vineyard. He would pay them a denarius for the day's work. Three hours later, he saw others standing idle in the marketplace. He told them to go work in his vineyard. They would be paid what was right. He went out again at noon and 3:00 and did the same. At 5:00 he went out and found others still standing idle because no one had hired them. He told them to go to his vineyard. When evening came the owner told his foreman, 'Call the workers; pay their wages from the last to the first.' The workers who were hired last were paid a denarius. When those who came first were paid, they expected more but each received a denarius. Grumbling at the landowner, they complained: 'These men who were hired last worked only one hour; you have made them equal with us who bore the burden of the work and the heat of the day.' He answered, 'I am not being unfair; you agreed to work for a denarius; take your pay and go. I want to give the man who was hired last the same as I gave you. I have the right to do what I want with my own money.'

'Rich man and Lazarus' (Luke 16:19-31)

There was a rich man dressed in purple and fine linen. He lived in luxury. At his gate, a poor beggar, Lazarus sought to be fed what fell from the rich man's table. Covered with sores, even the dogs came and licked his wounds. In time, the beggar died and angels carried him to Abraham's bosom. The rich man also died and was buried. In Hades, he was in torment. Looking up, he saw Abraham far away, with Lazarus at his side. He called out to Abraham for Lazarus to dip his finger in water to cool his tongue because he was in torment in the fire. Abraham told him he needed to remember in his lifetime he received good things; Lazarus received bad things. Now Lazarus was comforted while the rich man was in agony. Abraham also told him there was a great chasm that separated the two of them. Neither could cross over to the other. The rich man begged Abraham to send Lazarus to his father's house; he had five brothers. Lazarus could warn them so they wouldn't come to that place of torment.' Abraham replied, 'They have Moses and the Prophets, they must listen to them.' The rich man said, 'No, father Abraham, but if someone from the dead goes to them, they will repent.' Abraham said, 'If they don't listen to Moses and the Prophets, they will not be convinced even if someone should rise from the dead.'

These parables proclaim God's kingdom, present in wondrous ways to those with eyes to see: The Seed in Good Soil, the Pearl of Great Price, Treasure hidden in a field, Seed that produced the largest tree in the garden. These parables reveal God's kingdom cannot be observed with our physical eyes, but with Spiritual eyes. His kingdom is eternal, spiritual, to all with eyes to see, all who truly seek the Kingdom.

The parables of the Wicked Tenants, the Laborers in the Vineyard and the Rich man and Lazarus were spoken directly to Israel's leaders. They needed to understand the kingdom God had in mind. Jesus taught his own so they could understand and come to the kingdom he had prepared for them.

The 'Wicked Tenants', the temple leaders who stoned and killed God's servants, were the learned scholars of the Torah. They were sure they were the righteous seed of Abraham, God's Vineyard. Jesus told them his faithful servants would receive the blessings these learned men thought they rightfully deserved. The wicked tenants who killed his prophets, persecuted his messengers and killed his Son would receive God's judgment. His vineyard would be let out to faithful tenants who would give him the fruit in their season.

In the 'Laborers in the Vineyard'. the laborers hired early in the day were the children of the Sinai Covenant. The servants hired late in the day were Samaritans and Gentiles. They received the same denarius Israel received. The early laborers' complaint spoke their belief that God's Kingdom was only for Israel. They could not understand why these 'dogs' should receive the same wages as they had. The last worked only one hour but the landowner had made them equal.

The landowner responded, *Am I not allowed to do what I choose with what belongs to me?'* God's kingdom was available not just to faithful Israel, but even to faithful Samaritans and Gentiles.

In the 'Rich man and Lazarus', we may not be hearing a parable but a prophecy. Jesus spoke of the rich man and we might understand he spoke of Caiaphas, in purple and fine linen, the High Priest's garments. The poor man, Lazarus, was an unclean beggar, and as Israel believed, lived outside God's presence. Proud and arrogant, the rich man believed he deserved his wealth as Abraham's son.

Jesus spoke of Lazarus and the rich man. This is the only 'parable' where an individual is named and his name is 'Lazarus'. As a prophecy, the rich man and Lazarus have died.

Lazarus rests in 'Abraham's Bosom', in covenant with God. The rich man suffers in Gehenna's eternal fire, separated from God.

God's covenant promises are lost to him. Pleading with Abraham for a drop of water to cool his lips, he is told there is a chasm separating the faithless from God's promised kingdom. He asks Abraham for a sign to warn his brothers, to save them from torment.

History reveals Caiaphas had five brothers, or brothers-in-law: Eleazar, Jonathan, Theophilis, Matthias and Joseph Ananus, all sons of Annas the High Priest. All would become High Priests in their time. Caiaphas was told 'They have Moses and the prophets.' He responded, 'If someone goes to them from the dead, they will repent.'

Luke may be speaking of Jesus' foreknowledge that Lazarus, a beggar with open sores, would beg at the Temple gates at Caiaphas' feet for crumbs from God's Table. Lazarus would die, as would Caiaphas. Lazarus rested in Abraham's bosom. Caiaphas, in Jerusalem's inferno, was separated from God.

In John's Gospel, Jesus raised Lazarus from the dead. Caiaphas saw this sign, but could not believe. Though Lazarus was raised from the dead, Caiaphas could not be convinced of Jesus' power or resurrection of the dead. In Jesus' 'prophecy', Abraham said, 'If they don't hear Moses and the prophets, they will not be convinced even if someone should rise from the dead.'

As a prophecy, Jesus may be speaking of Caiaphas who would suffer and die, asking Lazarus to speak to his brothers, his brothers-in-law, to warn them of what was awaiting them. The risen Lazarus could save them from Hadean judgment. History reveals Caiaphas' brother-in-law, Ananus was killed by the Zealots in AD 66. Abraham told Caiaphas his 'brothers' had Moses and the Prophets; without them they would not be convinced, even if someone should rise from the grave.

Through Jesus' many parables, he taught his own of promises that would be theirs in his Kingdom. At the time of Jesus, the kingdom was small, but it was rapidly growing. Over the millennia, it has grown and is ever-growing. As the mustard seed becomes the largest tree, God's kingdom will be the greatest in the garden. Birds can lodge in its branches.

We have power from the Holy Spirit to spread the Good News. God's Kingdom, governed by the perfect law of the LORD, has come. We must seek his kingdom and his righteousness, making Jesus Lord of our lives. Seeking his Kingdom and his Righteousness, we can dwell with him in his Kingdom and his Presence forever.

Chapter 9

A 'CENTURY OF SILENCE'

Almost all Christians today believe and have been taught from childhood that Christ's 2nd Coming is a future event, something we must prepare for with great joy but also great fear and trepidation. We have been taught this by pastors and Biblical scholars for centuries and are assured our Bible declares this to be the unquestionable truth.

Our parents before us, their parents before them for countless generations, have been told we must watch and be ready. Our Lord will come as a thief in the night. If we are not watching and ready, we will be left behind when he returns for his glorious Bride.

Learned teachers and scholars assure us there has been absolutely no visible return of our Lord; he has not returned in judgment; the world still spins on its axis; sin still fills the earth. They assure us, "Scoffers say, 'Where is the coming he promised? Ever since our fathers died, everything goes on as it has since the beginning of creation'." 2 Peter 3:4 For two thousand years, scholars continue to preach this message to each succeeding generation until in the 21st century we still are taught our Lord has not returned. Totally ignoring Hebrews 10:37, "For in just a very little while, 'micron hoson hoson', **'a very, very little time'**, he who is coming, will come, and will not delay", we are told he continues to delay but we must watch and be ready.

Should we listen to all these scholars or from those who learned from Jesus of all that would happen in the Apostolic Age? What happened to the early church? How did it become Christ's Church that flourishes today? How did they celebrate their Lord's Presence with them? How did they honor this Glorious Holy Day? How are we to celebrate and honor our Lord? Is there anything we have overlooked or misunderstood to answer all our endless questions?

Our first step must be to learn what happened to the church after the Fall of Jerusalem. What happened in that horrendous event that brought Israel to the ground? Study of the history of the church post AD 70, suggests that from AD 70-150 there was absolutely no written record of the Christian faith in the land. No new epistles circulated. There were no messages from churches or converts, no writings whatsoever on the life and ministry of the triumphant, jubilant faith. Why has the message stopped after the time of the Apostles when just before all was passion, vibrancy and life? The church was growing dynamically then suddenly there was deafening silence. Why?

If our Lord's 2nd Coming was truly at the Fall of Jerusalem, why is there no historic record of his return? Why has history hidden this from us? The early church fathers in Rome, Corinth, Ephesus, Philippi, Galatia, Colossae, and Thessalonica were assured by Paul, the Apostles and their Lord, himself, that he would soon return. They all anticipated this glorious day. They should have been proclaiming the wondrous message to all the empire. We only learn all is silence. There is absolute unexplainable deafening silence.

All of Christendom appears still. There is no sound of the triumphant church after Jerusalem's fall. If their Lord has returned, if God's kingdom has truly come, these jubilant saints should have proclaimed the message at the tops of their voices. Instead of joyous triumphal celebrations, all we have is a century of silence. Where have all the Lord's faithful saints gone? Why are they so silent?

There are some who say we must remember the Jewish Christians were hiding in Pella, far from the violence of the war and the Jewish authorities who were trying to destroy their faith. Many were hiding from the Roman authorities who were persecuting Christians wherever they could be found. Churches throughout the empire worshiped 'underground', in people's' homes, far from anyone who could arrest and sentence them to barbarous deaths.

Scholars also suggest if any literature was written by the Christians after the Fall of Jerusalem, especially if it concerned Christ's return, it was suppressed or totally destroyed by the Jewish leaders. Rabbinic sources believe the remnant of the Jewish nation actively destroyed apocalyptic works, especially if they spoke of an 'imminent end of the world' after Jerusalem's destruction in AD 70.

Historical record confirms Jerusalem has fallen. The Temple is gone. Faithful Saints living in the Holy City have fled as their Lord had forewarned them but the war is over; the battles have stopped. It is safe to come out from the wilderness. Have they come out of Pella; have they resumed their lives? If so, why has the Church not blossomed and grown as before? Why aren't these joyous saints proclaiming the wondrous news that their Lord has returned, just as he promised, and His Kingdom has come? Something is missing.

Where are the triumphant saints, the faithful remnant who fled the wrath of God? Where is the proclamation of triumph? What has silenced God's faithful witnesses? They should be proclaiming victory. Why this deadly silence? There is surely something missing or misunderstood that must be uncovered.

Some suggest that if their Lord did return at this time in the history of the Church, perhaps we can see why there are no faithful saints carrying on their Lord's work, passing on knowledge of the Love of their lives. Perhaps, as believed by many faithful Christians today, they were taken, caught up to be with their Lord.

WERE THESE COUNTLESS SAINTS OF THE LORD 'RAPTURED' TO HEAVEN?

Some believe there was a sudden, unexplainable passing of a great multitude. Christ's faithful servants received their reward. The Bridegroom came, carrying them to heaven. In this passing, there were no saints to teach the multitudes, making disciples of all nations. They passed from this vale and abide with their Lord in all His Glory. In grief we cry: How did the faith survive if all the Lord's Saints are Gone?

We are convincingly told from AD 70 until about AD 150, there was no word from Apostles or followers of the faith. The Gospels were all written; the epistles had all been read but now there is silence. In this silence, we notice a mystery many have missed. The Gospel of Mark ends abruptly, almost in mid-thought. Many scholars suggest that the last verses were finished by another man's hand. The Acts of the Apostles also ends abruptly. There is no record of the continuing acts of the early church or Peter and Paul's martyrdoms. What silenced the voice of Mark? What ended the words of Luke on the lives of the Apostles and the mission of Christ's Church? Was it martyrdom or are we hearing in the silence of these sacred voices a Mystery of God?

Earnest Hampden-Cook, in "The Christ Has Come" sees in these days just before and immediately after the Fall of Jerusalem, the sudden disappearance of disciples, Apostles and churches, and asks the same questions. Peter, Paul, Timothy, and Barnabus have all 'disappeared'. The infant church, born in Jerusalem, has advanced through Paul's missionary journeys to Antioch, Ephesus, Corinth and Rome, and then it suddenly vanishes. *"Paul arrives in Rome and suddenly there is a profound night, lit only by the lurid fire of Nero's horrible festivities and the lightning flash of the apocalypse. The history of Paul's life and the apostolic age end and a grim brooding silence holds, in hushed expectation of the Day of the Lord, the awestruck breathless church."* (pp. 100-101)

From the Preface of J. S. Russell's "The Parousia," we learn of this awesome silence. We are asked to prove Matthew 24:31 and 1 Thessalonians 4:17's predictions were physically fulfilled. We have so many questions on removal of this multitude from this earthly plane. There must be a trace in history of the sudden disappearance of this vast body of believers that left a blank in history. *"Can we find in church history such a blank, silence, where a moment before all was life and activity? Ecclesiastical scholars say the light suddenly fails."* The Jerusalem Church has disappeared without a trace. Historians, marking the spot where record of early Christianity is most obscure, point to the Acts of the Apostles. Leaving the Apostolic Age, we lose sight of the Church in a historical chasm of 60-80 years. *"At the close of Acts, Luke's voice is stilled. Christian history is abruptly quenched."*

From F. W. Farrar, Chaplain of Queen Victoria and Canon of Westminster Abbey, in "Early Days of Christianity," we find this silence, the result of the terrible scenes in which the apostles perished. It was crucial for the survival of the entire Faith community that the Gospels, Epistles, the Acts of the Apostles and John's Revelation, when discovered by enemies or informants, not contain compromising, threatening record of Rome's hand in their persecution. It would surely have been compromising if Luke included the horrors of Nero's persecution, the deaths of Peter and Paul and the martyrdoms of countless saints who fell at his hands.

The sudden close of the Acts of the Apostles could be because Luke could not speak without drawing indignation and furor of the Emperor and Rome between AD 64-68, inflicting on innocent men and women atrocities known today only through historic record. *"Only through the disguise of cryptograms, with the meaning hidden to all but the few who truly understood the mystery behind the message, can we hear the cries of horror Nero's cruelties wrung from Christian hearts."* These cryptograms, coded, apocalyptic messages, revealed to the wise and understanding, the message silenced when Luke 'penned' the last words of Acts.

Understanding this, we must take the next step. Why didn't those living in Jerusalem notice God's faithful servants were gone? They should have questioned why so many no longer walked amongst them. They should have asked, 'What has happened to those foolish Christians?' We might think the questions were not asked. Why would so vast a multitude not be missed by so vast a multitude? Certainly someone must have noticed so many were suddenly gone but it appears no one asked, no one wondered.

We must remember Luke 17:21. The Coming of God's Kingdom would not be visibly observed. No one noticed or reported this glorious event. Only those who had a personal interest in the event, faithful believers would 'see' the Son of man coming in his kingdom. Those outside God's Covenant Kingdom would have no knowledge of the glory revealed. F. W. Farrar tells us that outside the faithful in the church, no one would see their Lord Return. The 'unwise virgins' missed their Lord's return. No one made or saw the report that:

"Countless Saints of the Lord Suddenly Disappeared"!

Scholarship says the glorious Bride and Bridegroom were nowhere to be seen; nothing can prove they celebrated this Glorious Day. Scholars assure us everything they were taught, everything they believed, was proved false. There was no wedding feast; the Bridegroom has not returned for his Bride. With their denial, disbelief and misunderstanding was born. Turning to prophesy, Isaiah 57:1 speaks of this passing of the righteous. *"The righteous perished; (vanished) no one ponders it in his heart. Devout men are taken away; no one understands. The righteous are taken away to be spared from evil."* Have God's righteous, faithful servants, his Faithful Remnant, been 'raptured', taken from calamity to enter God's Peace or, in obedience to their Lord, did they flee the abomination that causes desolation? Has their Lord snatched them from the judgment God brought against the faithless of his covenant? No one lays it to heart. No one understands.

Has this great multitude perished; have they truly been raptured or have they, as commanded by their Lord, fled without looking back? It appears those left behind, the

Zealots, their legions and the multitudes who remained did not, could not understand what became of them and did not let it concern them. Hundreds of thousands, perhaps more than a million died in the siege of Jerusalem. Countless others died of famine and pestilence. Others were carried away as prisoners of the state. These faithful sons and daughters of the Lord however, vanished. No one laid it to heart or saw any need to concern themselves.

We must realize there were not as many 'faithful saints' as we have been led to believe. Most of these saints were the poor, peasants, women and children, the 'unclean', those who would not be missed by most of Israel. So many had already been persecuted, martyred for their faith. As scripture repeatedly proclaims, God would provide a remnant, not a great multitude. This 'remnant' obeyed their Lord's command; they fled before their Lord's wrath fell upon the disobedient, before the Roman armies took vengeance against the Zealot forces.

It appears this faithful remnant has 'vanished' to Pella. Secured in the Shekinah Presence, God's wrath would not come nigh. These faithful saints did not vanish from this physical plane. They were not raptured, taken to Heaven. If we continue to believe these saints were raptured to Heaven, we truly miss the wonder of this glorious 'Day of the Lord'.

Paul promised the Thessalonians that those who were alive at the coming of the Lord would be caught in the clouds to meet the Lord in the air. They would be with the Lord forever. (1 Thessalonians 4:15, 17) 'Caught in the Shekinah Glory' they would meet their Lord in his Glory Cloud. Jesus declared the same truth. Before the generation to whom Jesus spoke had passed away, the Son of man would send his angels to gather his faithful remnant to him. (Matthew 24:31, 34, 40, 41)

Some suggest these words reveal the faithful saints were raptured, translated without any evidence of departure. If these faithful saints were 'raptured' to Heaven, we need not explain this alleged century of silence. No one remained to record the Lord's coming; therefore there is no written record to confirm it.

We are told of silence of saints and scripture. No praise or worship is heard in the land. We see lack of concern of the multitude after their departure. This possibly not so vast a multitude has vanished, but the vast multitude left behind are not concerned; they do not lay it to mind and we believe we understand. One last question must be asked however, and an answer is imperative. How did Christ's Church survive if all God's faithful servants were gone? If our Lord did return, if his disciples were taken in the twinkling of the eye, if all Israel was devoid of God's faithful witnesses, how do we stand in the 21st century claiming a part in this glorious faith?

To understand this mysterious silence of saints and scripture, we must hear Christ's prayer. Just before Jesus went to the cross, he spoke his priestly prayer. *My prayer is not that you take them out of the world but that you protect them from the evil one.* John 17:15 Praying to his Father, Jesus asked that his faithful disciples not be taken from the earth

THE HOLY DAYS OF GOD, THE HOLIDAYS OF MAN

but to be protected from the hand of the 'evil one'. Jesus asked his Father to keep them safe in the world. Their mission, before and after his Parousia, his coming in glory, was to bring all generations to the saving knowledge of God and his love for his own. Jesus knew they needed to remain in the world, not of the world. Answering Jesus' prayer, God secured his faithful sons and daughters in the hands of his Shekinah Presence.

Understanding our Lord's prayer for his own and His Father's answer to his prayer, we learn these faithful saints were not taken from the world; they were given sanctuary from 'the adversary', both Jewish and Roman. Secured from out of the world and the hand of the adversary, they were safe in their Lord's care.

For so long we have expected a physical, visible kingdom sometime in the future. We are told the Lord's saints will be raptured. We are assured Christ will return with these saints to reign on a physical earth, in a physical kingdom from physical Jerusalem. Some who believe Christ's 2nd Coming is past still suggest there was a rapture and the Lord's saints dwell in a heavenly kingdom, not on this earth.

Acknowledging these saints were not taken from the world does not mean we must explain this alleged 'century of silence'. We can rejoice in his coming, as they did, knowing they reigned with him in a Spiritual, Heavenly kingdom, not of this world, but in this world.

The early Church Fathers did not all deny the Lord's Coming. Eusebius' "Demonstratio Evangelica", Bk. 2, AD 312, spoke of unmistakable signs of Christ's coming. *"Among the Jews there were three offices of dignity, the kingship, prophet and high priesthood. Abolition and complete destruction of these offices would be the sign of the presence of Christ. Proof that the times had come would lie in ceasing of Mosaic worship, desolation of Jerusalem and its Temple and subjection of the whole Jewish race to its enemies. The holy oracles foretold that all these changes not made in the days of the prophets of old, would take place at the coming of Christ."*

He also believed 'the last days' spoke of destruction of the Jewish state. *"We must understand in the end of days, the end of national existence of the Jews, cessation of the rule of Judah, destruction of the whole race, failing and ceasing of their governors, abolition of the kingly position of the tribe of Judah and the rule and kingdom of Christ, not over Israel but over all nations, according to the Word. This is the expectation of the nations."*

St John of Chrysostom, in his Homily, AD 375, saw fulfillment in that generation. *"Was their house left desolate? Did all the vengeance come upon that generation? It is quite plain it was so; no man gainsays it."* Origen also saw the Abomination of Desolation fulfilled in the war with Rome under Nero, Vespasian and Titus.

"THE ODES OF SOLOMON"

This 'Century of Silence' is a fallacy. We have historical record of the triumphant church rejoicing in their Lord's appearing. While not inspired Scripture or apostolic writ, there is record of these saints shortly after Jerusalem's destruction, proclaiming his presence amidst them. Written by an anonymous Syrian poet in Antioch, the Odes of Solomon sing of redemption and fulfilled eschatology before the close of the 1st century, c. AD 88. Discovered in 1909 in a pile of ancient Syriac manuscripts, these 42 Odes may be the earliest Christian Hymnbook.

Discovery of these Odes reveals the remnant of the Jewish nation, seeking to destroy all evidence of the Coming of the Lord in his Glory, missed this glorious Hymnbook that sang the praises of our Lord's abiding presence with and in his people, the marriage of the Bride to her Bridegroom, death's destruction, Hadean release, immortality, and the bringing in of his Kingdom, not of the earth but upon the earth.

Ode 1, a beautiful hymn, speaks of our LORD's presence on Christ's head, like a crown. *"The Lord is on my head like a crown. I shall never be without Him. Planted for me is the crown of truth. It caused your branches to blossom in me. It is not like a parched crown that blossoms not. For you live on my head and blossomed on me. Your truths are full and complete. They are full of your salvation."*

In Ode 10, we hear Christ's voice and see the Gentiles gathered together, walking according to Jesus' life. Receiving salvation, they would forever be God's people. *"The Lord has directed my mouth by his Word and opened my heart by his Light. He has caused to dwell in me his immortal life and permitted me to proclaim the fruit of his peace, to convert the lives of those who desire to come to him and lead those who are captive into freedom."*

Continuing, we hear Christ's 'voice'. *"I took courage and became strong and captured the world. The captivity became mine for the glory of the Most High, and of God my Father. The Gentiles* (The ten tribes of Israel) *who had been dispersed were gathered together. I was not defiled by my love for them, because they praised me in high places. The traces of light were set upon their heart. They walked according to my life and were saved. They became my people forever. Hallelujah!"*

Ode 15 proclaims the coming of His Holy Day, death's destruction, the vanquishing of Sheol and the putting on of immortality through his name. *"As the sun is the joy of them who seek daybreak, so is my joy in the Lord. He is my Sun; his rays lifted me. His light dismissed all darkness from my face. Eyes I obtained in him, I have seen his Holy Day. Ears I acquired, and heard his truth. Thoughts of knowledge I acquired, and enjoyed delight through Him. I repudiated the way of error, went toward him and received salvation from him abundantly. According to his generosity, he gave me; according to his excellent beauty, he made me. I put on immortality through his name, and took off corruption by his grace. Death has been destroyed before my face. Sheol has been vanquished by the Word. Eternal life has risen in the Lord's land, declared to his faithful ones, given without limit to all that trust him. Hallelujah!"*

Ode 17 sees our Lord's crowning, and his people crowned with him. Crowned by God, he offered salvation to the faithful. Just as Mary Magdelene, the disciples going to Emmaus, and the disciples at the Sea of Tiberius saw Jesus but did not know him, he appeared as a 'Stranger' with the likeness of a New Man. *"I was crowned by my God, my crown was living. I was justified by my Lord, for my salvation is incorruptible. I have been freed from vanities and am not condemned. My chains were cut off by his hands. I received the face and likeness of a new person; I walked in Him and was saved. The thought of truth led me. I went after it and wandered not. All who saw me were amazed, I seemed to them like a stranger. He who knew and exalted me is the Most High in all His perfection. He glorified me by his kindness, and raised my understanding to the height of truth. From thence he gave me the way of his steps. I opened doors which were closed. I shattered the bars of iron; my own shackles had grown hot and melted before me. Nothing appeared closed to me, because I was the opening of everything. I went to my bound ones to loose them that I might not leave anyone bound or binding. I gave my knowledge generously, my resurrection through my love. I sowed my fruits in hearts and transformed them through myself. They received my blessing and lived; they were gathered to me and were saved. (Resurrection of the dead) Because they became my members and I was their Head. 'Glory to You, our Head, O Lord Messiah.' Hallelujah!"*

Ode 21, a glorious praise hymn, speaks of bonds broken, darkness cast away and the Lord's abiding presence. *"I lifted up my arms on high on account of the compassion of the Lord. He cast off my bonds from me, and my Helper lifted me up according to his compassion and his salvation. I put off darkness, and put on light. Even I myself acquired members. In them there was no sickness or affliction or suffering. Abundantly helpful to me was the thought of the Lord and his everlasting fellowship. I was lifted up in the light and passed before him. I was constantly near him, while praising and confessing him. He caused my heart to overflow. It was found in my mouth and sprang forth on my lips. Upon my face increased the exultation of the Lord and his praise. Hallelujah!"*

In the last Ode, Ode 42, Christ has released the captives from Sheol, granting them entry into his presence and glory. At verse 8, we hear: *"Like the arm of the bridegroom over the bride, so is my yoke over those who know me. As the bridal chamber is spread out by the bridal pair's home, so is my love by those who know me. I was not rejected, though I was considered to be so. I did not perish, though they thought it of me. Sheol saw me and was shattered; Death rejected me and many with me. I have been like vinegar and bitterness to it."*

"I went down with it as far as its depths. The feet and the head it released, because it was not able to endure my face. I made a congregation of the living among his dead; I spoke with them by living lips, that my word may not be unprofitable. Those who had died ran towards me, crying, "Son of God, have pity on us. Deal with us according to your kindness; bring us out from the bonds of darkness. Open for us the door by which we may come out to you; we perceive our death does not touch you. May we also be saved with you because you are our Savior." I heard their voice and placed their faith in my heart. I placed my name on their head because they are free and they are mine."

These Odes proclaim the glorious presence of God's Heavenly Kingdom where the redeemed of Israel and the Gentiles dwell. They were not raptured out of the world; they dwelt in the New Jerusalem with their Lord. **'Hallelujah'!**

We do not have to wait until we die before we can join them in the Presence of the Lord. We are amidst them; they are amidst us. We must rejoice! Our Lord and his saints remained on the earth. They continued to praise their Lord, drawing all nations, all peoples into the presence of the Lord. By the power of the Holy Spirit, the seed germinated and grew. Through their fervent prayers, it grew in those who heard the word through them.

Through the power of the Holy Spirit, through his faithful witnesses, the Word of God has been given us. We have heard the word, spoken and taught through the voices of those who were Left Behind. We are Children of the Left Behind. They were not left behind because they did not believe and missed the rapture. They were left behind so we could believe, dwell with them in the holiness of the Lord and praise his Holy Name.

Through God's Spirit, we are the greatest tree in the garden. We reign with our Lord in the New Jerusalem. We must thank God he did not Rapture his faithful servants. He left them behind, not left behind alone however, but with him in his glory. We must understand: without them, without our Lord with them, there would be no church in the 21st century.

All the faithful saints were dwelling in their Lord's Presence, praising him in his kingdom, heavenly, not physical or visible to the human eye, but revealed through Spiritual Eyes. Through their presence and witness, God's kingdom has triumphed. We have been promised, *"My word that goes forth from my mouth, will not return to me empty but will accomplish what I desire and achieve the purpose for which I sent it."* Isaiah 55:11

God's Church was not lost from this world for a moment, not an instant. God's Spirit was at work from the start. These saints remained on this plane of existence, to wake the sleeping saints who missed the Bridegroom's return, those 'without oil for their lamps', to teach and prepare them for their mission. They would wake those sleeping saints so they could learn their Lord had truly come. Rejoicing, they would join the feast and celebrate the Presence of their Lord in all his glory. Those faithful saints, and those who slept, sang the praises of their Lord and continued to teach the world so we in the 21st century and beyond could reign with our Lord in his kingdom.

The faithful saints obeyed his command. They made disciples of all nations, baptizing them in the name of the Father, the Son and the Holy Spirit. They taught them to obey all that Christ commanded. (Matthew 28:19) Following their Lord's command they taught their Lord's words, and as in the 'Odes of Solomon', continued to proclaim fulfillment of the promises of his kingdom. The rest was in their Lord's hands. God, our Father gave us His Son as our Savior. Jesus, our Lord taught us of His Father's love and gave His Spirit to them to teach them. The Holy Spirit taught the faithful saints who remained on earth after the Coming of Christ, and teaches us who received the Word through them. He filled them and fills us with his power. The Spirit of God is within us. We dwell in the Spirit and Power of Christ.

If we understand what has been revealed, we might see why so much of Christendom insists our Lord is yet to come. Though Scripture teaches us and Christ's faithful witnesses proclaimed the glory of His Coming, the message we have received was passed to us through the words of those who did not believe the glorious message. We have been taught by those who missed the mark. They heard the voices of the triumphant remnant; they heard the message of redemption but could not believe. They could not understand what they could not see with their physical eyes.

From the first days of the Kingdom, many could not accept God's Spiritual kingdom. From the Judiazers, many were taught of and expected a physical kingdom. They preached and taught postponement. The church heard both messages and had to choose which one to believe. Without spiritual eyes, many could not see, refused to see and refused to believe.

We must praise God. The Spirit was working God's purpose out. In the power of the Holy Spirit, some came to the knowledge of God in their lives but we must live with the knowledge that what we have been taught, what we teach others, we learned from those who were not quite ready to receive the promise. They could not see the Kingdom and their Lord amidst them. Not all who came after those faithful witnesses understood or believed. We can rejoice however. There always was God's Faithful Remnant!

Over the eons, we have heard the word preached from those who could not believe what they could not see. They preferred to live in the world, not step out and enter the heavenly, the invisible, the mysterious world. They were left to wonder when their Lord would return. They did not understand and could not believe.

Christ's saints dilligently taught them. God's faithful servants were watching and ready. Those who were not watching did not believe or understand that the Master of the House had returned. Our Lord and his disciples taught them, trying to reach them. Many believed and were ready. Others closed their eyes. Continuing to sleep, they could not believe.

His disciples rejoiced in their Lord's love and forgiveness. They wanted all to believe, gather at the wedding feast, celebrate with the bride and dwell with their beloved Bridegroom in the New Jerusalem. Through the 'Odes of Solomon', they continued to preach and sing the message. They 'sang' to all who would listen.

"He sent out His Angels and gathered his elect from the four winds,
from the Ends of the Earth to the Ends of Heaven." Mark 13:27

"Watch, therefore, lest He Come Suddenly, and find you asleep."
"What I say to you, I say to all, Watch!" Mark 13:36
But many were not watching.
They were not ready.

Chapter 10

THE BEST IS YET TO COME!

Revelation 22:12-17 speaks of the promise of the Kingdom of God. *"Behold, I am coming soon; my reward is with me. I will give to everyone according to what he has done. I am the Alpha and the Omega, the First and the Last, the Beginning and the End. Blessed are those who wash their robes that they may have the right to the tree of life and may go through the gates into the city. Outside are the dogs, those who practice magic, the sexually immoral, murderers, idolaters, everyone who loves and practices falsehood. I, Jesus, have sent my angel to give you this testimony for the churches. I am the Root and the Offspring of David, the bright morning star. The Spirit and the Bride say 'Come'; let him who hears say, 'Come'; whoever is thirsty, let him come. Whoever wishes, let him take the free gift of the water of life."*

A confusing vision is before us. John reveals God's glorious eternal kingdom. Through his voice, our Lord, the Alpha and Omega promised his faithful remnant that he was coming soon to repay everyone for what had been done. The saints' robes, 'their spirits' would be washed clean; they could come to the Tree of Life and enter the city through its gates.

The next words surely reveal this is not an earthly kingdom free of sin where peace surrounds the kingdom. Outside the gates are dogs, sorcerers, fornicators, murderers and idolaters, everyone who loves and practices falsehood. Who are these sorcerers, murderers, those who love and practice falsehood? Aren't we told God would remove all evil from the world before his kingdom comes? The Kingdom of God is supposed to be a kingdom of peace, with evil purged away. There will be no sin or sinners. These words leave us questioning all we have been taught.

Listening carefully, we hear our Lord calling to us. *"The Spirit and Bride say 'Come'; let him who hears say 'Come'."* Christ's Spirit, His Shekinah Presence, and His Bride, His Church, call us into the kingdom, to enter its gates, partake of the waters of life and dwell with our Lord. The Spirit and Bride dwell in God's glorious kingdom. We are called to join in Communion with those countless saints and their Lord.

The New Jerusalem is revealed in all its glory. God's faithful servants dwell in his presence. The Spirit and the Bride have invited us in to join all who already dwell with the Lord. Outside its gates are those who choose not to enter or do not realize they can be invited in. They remain outside the gates, separated from God and his Kingdom.

In Revelation 22:2, Ezekiel's prophesy is fulfilled. *"Fruit trees of all kinds will grow on both banks of the river. Their leaves will not wither nor will their fruit fail. Every month they will bear because the water from the sanctuary flows to them. Their fruit will serve for food and their leaves for healing."* Ezekiel 47:12

God's Living Waters flow through Christ, God's Sanctuary. He gives life to the leaves of the Tree of Life. Paul told the Romans they were to bear fruit for God. (Romans 7:4) The saints of the Lord, the leaves from the Tree of Life, offer fruit for the healing of the nations so they too can enter the gates of God's Holy City, into his presence and peace.

We live in God's eternal Kingdom with his saints, in his glory. Outside the gates are those who don't know the way in, refuse the invitation or do not know they are welcome. Abraham, Isaac and Jacob are with us. They would welcome them, giving God the glory. David and Solomon, kings of the ancient land, would welcome them, giving glory to the King who reigns. Peter, James and John, Paul and Silas, Aquila and Prisca, Timothy and Titus, Lois, Eunice, Phebe, the innumerable saints of the Lord would invite them in to rejoice in their Lord. They would offer God's balm, proclaim his power and give him the glory.

However, only we can invite them to dwell in God's presence. Only we can lead them in through the Kingdom's gates. We must offer God's holy balm, Christ, the Water of Life. We, the leaves of the Tree of Life, are to offer them Christ's Living Water, the Bread of Heaven and the fruit of the Kingdom. The Love of God can heal them. We must proclaim they may enter. God's love and forgiveness must be offered those outside the gates, all those he has called. We are in God's kingdom. Our Lord is on his throne. We must welcome all the Lord has called, all those with ears to hear. The Spirit and the Bride say COME! We must let them know they are welcome to enter the Glorious Kingdom! They can celebrate with us, with their Lord.

We serve a Victorious, Risen, Reigning King!
He is Reigning and will Reign Forever! 'The Best Is Yet To Come!'

We have nothing to fear. The prophets of doom are lying to us. They tell us, and have told us for generations, that there are untold horrors to face. The devil is out to destroy us. The world is on the brink of disaster. There is nothing we can do but wait for the Lord to return to take us from the great tribulation. When we are removed, great horrors will befall those left behind. Under the control of Satan and the Beast, they will face unimaginable torment. We are told, day in and day out, **The worst is yet to come!**

Not only do we have nothing to fear, we have nothing to mourn. So many Christians live in a state of mourning, waiting expectantly for their Lord, anticipating the glorious day when he will finally return. They claim joyous hope but grieve in endless waiting. They long for the day he will return in his glory. In songs and prayers they cry, longing for their Lord's return when they can finally abide in His Presence.

If we believe the Bible, understand all that history teaches and see all that has come to pass, we see Christ has fulfilled to the letter, all the Law and Prophets. We have nothing to fear or mourn. We do not need to fear the End of the World. God did not speak of the End of the World or the end of time. He taught about the Time of the End. He assures us The End has Come; The Beginning has already started.

There is no End of God's Glorious Kingdom.
Jesus was Lord at the Beginning. Jesus was Lord at the End.
Even Now He is Lord!
"Generations Come and Generations Go while the Earth Remains Forever"
Ecclesiastes 1:4

GOD'S KINGDOM HAS TRULY COME!

From earliest childhood we have been taught Our Lord's Prayer and have memorized its words, often repeating them without realizing what we are saying. If we truly believe God's kingdom has come and Jesus has proclaimed his Glorious Jubilee, we must seriously review what we have learned and rethink what we are praying. We also need to remember who it was who first asked ***"Lord, teach us to pray."***

"THE LORD'S PRAYER" MATTHEW 6:9-13

"Our Father who art in Heaven, hallowed be your name.
Your kingdom come, your will be done on earth as it is in Heaven.
Give us today our daily bread.
Forgive us our debts as we forgive our debtors.
Lead us not into temptation but deliver us from the evil one;
For thine is the kingdom, the power and the glory forever. Amen."

This prayer was first spoken in AD 30-31. The disciples understood God's kingdom was yet to come, God dwelt in Heaven, they still lived under the Old Covenant Law of Moses and awaited, with great expectation, God's promised Jubilee. Awaiting their redemption and salvation, they longed for the day when their prayer petitions would finally be fully realized.

We must proclaim the glorious truth. God's Kingdom has come; we dwell with him and know the truth of his Jubilee. Our debts have been cancelled; we are restored, secure in his Presence in his Holy Land. Our prayer must proclaim these glorious truths. We no longer live in expectation or anticipation. Our Lord dwells with us. We are in God's glorious kingdom. God's glorious kingdom is within us. As the disciples asked their Lord, we must ask: **Please Lord, Teach us to Pray.**

THE NEW LORD'S PRAYER

Our Father who dwells within us, Hallowed be thy name.
As your kingdom has come, let your will be done on earth as it is in Heaven.
Give us each day your Living Bread.
As you have forgiven our debts, help us forgive our debtors.
You have kept us from temptation and have delivered us from the evil one.
Blessed be Your Name and the glory of your kingdom forever. Amen

Baruch Shem Kevod Malchuto Le' Olam Va' ed.
Blessed be your name and the glory of your kingdom forever.

Chapter 11

POST-EXILIC HOLY DAYS

The post-Exilic Holy Days, though not directly fulfilled in Jesus' life and ministry, teach of God's Covenant promises to Israel and to us. Purim celebrates the biblical record of the Israelite victory against Haman's attempt to destroy the Jewish nation living in Persia following their Babylonian captivity, as found in the book of Esther.

Chanukah celebrates the Hebrew revolt and victory against Syria's King Antiochus Epiphanes who tried to destroy the nation's faith after the 2nd temple was built following their Babylonian exile. The Books of the Maccabees record their revolt and victory over the Hellenizing Syrian nation. Studying the history of this time in their lives, we find additional connections to the promised redemption revealed in our Messiah.

PURIM—THE FEAST OF LOTS

Purim, the Feast of Lots, celebrated on Adar 14-15, honors the victory of the Jews in Persia over Haman's plot to eliminate their people. The Book of Esther tells how Esther and Mordecai thwarted Haman's plans to massacre the Jews. After their Babylonian exile, the Hebrew people were living in Persia. Esther, a Jewish woman, became the Queen. In a moment however, their lives were dramatically changed. Haman, the Prime Minister, convinced the king to destroy the Jewish people. Because of this threat, the nation was on the verge of destruction.

The Jews were divided into two kingdoms, the ten tribes of Israel to the north, Judah and Benjamin to the south. Prophets tried to bring them together but they lived in violent opposition. Because they faced extinction, Mordecai called the people of Judah to turn to God for mercy. Haman determined the Hebrews were to be removed from the land. This would come about by execution. The day of extermination was decided by a lottery.

Their deliverance began with a beauty pageant. Vashti, the former queen, found disfavor with the king. He decreed a new queen needed to be found. In a beauty pageant, Esther was chosen as the Queen. She was loved by the king above all the other women. At the time before Haman, the Jews lived peacefully in Persia however, Mordecai, the king's advisor, warned her not to reveal she was a Hebrew.

The king had promoted Haman who demanded that all the king's servants should bow to him. Believing he was to worship only God, Mordecai refused. Full of jealousy, Haman devised a scheme to annihilate every Jew. He convinced the king that the Jews did not keep his laws and should be killed. The king decreed that the Jews were to be executed. By lottery, the date of the execution would be Adar 14th.

Clothed in sackcloth and ashes, Mordecai went to the city in repentance, urging the Jews to do the same. He sent Esther to go to the king and plead for her people. She told Mordecai to gather the Jews and fast for three days and nights; she would also fast. The 3rd day, taking her live in her hands, she went uninvited to the king and found favor in his sight. He asked what she wanted and promised he would give her anything, up to half his kingdom. She asked the king and Haman to attend a banquet where she would reveal her request.

At the banquet, the king asked about her request. Exposing Haman as the king's enemy, Esther begged the king to spare her people. The king commanded Haman be hanged on the gallows prepared for Mordecai. Esther did not wait for God to send his angels but trusted God. In humility the Jews were not willing to trust their own strength but implored God for help. The king could not cancel the law decreeing the Jews be killed but he gave a new decree. They could defend themselves. The day that was to be their destruction became the day of deliverance. The Jews showed devotion to the Holy Land; in thanks for their deliverance, they rebuilt the temple.

THE MESSIAH IN PURIM

The nation was saved physically at that point in history. Full, Spiritual salvation and fulfillment of God's prophesy to Abraham was drawing close. Five hundred years later, it was revealed in all fullness in Jesus, the Messiah, the greater Mordecai. Just as Mordecai, Jesus was condemned to die for his people, the supreme sacrifice of atonement for the sins of both Jews and Gentiles. All prophesies of the Hebrew Scriptures were fulfilled in Christ. The Torah declared that all nations of the earth would be blessed in him. (Genesis 18:18) Just as the Jews were rescued from Haman, we are redeemed by our righteous Messiah.

Mordecai and Esther knew Haman's decree was not an accident of history but was because of the sins and failings of the Jewish people. They knew God would bring judgment. That is why Mordecai clothed himself in sackcloth and ashes, urging the nation to do the same. He sent Esther to beseech the king and plead for his people. Esther was also repentant, asking Mordecai to gather the Jews to fast three days and nights.

SYMBOLISM OF PURIM

Aphrahat's "The Demonstrations" shows comparisons between Mordecai and Jesus:

1. Mordecai was persecuted by Haman, Jesus, by the rebellious people of Israel.
2. Mordecai delivered his people from Haman's hand. Jesus delivered us from Satan's hand.
3. Mordecai clothed himself in sackcloth, saving Esther and his people from the sword. Jesus clothed himself with a human body, saving the church and her children from death.
4. Because of Mordecai, Esther was pleasing to the king and went in, instead of Vashti, who did not do the will of the king. Because of Jesus, the church was well pleasing to God and stands before God, instead of the congregation who did not do his will.
5. Mordecai trod on the neck of Haman, his persecutor. All enemies have been put under Jesus' feet.

WE SEE IN CHRIST, GLORIOUS FULFILLMENT OF THE CELEBRATION OF PURIM

1. Purim is a shadow of the 3-day resurrection. Esther fasted three days and nights. On the 3rd day, she went before the king. In fulfillment, Christ, after three days, was resurrected and rose to go before God.
2. Esther's story is symbolic of Christ walking in the new life. Exposing Haman's plot was symbolic of our sins exposed. The old decree is symbolic of Jesus' triumph over the law of sin and death; the new decree, the New Covenant, triumphs. Once Haman was put to death, Mordecai received unlimited authority and command. Once our sins were put to death, Christ's Spirit was given unlimited authority and command.
3. The Jews would again be delivered from death from the hands of their final enemy on Nisan 16, at First Fruits, the same day deliverance from Egypt began, the same day the 1st century church celebrated Jesus' Resurrection. (Messiah in Purim)

CHANUKAH—THE FEAST OF LIGHTS

Chanukah is the Feast of Lights, celebrated for eight days. Chanukah honors restoration of Divine Worship in the Temple after it was defiled by Syrian king, Antiochus Epiphanes. Placing a Greek idol in the temple, Antiochus forced the Jews to worship his Greek gods. Any Jew who practiced any form of Judaism, studied the Torah or refused to sacrifice an animal to the Greek idols, was killed.

Between the Testaments, c.168 BC, Syria supported the spread of Greek culture and religion throughout Judea. The Maccabees wrested Judea from the Syrian rulers who were replacing their religious laws with Hellenized worship. Chanukah commemorated the recapture of Jerusalem and reestablishment of the Temple. The Maccabees restored holiness to the temple and ruled until Herod took power in 38 BC.

Antiochus' soldiers went through Judea, forcing the Jews to worship the Greek gods. Reaching Modin, the priest, Mattathias, threw the idol down, crying: *"Whoever is for the LORD, follow me"* Leading his five sons and followers, rebellion began and raged for three years. Through the power of God, the greatly outnumbered Jews won. In 165 BC, they finally recaptured Jerusalem.

Return of religious liberty and the Holy Temple was life from death. In celebration they kept an annual holiday from Kislev 25-Tevet 2. Chanukah's greatest lesson was the Power of the Spirit. *"Not by might or power but by my Spirit" says the LORD of hosts."* Zechariah 4:6

Chanukah centers around a nine branched menorah. The menorah in the temple had seven branches but the Chanukah menorah has nine, eight for the eight days of Chanukah and the Shamus in the center, to light the others.

The Messiah in Chanukah

Chanukah's theme is a miracle God performed for the Jews. Following their military victory against Syria, the Jews searched for oil to light the menorah candles, but only found a small jar, enough for one day. God provided his miracle; there was oil for each day, enough for each candle to be lit, celebrating their victory.

Jesus spoke of miracles at Chanukah. "It was at the Feast of Dedication at Jerusalem. Walking in the temple, he told the people that if he did not do the things of his Father they were not to believe him. If he did do them, though they didn't't believe him, they were to believe his works that they would understand the Father was in him and he was in the Father. (John 10:38) Jesus wanted the people to see his miracles and believe in him. His miracles pointed to his divinity and his Messianic identity. He is the message of Chanukah. Through his miracles, he has brought us His Light.

Jesus preached three sermons at Chanukah, declaring himself the Light of the World. *"I am the Light of the World; whoever follows me will never walk in darkness but will have the light of life." "While I am in the world, I am the light of the world." "You are going to have the light just a little while longer, walk while you have the light, before darkness overtakes you. Put your trust in the light while you have it so you may become sons of light."* John 8:12, 9:5, 12:35

At Chanukah, eight candles are lit celebrating the miracle God performed for Israel's deliverance. They moved from death and darkness into God's light. Each day celebrated

God's light in their lives. Chanukah can be honored as we understand God is our Light; Christ, our Lord is the Light of the world. We are lights shining in the darkness. God's light shines in Christ; we must shine for him.

"It was the Feast of Dedication; Jesus was in the temple. The Jews asked: 'How long will you keep us in suspense? If you are the Christ, tell us plainly.' Jesus said, 'I did tell you but you do not believe because you do not belong to my sheep. My sheep listen to my voice. I know them; they follow me. I give them eternal life; they shall never perish. No one can snatch them out of my hand. My Father, who has given them to me, is greater than all. No one can snatch them from my Father's hand. I and the Father are one." John 10:22-30

The Jews could not believe the disciples; now they faced Jesus and demanded an answer they could believe. They could not understand; they were not His sheep. His faithful followers believed. He gave them eternal life. No one could take them from him. Jesus is the Son of God, God's Anointed. He and the Father are One. Israel's lost sheep heard Jesus. Jesus validated himself as God's Messiah, proclaiming Chanukah, the Feast of Dedication, celebration of his divine origin as the Son of God, God's Messiah King.

CHRIST AND THE FATHER ARE ONE! 'ECHAD'!
EIGHT READINGS FOR CELEBRATING CHANUKAH

1. The LORD is Our Light.   Isaiah 60:19 Psalm 27:1

"The sun will no more be your light by day, nor will the brightness of the moon shine on you; the LORD will be your everlasting light; your God will be your glory." "The LORD is my Light and my Salvation, whom shall I fear?"

The LORD is our Light. He is all we need to see the glory of his kingdom. The Light of our LORD's love supplies everything we need. The sun and moon are not needed to bring us his light. Walking with him, we will not walk in darkness. God is our light. He faithfully leads and supplies us with his glorious light. There is no darkness in our Lord's glory. His faithful servants dwell in the light of his Kingdom. He is our light and provides our salvation. We have nothing to fear.

There is no darkness in his kingdom. We must bring his Light to all those outside the gates, all who search for light to guide them. Offering God's Glorious Light, they can enter the gates of his kingdom.

2. The Word is Our Light.   Psalm 119:105 Psalm 119:130

"Your word is a lamp unto my feet, a light to my path." "The unfolding of your word gives light. It gives understanding to the simple."

The Word of our LORD is our light. The Word of God, our Holy Scriptures, are the light that gives us knowledge to understand our LORD's love and salvation. The Word of God, Jesus Christ, is our Light. He dwells with us and gave his life for us; he is the Light of the World. He will be with us wherever we go, to guide and teach us. We will never walk in darkness if we keep our eyes on him.

The words of Scripture and Christ, the Word of God, assure us he has given us his kingdom; he dwells within us. We dwell in him, in his eternal kingdom. With the light of the Word of God to lead us, we can know and serve him. We can enter his kingdom and dwell in his light. We are to bring His Word and Light to all the world. With his light we can go wherever our Lord leads us and never fear the dark.

3. We should be a Light to Others.   Matthew 5:14-16 Luke 11:33

"You are the light of the world; a city set on a hill cannot be hidden. Neither do people light a lamp and put it under a bowl; they put it on a stand; it gives light to everyone in the house. Let your light so shine before men that they may see your good deeds and praise your Father in heaven." "No one lights a lamp, and puts it in a place where it will be hidden. He puts it on its stand so those who come in may see the light."

We are called to be a light for the world, reflecting our LORD's light so all may see his light in us, and be led to him, the True Light. If we let our light shine before the world, they cannot help but see the glory of God, the True Light. This world, lost in darkness, searches for a light to guide them. It is our solemn obligation by God to guide them out of the darkness and offer them his light. In Christ's kingdom, we must lead them through the gates of his Kingdom, and welcome them in. God's light shines on all who enter. Seeing his light reflected in us, the world can see their way into the kingdom to dwell with their Lord, the Light of the World.

4. The Light of the Body is the Eye.   Luke 11:34 Acts 26:18

"Your eye is the lamp of your body, when your eyes are good your whole body is full of light."

"I send you to open their eyes, and turn them from darkness to light, from the power of Satan to God."

To see the Light of God, we must open our spiritual eyes to see his presence and power; his light can't help but shine through. We must not close our eyes to him. With our eyes open, our Lord's light shines into our hearts and lead us out of darkness. With his light in us, we must open the eyes of those still in darkness. God calls us to open their eyes and lead them to Him, their light and salvation. In our Lord's light, they will see the glory of his kingdom, and understand they are welcome in his eternal kingdom.

5. The Messiah is the Light of the World.   John 1:4-5

"In Him was Life, that life was the light of men. The light shines in the darkness; the darkness has not understood it."

Christ's light has been shining in our world for two millennia and continues to shine. His world, 1st century Israel, could not put out God's light, neither can we. In their darkness, they denied his light, closing their eyes to his glory, but His Light continued to shine. The LORD's light will shine; His Son, our Lord, will reign in his kingdom; his kingdom will have no end. His light has overcome the world His Light continues to shine, calling us to come out of our darkness, out of our denial, into the light of His Eternal Kingdom.

6. Paul Saw the Light.   Acts 26:12-13, 18 Romans 11:11-12

"I was going to Damascus; about noon, O King, I saw a light from heaven, brighter than the sun, blazing round me and my companions." "I am sending you to open their eyes and turn them from darkness to light, from the power of Satan to God." "Because of their transgression, salvation has come to the Gentiles, to make Israel envious. If their transgression means riches for the world and their loss means riches for the Gentiles, how much greater riches will their fullness bring?"

God gave his light to the children of Judah, his beloved sons and daughters. He would be their light. He guided them, offering them his covenant promises. He would be their God; they would be his people. Living in blindness, they would not let God's light shine in their lives. God, in his love, mercy and grace, brought his light to the Gentiles. Through Paul, he revealed his light to them.

On his journey to Damascus, Paul was brought to the ground by a vision of God's Shekinah Presence. A light from heaven, brighter than the sun, shone around him and took his sight. Paul was blinded by this light. Led by the hand of God, he was given his mission, to lead the Gentiles out of their blindness.

The light of God was given Paul, so in his blindness he could see and guide the house of Israel living in the Gentile nations, out of their darkness, and through jealousy bring Judah into covenant with him, to dwell in his light. They all could enter into the light of God's glorious kingdom. Paul was sent to bring God's light to Israel, Judah and the Gentiles, so all would hear, believe, and see the glorious Light of God.

7. We are No Longer in Darkness.   Ephesians 5:8, 1 Thessalonians 5:4-6, 1 Peter 2:9

"You were once darkness, now you are light in the Lord. Live as children of light." "You brothers are not in darkness, so that this day should surprise you like a thief. You are all sons of the light, of the day; we do not belong to the night or the darkness" "You are a chosen people, a royal priesthood, a holy nation, a people belonging to God, that you may declare the praises of him who called you out of darkness."

Peter, Paul, and all the disciples were sent to the Jews and the Gentiles, to teach, guide and show them the light. They were not to live in darkness; they were to live in the light of Christ. Their Lord's Light would shine in their lives and the world's darkness would be destroyed. Paul led and taught them to walk as children of the light. They no longer were to live in darkness; they were to live in the light, as sons and daughters of the promise given Abraham, as sons and daughters of the Lord. His light would shine in their lives as they entered his glorious kingdom. They were promised they would see their Lord, in all his glory, and would dwell with him forever.

8. We Need to Shine.   Philippians 2:14

"Do everything without complaining or arguing, that you may become blameless, pure children of God without fault in a crooked and depraved generation, in which you shine like stars in the universe."

The Apostles and Jesus' faithful servants continued to teach the Jews and Gentiles, assuring them they were all part of his glorious kingdom. They were to step out of that crooked, perverse generation and enter into God's Glorious Light, to be his light. In his light, they would see God's promised kingdom coming to them. The glory, power and light of their Lord was shining in their lives. They were to prepare themselves and each other, for the kingdom they were promised was surely coming. They would dwell in their Lord's light, forever in his kingdom.

As we live in this generation, we must not sleep; we must stay alert. We must not let the Light of God go out. His light must continue to shine. We must reflect his glorious light to all in our generation who long to follow His Light, so all may know God's light shines on those who seek him. God's light will continue to shine. The world's darkness cannot put it out. The Light of God's Glorious Kingdom, where our Lord reigns as King, is shining on us. We have before us a great mystery. We are in the Kingdom of God. We are the Kingdom of God. The Kingdom of God is within us. God's light will continue to shine in his kingdom, in us, for all eternity. We must not let God's light go out, for we are assured:

He Shall Reign Forever and ever;
His Light Will Shine in the Darkness.
The Darkness Cannot Overcome It!
All God's People Say 'AMEN'!

Appendix 1

GOD'S FEASTS AND HOLY DAYS—
CHRIST AND THE BRIDE

THE THREE GREAT PILGRIMAGE FEASTS

Passover—Unleavened Bread, ***Pentecost***—the Feast of Weeks
and ***Sukkoth***—the Feast of Tabernacles,
The ***Feast of Trumpets*** and ***Yom Kippur***, the Day of Atonement
all speak of Jesus and his Bride.

| At the Last Supper | | Taking the cup, |

At the Last Supper

Taking the cup,
The Bride accepted the Ketubah,
The Marriage Contract.

Passover   Crucifixion of the Lamb
1. Unleavened Bread
                                                            Death of the Lamb
The Bridegroom paid the Bride's Price.
1st Day of Unleavened Bread   The Bride delivered from slavery to Sin
3rd Day of Unleavened Bread   First Fruits   Resurrection of Christ
7th Day of Unleavened Bread   Promise of Full Deliverance
                                                            when last enemy is Defeated

Counting the Omer   50 Days Between First Fruits and Pentecost
Betrothal of the Bride   —   Ascension of Christ   —   Departure of Bridegroom

2. Feast of Weeks   Pentecost   Maturation of the Bride
First-Fruits Harvest   Mikveh of Holy Spirit
Bridegroom goes to prepare   Gifts of Spirit Given
a place for the Bride while Bridegroom is away.
Bride made ready for Wedding

3. High Holy Days   Day of Trumpets   Return of Bridegroom
End of Israel's Sins.   Marriage of the Lamb
Israel Cleansed.   and the Bride

                                    Days of Awe   Bride and Bridegroom
                                  Great Tribulation   in Wedding Chamber
                            Satan's World a little time more

Yom Kippur—Day of Atonement
Satan removed as god of this world

Purification of Remnant
Final enemy is Defeated
Hadean death is defeated
7 Day Wedding Feast

Feast of Tabernacles
Final Harvest

New Jerusalem
New Heaven and Earth

Shemini Atzeret—Simchat Torah
8th Day of Assembly
Rejoicing in Christ
Eternal Kingdom of Messiah

Comparisons between the Old and New Covenants
Shadow to Fulfillment 1st and 2nd Exodus

1. In the Old Covenant is the Shadow, revealed in the Exodus.
    For persecuting Israel, Egypt faced God's judgment.
    God delivered Israel from Egypt's persecution.
    Israel began their journey to their promised land.
    After three days, Israel crossed the Red Sea.
    In fear and doubt, Israel rejected the Promised Land and refused to enter.
    From Passover & Unleavened Bread to Israel's entry into the Promised Land was forty years.
    After forty years, God's Faithful Remnant entered the Promised Land.
    Joshua, (Yeshua) brought them into the Land God promised them.

    In the New Covenant is Fulfillment in the 2nd Exodus, revealed in Christ.
    For persecuting Christ's servants and crucifying their Lord, Israel faced God's judgment.
    Jesus came to bring his people into his Kingdom.
    Israel was offered the Kingdom but they rejected it and crucified their Lord.
    After three days, Jesus was raised from the dead.
    In disbelief and lack of faith, Israel refused to enter God's kingdom.
    From the start of Jesus' ministry to the Destruction of Jerusalem was forty years.
    After forty years, God's Faithful Remnant was delivered from the persecution of Spiritual Egypt.
    Jesus (Yeshua) brought his Faithful Remnant into the New Jerusalem God promised Abraham.

2. We see the Shadow from the times of Moses and Joshua. (Yeshua)
    Until Israel's entry into the Promised Land,
    there was a forty year transition in the wilderness.
    Jericho stood in the way of entry to their Promised Land.
    Jericho was destroyed at the sound of the Trumpet of God.
    After the forty-year transition, Israel reached the Promised Land.
    The Kingdom was initiated, the Manna ceased, Rahab was saved by the Red Cord,
    and the Children of Israel were redeemed.

We see Fulfillment from the time of Moses' Law to Jesus. (Yeshua)
Until the Church reached the New Jerusalem,
there was a forty year transition, the Apostolic Age, AD 30-70.
The Temple stood in the way of the New Jerusalem.
The Temple and the Mosaic Dispensation were destroyed
at the sound of the Trumpet of God.
After the forty-year transition, the Church reached their Promised Land, the New Jerusalem.
The Kingdom was instituted, the Charismata ceased, the Church was saved by the Blood of Christ,
and the Church was redeemed.

3.   Old Covenant—The Covenant of Death—The Shadow

Passover to Shavuot
Fifty days after Passover, at Shavuot, the Law was given. Exodus 19:1
For worshiping the golden calf, three thousand were killed. Exodus 32:4

Slavery in Egypt------------------forty years in wilderness-----------------------Israel enters
Promised Land.

Throughout the Sinai Covenant, miracles revealed God's Glory, Presence and Power.

Israel crosses the Red Sea--Israel crosses the Jordan River

Their delwiverance is complete.   Their Salvation is complete.

New Covenant—The Covenant of Life—The Fulfillment

Pasha to Pentecost
Fifty days after the Resurrection, at Pentecost, the Holy Spirit was given. Acts 1:4
Hearing the message of God, three thousand were baptized, receiving life Acts 2:41

Slavery to sin   Church in New Jerusalem
In Spiritual Egypt------------------forty years Apostolic Age--------------Christ's Kingdom
End of Old Covenant Age

Throughout the New Testament, miracles revealed God's Glory, Presence and Power.

Christ's Ministry and Death   Church in
Church Crosses the Jordan at Pella   The New Jerusalem
Our Deliverance is Complete. AD 30------------to----------AD 70 Our Salvation is Complete.

Appendix 2

DATING THE MINISTRIES OF JOHN THE BAPTIST AND JESUS TO THE TIME OF HIS PAROUSIA

Accurately documented historic and archeological records and computer science can reveal the dates for ancient events, including the ministry of John the Baptist and the life and ministry of Jesus. In Murrell Selden's "Chronology of the Passovers Associated with the Ministries of Jesus and John the Baptist," we learn of the dating of John the Baptist's ministry and Jesus' life. In his work and Greg Kiser's "Kiser's Science," we can determine the time of their ministries, the date of the Passover when Jesus was crucified and the Rosh-Hashanah New Moon of AD 70.

Selden acknowledges that Israel's calendar was determined by the moon. There is a New Moon every 29 days, 12 hours, 44 minutes and 2.78 seconds, or 29.530 days. The Roman world dated events by the sun. A solar year is 365.2425 days long. With the use of computer programs we can look back 'many moons' or years for precise information about ancient events. From historical and Biblical records, we learn that John's ministry began before September, AD 29, fifteen years after Tiberius took the throne.

1. John began his ministry in Tiberius' 15th year. *"In the 15th year of the reign of Tiberius, the word of God came to John."* Luke 3:1-2 Augustus died on August 19, AD 14. Tiberius succeeded him to the throne on September 17th, AD 14. Fifteen years later, John's ministry would have begun in AD 29. Jesus' testing, probably at Teshuvah, would have begun on Elul 1, AD 29. His ministry would have begun forty days later, at Yom Kippur. Jesus' 3 ½ year ministry, beginning on Yom Kippur, places his crucifixion at Passover AD 33.

2. Jesus attended three Passovers in his ministry, John 2:13, after Jesus turned the water into wine, John 6:4, after Jesus fed the five thousand, and John 11:55, after Jesus raised Lazarus, the Passover of his crucifixion.

3. Historical and astronomical records help us determine when Jesus was crucified. Learning of Passovers from AD 30-35, and their connections with John the Baptist and Jesus' ministries, we can accurately determine the time of Jesus' ministry and crucifixion.

4. March 22nd, AD 33 was the Spring Equinox. March 19th, the Astronomical New Moon, was at 15 hours, 14 minutes. The Astronomical New Moon is not visible, so March 20th was Nisan 1. Passover, thirteen days later, was April 3^{rd,} AD 33. To the Jews, that was the evening of Thursday, April 2nd. After sunset, it was Friday, April 3^{rd,} Good Friday. It was the only time from AD 29-35 that Passover came at the time that correlated with Jesus' 3 ½ year ministry, which started in Tiberius' 15th year, September AD 29.

5. On April 3, AD 33, for 3/4 of an hour, at 3:00 PM, at Jesus' crucifixion, there was a total eclipse of the moon. Passover AD 30, Jesus 1st Passover, to his crucifixion in AD 33 was three solar years. Adding the half year before his first Passover, shows his ministry began in the fall of AD 29 and lasted 3 ½ years.

Daniel's Seventy Sevens

Daniel 9:24-27, essential to Biblical prophecy, is the only prophesy that speaks of the exact time of Jesus' birth and crucifixion. It is also the only prophetic passage that speaks of the Messiah. Isaiah speaks of the Root of Jesse, Isaiah 11:10, and the Prince of Peace, Isaiah 9:6. Jeremiah speaks of the Righteous Branch, Jeremiah 23:5, and 33:15. The title, Messiah, appears only in Daniel 9:24-27 where we learn of the years for the decree for Daniel's people and when God determined his Son, the Messiah, would be crucified.

"Seventy sevens are decreed for your people and your holy city. Know and understand: from the issuing of the decree to restore and rebuild Jerusalem until the Anointed One, the Ruler comes, there will be seven sevens, and sixty-two sevens; after the sixty-two sevens the Anointed One will be cut off and will have nothing. The people of the ruler who will come will destroy the city and the sanctuary."

At the time of Daniel, Jerusalem and the Temple were destroyed. From the decree to rebuild Jerusalem, there would be seven, seven year periods, and sixty-two, seven year periods until Messiah would come; after the 69th seven-year period, Messiah would be cut off.

The Hebrews and Babylonians used a 360-day calendar. These sixty-nine weeks of years equal 483 Babylonian years. 483 years x 360 days is 173,880 days. In the Gregorian calendar, this was 476 years, 25 days. The start of these Seventy Sevens was Artaxerxes' 20th year, 444 BC. Nehemiah 2:1-8 says his edict to rebuild Jerusalem was in Nisan, between Feb 27th and March 28th. 173.880 days from Nisan 444 BC is March 24^{th,} to April 22^{nd,} AD 33.

The Messiah would present himself to his people and be cut off sometime in Nisan AD 33. Jesus presented himself to his people on Palm Sunday, Nisan 10th. Five days later, on Nisan 14^{th,} as their Passover Lamb, he was cut off. On Nisan 16, April 5^{th,} he rose from the grave, all in the time revealed to Daniel.

The Messiah made a strong covenant with many in Israel for one week. (seven years, AD 30-37) After half the week (3 ½ years, AD 33) sacrifice and offering ceased; the Messiah offered the final, perfect sacrifice. Further sacrifices were no longer accepted. His mission to Judah, through his Apostles, continued for 3 ½ more years. The word first had to go out to Judah, bringing God's lost sheep into communion with him. 3 ½ years later, AD 37, and Philip's ministry (Acts 8:5) the word went to the Gentiles so All Israel would be saved.

The last words of Daniel's prophesy reveal *"the people of the prince who would come would destroy the city and sanctuary."* In the generation of Jesus' ministry, Jewish Zealots, the people of the Prince, Christ, had come. Determined to destroy Rome's oppressive yoke, they desecrated the temple, bringing the Abomination that causes Desolation. Because of their abominations, Jesus brought judgment upon his people.

Through Jesus' ministry and the Apostolic Age, we see completely fulfilled the answer to Daniel's prayer. Artaxerxes' edict to rebuild the Temple to the crucifixion and the Apostolic Age is accurate beyond question. Nisan 444 BC to Nisan AD 33 is exactly sixty-nine weeks of years. The last week, the 70th Week, divided in two, is the 3 ½ years of Jesus' ministry, AD 29-33, and the 3 ½ years of the Apostles' ministry to the Lost Sheep, AD 33-37. In AD 37, their ministry went to the Gentiles, completing Daniel's Seventy Weeks of Years.

The judgment against that generation is accurate as well. After Christ, the Anointed One, was cut off, the *"people of the prince who was to come destroyed the city and sanctuary."* The Zealots were already present in Jesus' ministry. No time is given between these events but Daniel was told that at the end there would be war; desolations were decreed.

Because of the Zealots' abominations, one would come to make desolate until the decreed end was poured out on the desolator. This abomination, the profaning and desecration of the Temple and the desolation brought on by Christ, their Prince, through the hand of Rome, speaks of the years leading to the Destruction of Jerusalem and the desolation of the Holy Temple. Christ's judgment was, in truth, the decreed end poured out on the desolator, the Zealots who brought the abomination that causes desolation.

THE NEW MOONS OF AD 70

From "Kiser's Science", we learn of the New Moons of AD 70 and discover God's Ultimate Jubilee. As Rosh-Hashanah falls on Tishri 1, at the New Moon, we see God's Ultimate Jubilee was celebrated on Tishri 10, Yom Kippur, October 2nd, AD 70.

Universal Time	Date		Universal Time	Date		
01/01/70	08:20	Shevat	07/26/70	01:31	Ab	Temple destroyed 9th of Ab
01/30/70	22:36	Adar	08/24/70	12:23	Elul 1	Start of Teshuvah
03/01/70	10:15	Adar 11	09/23/70	10:30	Tishri 1	Rosh-Hashanah
03/30/70	19:40	Nisan	10/22/70	19:44	Chesvan 1	
04/29/70	03:24	Iyyar	11/21/70	16:57	Kislev 1	
05/28/70	10:14	Sivan	12/21/70	10:30	Tevet 1	
06/26/70	19:12	Tamuz				

From all we have learned from Hebrew Scripture's prophecy and its fulfillment in the New Testament, we see the accuracy of the time of Jesus' life and ministry. Jesus was born on Tishri 1, 3 BC, his 3 ½ year ministry was from Tishri 10, AD 29 to his being crucified on Nisan 14, April 3rd. AD 33. He rose from the grave on Nisan 16, April 5th. AD 33. His mission to the Gentiles began in AD 37, after the Lost Sheep of Israel had seven years to receive his message.

His Parousia, his Coming in judgment against that generation and the Wedding of the Bride and Bridegroom was Tishri 1, AD 66. After the Great Tribulation, lasting 3 ½ years, Atonement and God's Ultimate Jubilee was celebrated on Yom Kippur, Tishri 10, October 2nd, AD 70. The Feast of Tabernacles was Tishri 15-21, October 7-13, AD 70. Shemini Atzeret, the 8th Day of Assembly, and Simchat Torah, Rejoicing in the Torah, were October 14-15, AD 70. All came to pass, exactly as Daniel spoke.

All is fulfilled; We dwell with him in His Glory,
His Kingdom and His Presence.

Appendix 3

THE RETURN OF ELIJAH— THE RETURN OF CHRIST

Scripture reveals that without facing death, Elijah ascended into heaven in a fiery chariot. A chariot of fire, the Shekinah Glory, and horses of fire separated Elijah and Elisha. Elijah went up in a whirlwind to heaven. (11 Kings 2:11) Malachi 4:5-6 prophesied that God would send Elijah the prophet before the great and terrible day of the Lord. He would turn the hearts of the fathers to the children and the hearts of the children to the fathers. If his people did not come together to their LORD, he would strike the land with a curse.

Elijah ascended to heaven in the fire of the Shekinah Glory. Many prophets were present but only Elisha witnessed his departure. About 450 years later, at the time of Christ, the Jewish people, even Jesus' disciples, believed scripture declared Elijah would literally, physically return from heaven before the Messiah would appear. Since they witnessed no visible chariot of fire appearance of the great prophet, the Jews rejected Jesus as their Messiah. They were sure scripture affirmed Elijah would return before Messiah would come.

No one saw Elijah return from heaven. They expected to see Elijah literally, physically descend from heaven in the same fiery chariot that took him to heaven. Soon after his reappearance, the Messiah would appear. They were sure that at his appearing they would be freed from Roman oppression. Israel would rule the world; the Messiah would be their king and reign visibly, physically in Israel, his kingdom on earth.

ELIJAH HAS ALREADY COME!

The disciples asked Jesus why the scribes said Elijah must come first. The scribes had argued with them saying Jesus could not be the Messiah; Elijah had not returned. Unable to answer, the disciples asked Jesus. He told them Elijah had already come. The scribes did not know him but did whatever they pleased to him. Jesus told them the Son of man would suffer at their hands as well. The disciples understood he was talking about John the Baptist. (Matthew 17:11-13)

The leaders of ancient Israel felt they were the greatest experts of Judaism in the world. They 'knew' the prophets and the signs of Messiah's appearance. John the Baptist could not be Elijah; Malachi did not say Elijah would return in another man's body. It was the prophet Elijah who would return. He ascended into heaven in a chariot of fire and would return in the same way, visibly, physically in the flesh. Every eye would see him. There could be no argument.

The scribes did not believe Jesus. John the Baptist could not be Elijah. They 'knew' Elijah would return visibly. We might even believe as the Chosen of the LORD, his Holy Nation, these Rabbis, learned leaders of Israel, would be the first to welcome him when he returned. We would be sure a Prophet of God, returning from heaven in a chariot of fire, would not be missed by all those learned 'Men of God'.

The Return of Christ from Heaven

As Jesus prepared to ascend to the Father, Luke said, *"When he had led them out to the vicinity of Bethany, he lifted up his hands and blessed them. While he was blessing them, he left them and was taken up into heaven. They returned to Jerusalem with great joy; they stayed continually in the temple, praising God."* Luke 24:50 In Acts 1:9-11, Luke adds: *"As they were looking intently up into the sky as he was going, suddenly two men dressed in white stood beside them saying, 'Men of Galilee, why do you stand here looking into the sky? This same Jesus, who has been taken from you into heaven, will come back in the same way you have seen him go into heaven'."*

Our Lord ascended into heaven in the clouds of glory. While others may have been present, only the disciples witnessed it. Two thousand years later, faithful saints expect to see Jesus literally return, descending back to Jerusalem. Jesus will return, just as they believe the disciples saw him leave, 'in the clouds'.

As there has been no visible cloud-coming return of our Lord, his faithful followers cannot believe Jesus has already returned. They are sure Scripture confirms He will return in the clouds. Every eye will see him. There is no way they can believe Jesus has already returned. They are sure they will see Jesus literally, physically descend from heaven, in the clouds, just as he ascended into heaven. Soon after his return, he will bring in his glorious kingdom and physically, visibly reign with his faithful disciples. He will destroy all the faithless, unbelieving nations. The physical Heaven and Earth will be destroyed; the New Jerusalem will descend from Heaven. We will witness the End of the World; his kingdom will be revealed in a New Physical World.

Christ has Already Come!

Many Christian leaders ask us how we can believe Jesus has already returned. As the greatest experts of Christianity in the world, they 'know' what prophesy says and what will happen when Jesus returns. Jesus can't have already come. He will return visibly, physically, in the flesh. There can be no argument.

These Christian leaders do not believe Jesus' explanation. He could not have returned before the end of his generation. He will physically, visibly return 'in the clouds'. Until we see him return, we must stay ready and watching for the signs he promised would be seen.

These learned scholars are also sure Elijah must return before the Great and Terrible Day of the Lord. He will return in his chariot of fire to bring this awesome, glorious Day of the Lord. We might even believe, as the Chosen of the Lord, Christ's faithful followers will witness Elijah's return and be the first to welcome Jesus when he returns. The Son of God, descending from Heaven on the clouds, could not be missed by all these wise and learned 'Men of God'.

"MY KINGDOM IS NOT OF THIS WORLD."

From the very start of Jesus' ministry he was confronted by the Jews concerning his Messiahship and his promised kingdom. The 1st century Jews rejected Jesus as the Messiah. Not only did they disbelieve because 'Elijah' had not returned as expected, but Jesus did not meet their expectations concerning the kingdom they believed was promised. Jesus came to bring a Spiritual kingdom; they were waiting for and truly expected a physical kingdom. They expected that at his coming they would reign with their Messiah in Jerusalem. He would set up his throne in Israel, destroy the power of Rome and defeat all their enemies. He would rule the physical world; reigning on David's Throne and they would reign with him.

When brought before Pilate and questioned about his kingship and kingdom, Jesus told him, *"My kingdom is not of this world. If it were, my servants would fight to prevent my arrest by the Jews."* John 18:36 The Jewish nation and their leaders could not accept Jesus as their Messiah; he promised a Spiritual kingdom, not the earthly kingdom they had been dreaming of, and truly expected.

It looks like we have learned nothing in all this time. We live with the same expectations and mistakes of the 1st century Jews. Much of Christianity today still believes Elijah must return to prepare the way for the Great and Terrible Day of the Lord that is still to come. Jesus has not brought a Spiritual Kingdom. Jesus will return, setting up a physical kingdom on earth. All our enemies will be defeated. It is what many Christians have long been dreaming of, and truly expect; but now, Christians will reign with their Messiah, reigning in Jerusalem over all the physical world.

Many Christians today cannot accept the Spiritual Kingdom Christ has brought. It does not meet their expectations for the kingdom they believe he promised. Just as the children of Israel believed, many Christians believe our Messiah will destroy all our political enemies, ushering in a physical kingdom of peace on earth. He will reign literally, visibly in physical Jerusalem, reigning over an Earthly Kingdom and we will reign with him.

Must we continue to let ourselves be blinded and deceived by scholars and religious leaders who continue to teach deception? Must we make the same mistakes the 1st century Jews made or can we honestly believe what Jesus taught his followers and what he continues to teach us?

"My Kingdom is Not of This World!
If My Kingdom were of this world, My Servants would fight."

Isn't it Strange? Have we Learned Nothing?
The Jews would not Believe. Must we do the Same?

Appendix 4

THE PRIESTHOOD OF CHRIST

If we are to understand Christ's Kingdom and whether it will be earthly and physical, or is heavenly and spiritual, we must learn of his Priesthood. The 1st century Jews anticipated an earthly kingdom and believed their Messiah would rule as Israel's King. They were assured this was promised from their Scripture. Much of Christianity today still believes Christ will return to set up his kingdom physically, visibly on earth. He will reign as King and serve as High Priest, as taught in Biblical record.

Understanding Torah Law, to be a priest, you had to prove your lineage back to the house of Levi. Jesus was not of the house of Levi. His lineage can be traced back to the house of Judah. For Jesus to be an earthly priest, understood in Hebrew Scripture, the Torah demanded proof of his lineage back to the house of Levi.

Matthew and Luke trace Jesus' lineage. Matthew 1:2-16 traces his royal lineage through Joseph, to Abraham, the father of Isaac, the father of Jacob, the father of Judah. Luke 3:23-38 traces his blood lineage from his mother, Mary, to her father, Heli, to Adam. This line also connects to David, through his son Nathan, back to the house of Judah. These ancestral lines were given to confirm Jesus' right to the throne of David and his right to serve as the King of the Jews.

To understand Jesus' Priesthood, we must study Hebrews 7:11-21. *If perfection was attainable through the Levitical priesthood, there would be no need for another priesthood of the order of Melchizedek rather than of the order of Aaron. When there was a change in the priesthood, there was also a change in the law. The one of whom those things were spoken belonged to another tribe from which no one has ever served at the altar. It is evident our Lord was descended from Judah.*

In connection with that tribe, Moses said nothing about priests. This is even more evident when we learn of another priest of the order of Melchizedek, who became a priest not according to bodily descent but by the power of an indestructible life. It was said of him, 'You are a priest forever after the order of Melchizedek.' A former commandment has been set aside because of its weakness; the law made nothing perfect. A better hope has been introduced so we can draw near God. It was not without an oath. Those who had become priests took their office without an oath but this one was addressed with an oath. 'The Lord has sworn and will not change his mind.'

"THOU ART A PRIEST FOREVER"

David spoke of the Kingdom of our Lord and Priest King. *"The LORD says to my lord, 'Sit at my right hand until I make your enemies a footstool for your feet. The LORD will extend your mighty scepter from Zion; you will rule in the midst of your enemies. Your troops will be willing on your day of battle, arrayed in holy majesty."* Psalm 110:1-3 The oath in Hebrews 7:22 was seen as well when David spoke of that Priest King. The LORD swore and would not change his mind. Christ was a Priest forever, of the order of Melchizedek. (Psalm 110:4)

Our Lord speaks of this Psalm in Matthew 22:41-45, asking if David, inspired by the Spirit, could call him Lord, if he was his son. Jesus would serve as High Priest and reign as King. These verses from Hebrews and Psalms leave us with several questions. Who was Melchizedek? How is Jesus of the order of Melchizedek? If Jesus was not of the tribe of Levi, unable to serve as an earthly priest, how can his kingdom be an earthly kingdom where he will reign as King and serve as our High Priest?

We learn of Melchizedek in Genesis 14:18-20 After defeating Chedorlaomer, Melchizedek met Abram at the Valley of Shuveh. Melchizedek, the king of Salem, brought him bread and wine. Melchizedek was the priest of God Most High. He blessed Abram and Abram gave him a tenth of everything.

Who is Melchizedek? The writer of the Epistle to the Hebrews tells us that Melchizedek was the king of Salem, the priest of God Most High. By translation of his name, he is King of Righteousness, also King of Salem, King of Peace. Without father or mother or genealogy, he has neither beginning of days nor end of life. Resembling the Son of God, he continues as our priest forever. (Hebrews 7:1-3)

These verses describe this King of Peace. "Being without father or mother or genealogy" implies a vision of Christ, before his incarnation. "Having neither beginning of days nor end of life" also speaks of his eternality. "Resembling the Son of God" also speaks of Christ's pre-existence. This description reveals this Priest of God Most High was not as the priests of Levi who could trace their lineage and genealogy to Aaron and the house of Levi. These sons of Aaron, of the house of Levi, knew their genealogies. They knew their 'fathers and mothers'. This priest of the Most High God was of a superior priesthood, not of flesh and blood descendency. His parentage was unknown, his 'being' eternal, without beginning or end. All that is known is he was the Priest of the Most High God and his priesthood would continue forever.

Learning who Melchizedek was, we must understand what was meant by Christ being of the order of Melchizedek. In the Torah, the Mosaic Law required that all priests prove their descent from Levi. Those who were not of Levi could not serve as priests. Melchizedek is revealed in Genesis but nothing is known of his ancestry or his past. Under Mosaic Law, he was not qualified to serve as a priest however, without knowledge of his genealogy, Melchizedek was the recognized priest of the whole human race. Before the sons of Jacob, before Levi, Aaron or the priests of Israel, Melchizedek was already the Priest of the Most High God.

Eusebius' "Church History" Book 1 Ch. 111, 18 says: *"History does not relate he was announced corporeally by the Jews or that he belonged to the lineage of priests. He came into existence from God, Himself, before the morning star, before the organization of the world. He obtained an immortal undecaying priesthood for eternal ages."*

The Epistle to the Hebrews reveals Christ's priesthood was of the order of Melchizedek, not of Levi, under Mosaic Law. His would be a superior priesthood for all humanity, both Jews and Gentiles. Under Levitical Law, the Levites could only serve as priests to Israel. Christ would serve as Priest for all, both Jews and Gentiles. He is the final, perfect revelation of God. Jesus' priesthood is different from the Levitical order which proved to be a failure. The Levitical order and Mosaic priesthood were incapable of securing victory over sin and offering full communion with God.

The Gospels and Epistle to the Hebrews proclaim Jesus was fulfillment of Psalm 110. He was of the house of Judah, outside the Levitical priesthood. Of the house of Judah, he was proclaimed King. Of the order of Melchizedek, he was proclaimed High Priest of the Most High God. Our eternal Priest is an eternal King. Jesus, the Christ, is the King of Righteousness. Jesus, the Christ, is the King of Peace, a priest forever after the order of Melchizedek.

In Jesus' earthly life, he never served as a Priest. Entering the temple, he taught as a prophet. As he was not of the tribe of Levi, he could not enter the Holy of Holies to sacrifice or burn incense as a priest. For him to return to an earthly priesthood would be to fall back to Old Covenant concepts which have been 'formally annulled'.

The physical, earthly priesthood has been put away in Christ. Now, in Christ, all believers are a Holy Priesthood. 1 Peter 2:5 says, *"You, like living stones, are being built into a spiritual house, to be a holy priesthood, offering spiritual sacrifices acceptable to God through Jesus Christ."* Revelation 1:6 and 5:10 proclaim *"He has made us to be a kingdom and priests to serve his God and Father." "You have made them to be a kingdom and priests to serve our God. They will reign on the earth."*

We are Christ's Kingdom, his holy, Royal Priesthood. As the Temple of God, as Living Stones, we reign and serve on this earth as a Spiritual House, as Christ's Holy Priesthood. We do not offer 'physical sacrifices'; we are to offer 'Spiritual sacrifices' to God, through Christ, our High Priest.

Jesus is High Priest of the Order of Melchizedek; his kingdom and priesthood are eternal. It will not and cannot be a physical, earthly kingdom. The Old Covenant and Mosaic Law have been fulfilled in the New Covenant.

Our Lord, our Christ, reigns as our King and serves as our High Priest of the order of Melchizedek. His Kingdom is an eternal kingdom, not of this earth where it could pass away or be taken by another man's hand. His Kingdom and Priesthood, on this earth, are Spiritual, Heavenly and Eternal. We are the Kingdom of God, his Royal Priesthood. We will reign with our Lord and serve with our High Priest Forever! We have been promised and are assured:

Christ the King Will Reign Forever.
Christ our High Priest Will Serve Forever.
As 'Living Stones', we are His 'Spiritual House',
A Kingdom and Priesthood to Serve our Lord and King Forever.

Appendix 5

SIGNS JESUS GAVE INDICATING THE END OF THE AGE.

("ADAM CLARKE AND MATTHEW 24")

Many of today's 'prophets' believe the End of the World will come in our lifetimes or sometime in the near future, in current events with signs that have never been seen before. We must recognize the signs we see today are not the signs our Lord spoke of. To know the truth we must learn of all that happened in the Fall of Jerusalem. Josephus, Tacitus and Eusebius all speak of the destruction of Jerusalem and the Temple, totally validating God's prophets' and Jesus' warnings of the Great and Terrible Day of the Lord. He assured them tribulation would shortly occur.

Matthew 24:4-5 "Watch out that no one deceives you. Many will come in my name, claiming, 'I am the Christ' and will deceive many."

False Messiahs—**1.** In AD 35, Dositheus, a Samaritan disciple of John the Baptist said he was the Messiah Moses had prophesied. **2.** Simon Magus, a student of Dositheus, deluded many saying he was the Great Power of God and the Christ. *"Simon practiced magic and amazed Samaria saying he was someone great. They gave him heed saying, 'This man is the power of God which is called Great'. He amazed them with magic."* Acts 8:9-13 **3.** A Samaritan impostor led many away saying he would show them the sacred utensils Moses had deposited in Mt. Gerizim. A multitude believed the Messiah had come. Pilate defeated them, slaying their chief. **4.** Theudas deceived many while Cuspius Fadus was procurator in Judea, c. AD 45. *"Theudas arose giving himself to be somebody. Four hundred men joined him but he was slain. All who followed were dispersed and came to nothing."* Acts 5:36 Many, taking all they owned, followed him to the Jordan, assured it would part at his command. Fadus pursued them, killing many, including Theudas. **5.** In the days of the census, c. AD 46, Judas the Galilean, drew many away in disbelief. His followers were scattered; he was killed. (Acts 5:37) Deceivers constantly tried to bring authority to themselves. Many were drawn into the wilderness to witness magnificent signs performed by God. **6.** In AD 55, Felix, an Egyptian, persuaded 30,000 to follow him to the Mount

151

of Olives, saying Jerusalem's walls would fall at his command, leading to the capture of the Roman garrison. They would possess the city. **7.** In AD 66, Menahem bar Hezekiah went to the Temple to be crowned as the Messiah. With eighty couples of the Disciples of the Law, he went in with golden armor crying *Write on the horn of the ox, 'Ye, yielding Pharisees have no share in the God of Israel.'* Because of his tyranny, he was slain by rivals in his own party. **8.** Simon Bar Giora, a leader of the Jewish revolt, attracted 40,000 soldiers, promising liberty for slaves and rewards to the free. In the spring of AD 69, he ruled as King until he was forced to surrender to Rome. He was executed in AD 70. **9.** In AD 68, John of Gischala, the 'man of sin', taking on Monarchial power, declared himself as a God-sent ambassador, truly the greatest false-Messiah of the Great War of AD 70.

Our Lord prepared his disciples for all they would witness; we need not search for impostors. Jesus taught his disciples, to protect them from all that would befall that perverse, sinful generation.

Matthew 24:6 "You will hear of wars and rumors of wars; see to it that you are not alarmed; such things must happen but the end is still to come."

Wars and Rumors of Wars—Wars are usually preceded by fears of war. **1.** In AD 35, war broke out between Herod Antipas and his father-in-law, Aretas, king of Arabia Petraea. When his wife learned Herod had committed adultery with Herodias, she returned to her father's home. In retaliation, war broke out. Aretas' army completely destroyed Herod's army. **2.** In AD 37-41, Caligula ordered his statue placed in the temple. The Jews refused to permit this sacrilege but the nation was terrified by the thought of opposing his commands and the possibility of war. In dread, they neglected to till their land. However, war did not come. Jesus had prophesied, "The END was not yet."

Matthew 24:7 "Nation will rise against nation and kingdom against kingdom."

Nations against Nations, Kingdoms against Kingdoms—**1.** In Caligula's reign, AD 40, great pestilence struck Babylon. Many Jews fled to Seleucia; Greeks and Syrians living there went to war against them, killing many. **2.** In AD 45, there was a battle between Jews in Perea and the Philadelphians. Many were killed. **3.** About AD 45, under Cumanus, the Jews in the temple area were outraged by a Roman soldier. The Romans approached in great force; 10,000 were killed as they fled. **4.** In AD 50 the Jews made war, ravaging Samaria. The Samaritans murdered a Galilean going to Jerusalem for Passover. The Jews took revenge against the land. **5.** At Caesarea, the Jews went to war but were repelled. 20,000 were slain. Wherever Jews and Syrians lived together there was bloodshed and violence. **6.** At Damascus, Tyre, Ascalon, Gadara and Scythopolis 13,000 died. At Alexandria, the Jews suffered under Roman oppression, 50,000 died. **7.** Finally, the whole of Israel went to war against Rome, bringing dreadful slaughter. After seven years, Judea was covered in blood. Jerusalem was a smoldering ruin.

We need not watch for nations or kingdoms to rise against each other. There have been countless wars in history. War will inevitably continue. Nations continue to invade, assault and overcome other nations that threaten them with equal fury. Our Lord warned his disciples of wars they would see, not wars that would never involve them.

Matthew 24:7-8 "There will be famines and earthquakes in various places. All these are the beginning of birth pains."

Earthquakes—**1.** In Claudius' reign, AD 41-54, Tacitus recorded an earthquake at Rome and Apamea, Syria where many Jews lived. **2.** Philostatus recorded an earthquake in Crete. **3.** Additional earthquakes were recorded at Smyrna, Miletus, Chios and Samos, all with Jewish settlements. **4.** Tacitus, Eusebius and Orosius recorded an earthquake in Laodocea in Nero's reign, AD 54-68 **5.** Hieropolis and Colossae were overthrown by an earthquake. **6.** Tacitus recorded an earthquake in Pompeii and Campania in Nero's reign, and at Rome in AD 69 in Galbo's reign. **7.** During the War of the Jews, there were several earthquakes in one night. Josephus recorded a heavy storm with violent wind, rain, lightning, and violent thunderings, followed by dreadful earthquakes. Josephus saw and understood these quakes as 'nature possessed for destruction of all mankind', truly signs of destruction never seen in history.

Famines—**1.** In the 4th year of Claudius' reign, AD 44, an excessive famine spread in Greece, Italy and Judea. Many died for lack of bread. *"Agabus foretold by the Spirit that there would be a great famine over 'all the world'. This took place in the days of Claudius."* Acts 11:28 **2.** In Claudius' 1st year, AD 40, Dion Cassius recorded a famine at Rome and throughout Italy. **3.** There was another in Claudius' 11th year. Galilee and Judea were afflicted by additional famines. **4.** Concerning the famine in the Jewish War, Josephus said, '*the Jews were compelled to eat belts, sandals, skins of their shields, dried grass, even ordure of oxen.*' In the depth of privation, '*a Jewess, of noble family, killed her infant son and prepared it for a meal.*' We remember our Lord wept over Jerusalem as he was led to Calvary. His words proclaimed foreknowledge of the grief these women would face. *"Daughters of Jerusalem, weep not for me but for yourselves and your children; the days are coming when they will say 'Blessed are the barren, wombs that never bore, breasts that never gave suck'."* Luke 23:29

Pestilences—Pestilence is usually the result of famine, but twice pestilences occurred before the start of the Jewish War. **1.** In AD 40, at Babylon, there was a massive pestilence. Many Jews fled to Selucia for safety. **2.** In Rome, in AD 65, a pestilence left great multitudes dead. **3.** In the Jewish War, Jerusalem was surrounded by Titus' army. Pestilence and disease overcame the entire nation, adding to the horrors of the siege. This pestilence came because of the multitudes who had gathered in Jerusalem for Passover, the horrors from the unburied dead and the spread of famine.

Countless 'prophets' continue to warn us of the approaching end of the world. Whenever there is an earthquake or great disaster, they claim these as signs of God's judgment and the end of the world. However, just as wars continue, earthquakes, famine and pestilence will be seen. We must not let natural destructions convince us these are signs of God's final judgment. The Lord prepared his disciples for what they would witness so they would be ready for what was to occur before the 'End of the Age'.

Matthew 24:11, 23-24 "Many false prophets will appear and deceive many people." "If anyone says, 'Look, here is the Christ!' or 'There he is', do not believe it; false Christs and false prophets will appear and perform great signs and miracles to deceive even the elect, if that were possible."

False Prophets—In the final days of the siege of Jerusalem, a false prophet, claiming divine commission, said that all who went to the temple would be delivered. About 6,000, mostly women and children gathered, anticipating a miracle. When the Romans set the gallery afire, the multitude fell into the fiery ruins. (Wars, Bk. 6, 5, 2)

Just as Jesus warned of false Messiahs, he was concerned that his beloved disciples not be led astray by false prophets who would pretend to show great signs and wonders, leading the very elect away.

Matthew 24:29-30 "Immediately after the distress of those days, the sun will be darkened, the moon will not give its light, stars will fall from the sky and the heavenly bodies will be shaken."

Fearful Sights and Signs from Heaven—The LORD consistently revealed destruction of the elements of the heavens and the earth, destruction of the very makeup of the universe. The sun being darkened, the moon not giving light, stars falling from heaven, all apocalyptic visions, showed the control God possesses. His wrath, his judgment was total; everything would be destroyed. While many believe this speaks of destruction of the universe, God's judgment was against peoples, nations and kingdoms. God's judgment, the sun darkened, the moon not giving its light, speaks of God's power over these nations' 'heavens and earths' for their disobedience to God. God would bring every last one to destruction, physical and Spiritual, for refusal to obey his commands. God is in control; his judgment would be physical and Spiritual. God's Holy Wrath and judgment reveal all he would do to purge his creation of the sinful apostate nations that turned from him in disobedience. The words 'world' or 'earth' were understood in Hebrew as the 'land of Judah', or the lands of those who faced God's judgment. The way we understand them is not as they were understood by those who first heard them; the apocalyptic language was clearly understood by those who faced the destruction and desolation.

1. Micah 1:2-3 foretold God's judgment against Judah. *"Hear, O peoples, all of you, listen O earth and all that are in it that the Sovereign LORD God may witness against you. The LORD is coming from his dwelling place. He comes down and treads the high places of the earth. Mountains melt under him; valleys split apart like wax before the fire.* All this is because of Jacob's transgressions, because of the sins of the house of Israel." No one saw God come down from Heaven but, by the hand of God, Babylon destroyed Judah; Jerusalem was razed. God destroyed the whole of Judah's Heaven and Earth. *'Mountains will melt under him, valleys will be cleft like wax before the fire,'* reveals fire brought the destruction. Though Babylon took the people into exile, God's hand was over Nebuchadnezzar, God's instrument of judgment. **2.** Nahum 1:4-9 prophesied Nineveh's destruction. The LORD took vengeance against the city for its sins. *"He rebukes the sea and dries it up, he makes all the rivers run dry; the mountains quake, the hills melt away'."* While these words are truly apocalyptic, we can be sure to Nineveh their land melted away. 'Their heaven and earth', the nation and its people were laid waste. **3.** Isaiah 13:9-13 speaks of God's judgment and Jerusalem's destruction under Nebuchadnezzar, the same description of 'destruction of the universe' revealed in Matthew. *"See, the day of the LORD is coming, a cruel day, with wrath and fierce anger, to make the land desolate and destroy the sinners within it. The stars of heaven and their constellations will not show their light. The rising sun will be darkened; the moon will not give its light. I will punish the world (the land and people of Israel) for its evil and the wicked for their sins. I will make the heavens tremble. The earth will shake from its place at the wrath of the LORD Almighty in the day of his burning anger."*

The Holy City, Jerusalem and the Temple were known as Israel's Heaven and Earth. In these words we see God's total judgment against his people. Their 'Heaven and Earth' were totally laid waste. To get his people to understand, the prophets warned of the wrath God would bring down upon their Heaven and Earth. Telling them Babylon would overtake and destroy them would have meant nothing. In their haughty strength, they were sure they could overcome this enemy. God would never destroy the Sons of Abraham.

Isaiah's words that the stars would not give their light, the heavens would tremble, the earth would be shaken, revealed God's message. The hand and power of the Almighty would 'shake' the nation. Their Heaven and Earth would 'tremble'. Babylon would surely take the credit, but it was the LORD, through the hand of Nebuchadnezzar, his instrument of Divine judgment, who brought the nation to its knees.

These prophesies reveal God's wrath and judgment against sinful nations, especially God's own. Understanding the destruction seen by those who lived through the events, we see all the Lord foretold was fulfilled. The earth, the land of Judah, was left a desolation; the stars of the heavens did not give their light. The Heavens and Earth, the nation and people of Israel trembled.

Matthew's words were symbolic of the Bible's apocalyptic language, but we might see these words fulfilled literally as well. "The sun darkened, the moon not giving its light," could be visible signs in the heavens. At the Destruction of Jerusalem, there were massive earthquakes which could have caused a tilt of the earth on its axis, causing the sun to move in the sky, causing darkness. At the full moon, a lunar eclipse gives the moon a red color. The Blood Moon, the moon at full eclipse, was seen at the crucifixion, and could have been seen in AD 70, helping us understand these signs in the heavens were spiritual and also physical.

The astrological signs at Jesus' birth, the Eta-Draconid meteor showers, recurred in AD 69-70. These meteor showers would surely have been seen, symbolically, through Matthew's eyes, as stars falling from heaven; the powers of the heavens were shaken. Our 21st century minds see them as meteors falling through space, but for 1st century minds, these visions held much mystery and wonder. Their appearance at such momentous times, truly spoke, apocalyptically, of God's judgment against them.

Matthew 24:30-31 *"At that time, the sign of the Son of man will appear in the sky, all the nations of the earth will mourn. He will send his angels with a loud trumpet call and gather his elect from the four winds."*

The Sign of the Son of man in Heaven—After descriptions of the tribulation, we read of our Lord's return in his Father's Glory. All would see this 'sign', Divine Assurance of the Son of man *'Coming in the Clouds of Heaven'*. His angels would gather his elect from the four winds. All the tribes of the earth, all Israel would mourn. Many believe this glorious event will be visible and literal. Others see it as total symbolic imagery, showing the glory of our Lord's return. However, there is accurate historical record of these events, the coming of the Lord in righteous judgment with his saints in His Father's Glory and Resurrection of the dead. In Jerusalem's destruction, Josephus and Tacitus recorded visions in the skies, 'Great Signs and Wonders.' **1.** Josephus said: *"Shortly after Passover, through different parts of the country, before sunset, there were visions in the clouds, chariots and troops of soldiers in armor. This spectacle occurred before the setting of the sun in various parts of the country, witnessed by various individuals."* **2.** He also recorded an event in the temple. *"At Pentecost, while the priests were going by night into the inner temple to perform their duties, they felt a shaking followed by murmuring voices, a great multitude saying in an earnest manner 'Let us depart hence'. (War Bk. 6, 5, 3, 297-300)* **3.** Tacitus recorded: *"Prodigies occurred which this nation, though prone to superstition, did not deem lawful to expiate by offering and sacrifice. There were hosts joined in battle in the skies, fiery gleam of arms, the temple illuminated by a sudden radiance from the clouds. The doors of the inner shrine were suddenly thrown open; a voice of more than mortal tone was heard to cry that the gods were departing. At the same instant, there was a mighty stir of departure."* (Histories, Bk. V)

THE HOLY DAYS OF GOD, THE HOLIDAYS OF MAN

Some believe this stir of departure and voices crying, *"Let us depart hence"* speak of God's presence, with his angels, departing the Holy of Holies. However, Scripture reveals the Shekinah Presence departed the Temple at the start of the War in AD 66. As Tacitus and Josephus recorded hosts joined in battle in the skies just before the time of these voices crying, these voices were not the sound of the Shekinah Presence departing the temple. Others believe they were the 'voices' of souls imprisoned in Hades.

'Everyman's Talmud' says the temple, the focal point of Heaven and Earth, was where the earth and the under-world met. The rock on which the temple was built was the capstone of Sheol where souls of the dead were imprisoned. The voices crying: *"Let us depart hence"*, could be the great multitude of God's saints released from beneath this capstone, ascending in resurrection life, voices of the Sinai Covenant saints and redeemed martyrs, receiving their 'incorruptible resurrection body', Christ, in the unseen realm.

Josephus and Tacitus recorded wonders in the 'heavens and earth', the same wonders Paul revealed in 1 Corinthians 15:52 These visions reveal everyone, all Jerusalem, 'every eye', saw the Sign of the Son of man on the Clouds of Heaven coming with power and glory, and the redeemed of the Old Covenant, martyrs of the New Covenant rising in resurrection life to their Lord in his Glory.

Matthew 24:9-11 "You will be handed over to be persecuted and put to death; you will be hated by all nations because of me."

Persecution of Christians—In the Church's infancy there was unprovoked cruelty against Christians. **1.** John the Baptist and our Lord were put to death. **2.** Peter and John were imprisoned and with other apostles were scourged by the Jewish council. **3.** Ignoring the 'Jus Gladii', Stephen was stoned to death c. AD 36; James, Jesus' brother, was thrown from the temple wall and stoned by the Pharisees in AD 62. **4.** Herod Agrippa beheaded James, the brother of John. **5.** He imprisoned Peter, planning to put him to death. **6.** Paul pled before the Jewish Council in Jerusalem and the Roman governor. **7.** With Silas, he was imprisoned, scourged, beaten with rods and stoned. **8.** In AD 64, Nero's persecution began. Multitudes faced martyrdom. Peter was crucified; Paul was beheaded.

Persecutions surely continue. Terrorism and hatred lead many to believe these are signs of our Lord's judgment against us. We must remember who our Lord spoke to when he gave these warnings. The early Christians knew what they would endure before their Lord came in judgment against that sinful generation.

Matthew 24:10 Many will turn away from the faith and will betray and hate each other."

Falling Away and Betrayal—**1.** Paul's Epistles clearly spoke of Christians falling away from the faith. Hearing the words of the Judiazers, betraying their Lord, many turned back to the Law of the Old Covenant. **2.** Speaking of Nero's persecution of the Christians,

Tacitus said that many who confessed responsibility for the Great Fire of Rome in July, AD 64, were seized. By their testimony, a great multitude was convicted and executed. *"An arrest was made of all who confessed. An immense multitude was convicted, not for arson but for hatred of the human race."* (Tacitus' Annals XV)

There is no difference between their time and ours. Betrayals among brethren continue but these are not the signs of our Lord's judgment against us. God's judgment against those who killed his messengers, scourged his followers and crucified His Son was brought against that sinful generation to the utmost.

Matthew 24:14 "This gospel of the kingdom will be preached in the whole world as a testimony to all nations. Then the end will come."

Gospel of the Kingdom preached to whole world.—**1.** Speaking to the Romans, Paul assured them: *"Isaiah says, "LORD, who has believed what he has heard from us?" Faith comes from what is heard, what is heard, from the preaching of Christ. Have they not heard? They have,* **'their voice has gone out to all the Earth, their words to the ends of the earth'.** *"* Romans 10:16-18 **2.** *"To him who is able to strengthen you according to my gospel and the preaching of Jesus Christ, according to the revelation of the mystery kept secret for long ages, now disclosed through prophetic writing,* **is made know to all nations."** *Romans 16:25* **3.** *"The gospel, which has come to you, in the whole world is bearing fruit and growing; provided you continue in the faith, stable and steadfast, not shifting from the hope of the gospel, which you heard,* **which has been preached to every creature under Heaven."** Colossians 1:5, 23

Paul was commissioned to preach the Gospel to the Gentiles. God's word had to spread to the whole of the Roman Empire, to the ends of the earth. All the World, Jews and Gentiles, had to hear the gospel preached as a witness and promise of fulfilled prophesy. As the Roman Empire grew, many within the Jewish faith had spread throughout the lands. Many others, driven from their homeland centuries earlier, were still separated from their homeland. Outside their Promised Land they were outside the covenant, alienated from their people and their God.

To ensure that all the people of Israel heard the Gospel, the Gospel had to be preached to all the Gentile nations. The Word had to go out 'to the ends of the earth'. Until the 'whole world', 'all the House of Israel' heard the message, the apostles' mission was incomplete. They were to make disciples of 'All Nations'.

Only Then Could The End Come!

The ten Lost Tribes, exiled out of their land, living in those Gentile nations, were considered Gentiles by the Jews. They needed to hear, believe, and return to the God of Abraham. Paul's mission, to preach to the Gentiles, would bring to completion all God's promises to the people of Israel, so 'All Israel' could be saved. Paul declared, *"The Word has gone out to the ends of the earth."* Paul proclaimed God's Word, His Gospel, had gone to the Ends of the Earth, to all the Lost Sheep of Israel. With that proclamation, both houses, All Israel, the 'Faithful Remnant' knew Salvation!

"ALL ISRAEL WILL BE SAVED!"

Paul's message, in Romans 11:26-27, speaks of God's promises to Israel and Judah, spoken by God's holy prophets. *"I do not want you to be ignorant of the mystery, brothers, so you may not be conceited. Israel has experienced a hardening, in part until the fullness of the Gentiles comes in. So then All Israel will be saved."* The Houses of Israel and Judah would be reunited as one nation, one people. *Hebrews 8:8 prophesied, "The time is coming, declares the Lord, when I will make a new covenant with the house of Israel and the house of Judah."* Though many scholars say the House of Israel, exiled from their Land and their God, is lost, forsaken, forgotten, God did not forget his own. He had not abandoned his faithful remnant, the ten northern tribes, the house of Israel.

We are also told the fullness of the Gentiles has not yet been revealed in completeness. We are told by many 'false prophets' and scholars that Israel, in 1948, finally was restored to the land and the fullness of the Gentiles is about to be fulfilled. In their understanding, Paul's words are ready to come to fulfillment. They assure us that only when the Fullness of the Gentiles comes in will All Israel be saved.

Ezekiel 37:15-28 speaks the truth of God's promise to both houses. Ezekiel took a stick and wrote, "To Judah and the Israelites associated with him." He took a second stick and wrote, "Ephraim's stick belonging to Joseph's house." He joined them together in his hand and they became one stick. God promised that he would take the Israelites out of the nations where they had been driven and bring them to their own land. He would make them all one nation and they would have one King over them. They would never again be divided into two kingdoms. God would cleanse them from all their sins and purify them. They would be his people; he would be their God.

God took Israel out of the nations where they had gone and gathered them with Judah into Christ, into their own land, a Spiritual Land. As one people with one King, they would never be separated from their land or their God. All the nations where they had been driven would know God made Israel holy, when they saw the twelve tribes, all Israel, and Christ, the LORD's sanctuary among them forever.

In Israel's exile to Assyria, the King of Assyria brought the people from Babylon, Cuthah, Avva, Hamath and Sepharvaim into Samaria to settle there and drove the people of Samaria into their lands. (11 Kings 17) The children of Israel were still living in those Gentile lands when Paul wrote to the Romans about All Israel.

These people were no longer Israel. Hosea 8:8 says "Israel was swallowed up. She was among the nations like a worthless thing." 'Nations' in Hebrew is 'Goyim' or Gentiles. Driven from their land, living in the Gentile nations, the children of Israel had become Gentiles. Paul's mission was to preach to the Gentiles to provoke Judah to jealousy so she would come to Jesus as her Lord. The fullness of his mission however, was to the Gentiles, to preach the Mystery of the Gospel, to bring in the fullness of the Gentiles so All Israel would be saved.

In Genesis 48:13-19, Joseph took his sons to Jacob to receive their blessings. Jacob put his right hand on Ephraim, though Manasseh was the elder, saying the younger would be greater than the elder. Ephraim would become a multitude of nations. Multitude is 'melow' meaning fullness. Nations is 'goyim', Gentiles. Jacob prophesied that Ephraim's descendants would be the 'Fullness of the Gentiles'. Ezekiel prophesied Ephraim's stick, joined with Judah's stick, would be One Stick, One people, One nation. When the fullness of the Gentiles came in, Judah and Israel would be One.

Paul spoke a mystery, partial hardening of Israel. Judah would be hardened until the fullness of the Gentiles came in. The fullness of the Gentiles does not speak of the End of Time, with Israel no longer trodden underfoot by the Gentile Nations. It speaks of the bringing in of all Gentile nations, as Paul was commissioned to do. 'All Israel' does not speak of all Israel in number or the physical Nation. Paul would bring in the Fullness of the Gentiles so all Israel, both Houses, would be saved. Israel and Judah would be One. Jews and Gentiles would be One. With One King they would dwell with their Lord forever.

Seeing many of these Gentiles as exiles of the House of Israel, we understand Paul's mission to the Gentiles. God's eternal plan from the foundation of the world concerned the House of Israel. Paul preached the Gospel to the Gentiles, in part, to cause jealousy in Judah so she would repent and come to the Lord. He was also sent to bring in the Fullness of the Gentiles so All Israel would be saved.

In Israel's salvation, Paul's mission brought All faithful Gentiles to God. All nations would be God's people and know His Salvation. Hosea prophesied, 'Great would be the Day of Jezreel', God's Final Harvest. Israel was brought out from exile, into covenant with God, no longer separated from her land or from her God. The faithful of Judah repented and turned to God. Faithful Gentiles were also brought in. Israel and Judah were reunited as One with their Lord. Jews and Gentiles were brought together as One. They have One Lord, One King, and dwell forever in his Kingdom. They dwell in a Heavenly, Spiritual Kingdom, their New Holy Land, the New Jerusalem where righteousness dwells. They will never be separated from each other or from God.

Hosea reveals a glorious day of deliverance and restoration. *"I will heal their waywardness and love them freely, for my anger has turned away from them. I will be like the dew to Israel; he will blossom like a lily, like the cedar of Lebanon, he will send down his roots; his young*

shoots will grow. His splendor will be like an olive tree, his fragrance like a cedar of Lebanon."
Hosea 14:4-7

The Lord promised: *"In that Day, says the Lord, you will call me 'my husband. You will no longer call me 'my master'. I will remove the names of the Baals from her lips; no longer will their names be invoked. In that day, I will make a covenant for them with the beasts of the field, birds of the air and creatures that move along the ground. Bow and sword and battle I will abolish from the land so that all may lie down in safety.*

I will betroth you to me forever, in righteousness and justice, in love and compassion. I will betroth you to me in faithfulness. You will acknowledge the Lord. In that day, I will respond to the skies; they will respond to the earth, the earth will respond to the grain, the new wine and oil; they will respond to Jezreel. I will plant her for myself in the land. I will show my love to the one I called 'Not my beloved one'; I will say to those called 'Not my People', 'You are my people' and they will say, 'You are my God' Hosea 2:16-23

Paul reaffirms this oneness. *"The scripture foreseeing that God would justify the Gentiles by faith, preached the Gospel beforehand to Abraham, saying 'In you shall all the nations be blessed'. Those who are men of faith are blessed with Abraham who had faith." "Now that faith has come, we are no longer under a custodian; in Christ Jesus you are all sons of God through faith. For as many of you as were baptized into Christ have put on Christ. There is neither Jew nor Greek, slave nor free, male nor female. You are all One in Christ Jesus."*
Galatians 3:8, 25-29

"If you are Christ's, then you are Abraham's seed."

"GREAT IS THE DAY OF JEZREEL!"
"GREAT IS THE DAY OF THE HARVEST!"

161

Appendix 6

BIBLICAL PROPHECY AND HISTORICAL FULFILLMENT

S tudying Scripture's prophetic, apocalyptic messages, we might be surprised to see historic fulfillment of John's words. We certainly should not look at all scripture as literal events but we might be surprised to discover historic reality in many of the messages given in apocalyptic form. Studying the events in the destruction of Jerusalem, we discover credible physical evidence of the voice and hand of God confirmed in historic record.

1. In Revelation 8:13 we see symbolic mysteries and try to understand their meaning. "*I heard an eagle, flying in mid-air, call out in a loud voice: 'Woe, woe to the inhabitants of the earth.'*" In all reasoning, these words are totally symbolic of the destruction that was about to befall Jerusalem. God's wrath would fall on the land and its people; God's 'creation' cried out in despair over what was coming.

Josephus heard this 'eagle' crying, a visible witness of God's awesome power. "*There was a man named Jesus, the son of Ananus, a plebeian and husbandman who, four years before the war began, when the city was in peace and prosperity, came at the time of the feast of Tabernacles and began to give a sudden cry. 'A voice from the east, a voice from the west, a voice from the four winds, a voice against Jerusalem and the holy house, a voice against bridegrooms and brides, a voice against this whole people'!*" He cried in divine fury. Many whipped him but he made no response. Taken to the procurator, he was whipped repeatedly but he never pled for mercy; he just continued to cry "*Woe to Jerusalem!*"

Until the start of the war, he continued his lament. He did not speak against those who whipped him nor kindly to those who offered comfort; he only cried of all that was falling on the beloved city. He cried loudest at the feasts and continued seven years and four months until the start of the siege that gripped the city. Then he cried more grievously: '*Woe to the city, the people, the whole house!*' At the end, he cried 'Woe to myself also!' At those words, a stone from an engine struck him, killing him." (War 6, 5, 3)

We hear a man in agony, crying the approaching doom on the beloved city. We hear in his voice, the agony felt in the heavens, a symbolic eagle crying the horrors befalling the nation and people of God. God's prophesy, in symbolic form, is seen fulfilled in Josephus' words. John revealed God's word to his children; Josephus revealed them as well. The visions John saw and Josephus revealed, proclaimed the woe that was about to befall the land.

2. Joel 2:30, Matthew 24:29-30, and Revelation 6:12-13, 12:3-4 speak of wonders that would be seen in the heavens at the End of the Age. Joel prophesied: *"I will show wonders in the heavens and on the earth. The sun will be turned to darkness, the moon to blood before the coming of the great and dreadful day of the Lord."* Matthew gave Jesus' warning. *"Immediately after the distress of those days, the sun will be darkened; the moon will not give its light; stars will fall from the sky; heavenly bodies will be shaken."*

John spoke fulfillment of Joel and Matthew's words. *"The sun turned black like sackcloth. The whole moon turned blood red; stars in the sky fell to earth."* He also revealed: *"Another sign appeared in heaven, an enormous red dragon, with seven heads, ten horns and seven crowns on his heads; his tail swept a third of the stars out of the sky and flung them to the earth."*

This heavenly portent proclaimed our Lord's completed mission to his people. The great red dragon's 'seven heads and seven crowns on his head', spoke of Lucifer's crowning spiritual dominion, authority and control; the 'ten horns' spoke of his physical assault against Christ, his persecution of the Lord's faithful remnant and his attempts to bring division, sedition and destruction to God's faithful flock.

This second portent foretold a meteor shower from the Eta-Draconid constellation, 'a great red dragon'. The Draconid constellation has four stars of the second magnitude, with one in the tail. In this physical meteor shower, his tail swept 'a third of the stars from the heavens', casting them to the earth. Metaphoric of the Old Covenant Heaven and earth, God's Spiritual meteor shower brought the Mosaic Covenant's Heaven and Earth to an end.

"Jesus' Birth Decoded" and "Introduction to Jupiter-Regulus Conjunctions" show the Draconid meteor showers and Jupiter-Regulus triple conjunctions appeared at Christ's birth and Return, correlated with the rising and the casting down of Lucifer, the Great Red Dragon. As these meteors fell from the skies, as seen in the acts of Herod and Nero, Lucifer and his legions rose in spiritual warfare against Christ. At Christ's physical appearing, Lucifer sought to conceal or prevent the Lord's suffering; at His Spiritual Appearing, Lucifer sought to overcome Christ's victorious saints but Christ's judgment forever cast Lucifer and his legions from their place of honor.

Christ's Kingdom has Come!   His Saints are Victorious!

Many of the Jupiter-Regulus triple conjunctions occurred at critical moments in Israel's life. They were seen at Josiah's reforms, in 620-619BC, and at his death, c. 608-607 BC, during Daniel's Four Kingdoms, at Jerusalem's Babylonian captivity, 597-595 BC, at the end of Judah's captivity, 525-524 BC and at the times of Cyrus, Artaxerxes, Alexander the Great and Antiochus Epiphanes. They also appeared at Jesus' birth, in 3-2 BC and at the destruction of Jerusalem, AD 69-70, all revealing the Hand of God over Creation. Josephus even saw a star resembling a sword, a comet lasting a whole year and chariots running among the clouds. (War 6, 5, 3 288-298) Pliny described a comet, a Torch-star, possibly Halley's comet which appeared in AD 66 at the start of Rome's invasion, 3-years before Jerusalem's destruction. (Nat'l History Bk. 11 xx 11.90)

Balaam's prophesy: *"A star will come out of Jacob; a Scepter will rise out of Israel"* in Numbers 24:17, was fulfilled in the recurrence of the triple conjunction of Jupiter and Regulus in Leo which began October 16th, AD 69, bringing the destruction of Jerusalem and a 'New Beginning', the triple crowning of Regulus, Coronation of Heaven's King! Josephus' star resembling a sword, or scepter, Pliny's 'torch-star' and Balaam's Scepter proclaim Yeshua YHWH, the LORD's Salvation, at His Coming has retaken the Scepter and Reigns as LORD and Christ.

3. John's Apocalypse reveals a vision of invading locusts. Out of the smoke, locusts came down on the earth with power like scorpions. They were not to harm the grass, plants or trees, only those who did not have the seal of the Lord on their foreheads. They were permitted to torture them for five months but to assure a righteous remnant, they were not to kill them. *"The agony they suffered was like that of the sting of a scorpion."* Revelation 9:3, 5

This was surely not a literal siege of locusts, but apocalyptic language revealing truths fulfilled in historic record. In the siege of Jerusalem, from April to September AD 70, we learn of Rome's last assault against Jerusalem. This siege against the children of Israel was seen as scorpions burning them physically and spiritually as their beloved city and temple were leveled and destroyed.

In the last five months of the siege, Rome, the 'Scorpion of the earth', brought down this mighty nation. From historic record we learn of the timetable of these five months. From April to September AD 70, these 'locusts' these legions of Rome, tortured the land and children of the land with demonic power, like the torture of a scorpion's sting, burning their temple and their nation. While Revelation's scorpions are truly apocalyptic imagery, Israel would have had no problem convincing us Rome's legions were truly a 'demon force' to the utmost.

FIVE MONTHS' ASSAULT OF 'LOCUSTS'

April AD 70	The assault began forty years from the start of Jesus' ministry to his people.
May 25th	Rome breached the 3rd Wall and captured the New City.
May 30-June 2	They entered the 2nd Quarter. The Jews withdrew behind the 1st Wall. The Wall of Antonia fell. Rome built a siege wall around the city.
July 22nd	Rome renewed its assault on Antonia; the fortress fell to Titus. Rome burned the gates and entered the Temple Courtyard.

August 10ᵗʰ   The Temple was destroyed by fire.

September 26ᵗʰ   The lower city was burned. Herod's palace was assaulted. Rome entered the Upper City.

THE RESISTANCE ENDS.

4. These locusts only harmed those who did not have the seal of the Lord on their foreheads; the faithful saints of the Lord were not harmed by this 'demonic force'. This again is validated by historic record. Matthew and Luke spoke of the Desolating Sacrilege and our Lord's warning to his disciples to flee when the abomination stood in the temple and Jerusalem was surrounded by armies.

Eusebius reveals that Jerusalem was totally abandoned by the Christians. By AD 69, the Jerusalem Church was deserted. Jesus' faithful servants fled before desolation approached the beloved city. The saints, with 'the seal of the Lord on their foreheads', were safe from the scorpion's sting. They were warned that when they saw the desolating sacrilege standing in the temple those in Judea were to flee to the mountains. There would be great tribulation like nothing ever seen before or ever seen again.

Our Lord wanted his disciples to understand the urgency of flight before it was too late. The disciples understood Daniel's vision of the desolating sacrilege. The temple was not to be desecrated by unholiness. Jerusalem, the Beloved City, was holy to the Lord. Jesus' disciples were all witnesses of the Zealots' atrocities upon their Temple, their city and their God. The Holy Temple, the Dwelling Place of God, was desecrated, covered in blood. Nothing could restore its holiness; it was thoroughly defiled. God's Shekinah Presence could no longer abide within its walls. Their House would be left Desolate.

Seeking to end Rome's oppression, the Jewish Zealots brought upon themselves the Abomination that caused Desolation. They had murdered priests and temple guards and killed great multitudes, defiling the Temple and the Holy City. They covered the temple courts with dead bodies and blood, defiling the Temple, bringing on the desolation. Jesus followers understood that when they saw this sacrilege standing in the Holy Place, when they saw Jerusalem surrounded by armies, they were to flee without looking back.

With all the Zealots' assaults, Rome knew they needed to act quickly to bring order back to the land. By November 14, AD 66, Cestius Gallus, Governor of Syria, had pursued the rebels to Jerusalem. By November 17ᵗʰ, he was advancing toward the city. Invited into Jerusalem by the Pro-Roman men, he delayed. In his delay, the Zealots attacked, murdering their leaders. Five days later, the Romans, ready to undermine the wall, were preparing to set the temple gates ablaze. However, on November 22ⁿᵈ Gallus suddenly gave up, retreating, with no reason in the world.

Cestius' unexpected withdrawal gave the Zealots a false sense of victory. After his retreat, they lived in an atmosphere of peace and safety, assured of triumph. Writing to the Thessalonians, Paul prophesied their false security. *"You know very well that the day of the Lord will come like a thief in the night. While people will say, 'Peace and safety', destruction will come on them suddenly.'* 1 Thessalonians 5:2-3

The Thessalonians were given signs to watch for, to warn them of Jerusalem's coming destruction. Destruction would come without warning on those who lived with that false perception of peace and safety. The faithful remnant were not living in darkness. They understood their Lord's words. Watching for these signs, they were not living with a vain hope of victory over the hand of Rome.

We are told that Cestius fled without any reason in the world. We might discover there was reason, though history will not reveal it. With God's wisdom and power, he prepared Cestius and his faithful remnant. The Shekinah Presence, dwelling over Jerusalem, watching over his own at the Mount of Olives, was ready to draw his people to himself, preparing for his Bride to escape this Great Tribulation. Cestius and his legions were ready to undermine the wall and set fire to the temple gates. Seeing the desecration of the Temple, seeing the Idumaeans entering the Temple and Cestius' armies ready to invade Jerusalem, the Lord drew his faithful Bride to Himself.

The Desolating Sacrilege had been seen. The Roman armies were on the verge of entering the city. Escape was possible; the Lord's beloved Bride would survive if she followed his warnings and did not delay. They recognized the Zealots abominations; they saw the Idumaean armies advancing, joining the Zealots, desecrating their Holy Temple. They understood Cestius was preparing his armies for their assault. They knew they were to flee; their Lord's vengeance was ready to fall upon the land.

The faithful remnant knew they could wait no longer. They saw the fulfillment of their Lord's words and remembered Luke's warning. *"Let those who are in Judea flee to the mountains; let those who are in the city get out; let those in the country not enter the city. This is the time of punishment."* Luke 21:20-23

The Zealots were the abomination; Cestius' army was God's desolating force. Desolation and destruction were rapidly drawing near. There was no time to delay. Their Lord's words were being fulfilled right before their eyes. They were ready to flee before the Great Tribulation. Cestius was preparing to destroy the city. Jesus' faithful disciples understood the signs. Seeing the desolating sacrilege, the armies surrounding the city, and knowing their Lord's warnings, his faithful Bride was ready to flee. Not living in darkness, she was watching and waiting, assured of her Lord's faithfulness. Hearing the sound of the Shofar and the shout of their Lord, with their Beloved Bridegroom guiding them, every Christian in Jerusalem fled without looking back, as Hosea 2:14-16 and Revelation 12:6 had prophesied.

The Lord's faithful Saints heard the Shofar proclaiming Rosh Hashanah. Yom Ha' Keseh, the Day of Concealment had come. The Bridegroom shouted out to his Bride; he was coming to carry her to the Wedding Chamber. She would be joined with her Lord as his beloved Bride. They all sang *'Baruch Haba B' Shem Adonai'*. Their Lord was coming for his Bride. Secure in his arms, they knew fulfillment of all he promised.

Not one Christian was in Jerusalem when Titus' legions entered the city in April AD 70; not one Christian was killed in the destruction of the city. By AD 69, the Jerusalem Church was abandoned. The faithful Bride of the Lord had fled to Pella, the Bridal Chamber.

In "Ecclesiastical History Eusebius reports: *"The people of the Church of Jerusalem had been commanded by a revelation vouchsafed to approved men before the war, to leave the city and dwell in a town of Perea, called Pella. When those that believed in Christ had come from Jerusalem, as if the royal city of the Jews and the whole land of Judea were entirely destitute of holy men, the judgment of God at length overtook those who committed such outrages against Christ and his apostles, and totally destroyed that generation of impious men."* These 'holy men', the Lord's Bride, without looking back, fled in their Lord's Shekinah Presence. They were assured tribulation would not come nigh.

5. From Revelation, we see our Lord's foreknowledge of God's wrath poured on all who had forsaken him. *"There were thunders and lightnings and a great earthquake such as was not since men were on the earth. There fell on men great hail out of heaven, every stone about the weight of a talent."* Revelation 16:18, 21 KJV

Josephus speaks complete fulfillment of this prophesy. *"On one night there was a prodigious storm with utmost violence, very strong winds, largest showers of rain, continual lightning, terrible thundering, amazing concussions, bellowing of the earth in an earthquake."* (Wars 4, 4, 5)

These natural assaults fully confirm John's vision. Though these hailstones cannot be literally interpreted, Josephus validated this 'hailstorm' as well. In the siege, *'the 10th legion constructed balistae of enormous magnitude and power, discharging vast stones into the city. These stones were of peculiar excellence; their scorpions were of greater power; their stone-projectors were larger. The stones used were the weight of a talent. The Jews at first could guard against the stones for their approach was intimated by their whiz but also being white, they were visible to the eye for their brightness.'* (War Bk. 5, 6, 6) These stones, the weight of a talent, white in color, match the 'hail as heavy as a talent, falling from heaven'. With acute accuracy, Josephus validates Scripture's account of this great hailstorm, metaphoric of God's wrath falling from heaven against that unrepentant nation.

Serious study of Josephus' "War of the Jews" reveals the complete desolation Jerusalem faced. His words validate all that we read in the Gospels, Revelation and the Old Testament Prophets and all we have been taught of Christ's Glorious Appearing.

THE WORD OF GOD   THE WAR OF THE JEWS BY JOSEPHUS

The Greatest of all Wars Matthew 24:21 (Preface War of the Jews and Bk. 6, 9)

Responsibility of the Jews for the Desolation Daniel 9:26 (Preface 4, 11)

The 'Wicked Generation' Matthew 17:17 (Bk. 3, 10, 9)

The Ceasing of the Daily Sacrifice Daniel 9:27 (Bk. 6, 2, 1)

False Prophets Matthew 24:5, 11:23-24, Mark 13:5, 21-22 (Bk. 2, 13, 4-5; 6, 5, 2-3)

Desolating Sacrilege Matthew 24:15, Mark 13:14, Luke 21:20 (Bk. 2, 19, 2-7)

Great Tribulation Matthew 24:21-22 (Bk. 3, 1-2, Bk. 4,1-3, Bk. 5, Bk. 6

A quart of wheat, three quarts of barley for a denarius Revelation 6:5-6 (Bk. 5, 10, 2)

Harming the oil and wine Revelation 6:6 (Bk. 5, 13, 6)

Famine and Pestilence Matthew 24:7b, Mark 13:8b, Luke 21:11 (Bk. 5, 1, 4; 5, 10, 2-3)

The Two Beasts, Nero and Gessius Florus Revelation 13 (Bk. 2, 13, 1-2; 2, 14, 2-9)

Lakes and Rivers of Blood Psalm 78:44, Revelation 8:9, 14:20, 16:3-4 (Bk. 2, 10, 9; 4, 7, 6)

Signs preceding the destruction Joel 2:30, Matthew 24:29-30, Revelation 6:12-13 (Bk. 6, 5, 3)

Hailstones the weight of a talent Revelation 16:21 (Bk. 5, 6, 3)

Violent storm, earthquake Revelation 16:18 (Bk. 4, 4, 5, (286-287)

Not one stone upon another Matthew 24:2 (Bk. 7, 8, 7 (376)

Babylon is Fallen Malachi 4:1, Revelation 11:8, 14:8, 16:19, 17:5, 18:24 (Bk. 6, 6-10)

These signs of God's foreknowledge, revealed through Scripture, are recorded by Josephus, fully confirming all we have been taught from Biblical studies, validating the 1st century Coming of Christ in judgment of the wicked and atonement of God's faithful remnant.

We Must Proclaim

Christ was Born. Matthew 1:23-25 Christ Died. Luke 23:44-46

Christ Arose. John 20:1-10

Christ Has Come Again! Revelation 22:6-7

"These words are trustworthy and true.
The Lord, the God of the Spirits of the Prophets,
sent his angel to show his servant what must soon take place."

"Behold, I am Coming Soon!"
"His Kingdom will have No End!"

Appendix 7

THE LORD'S SUPPER, UNTIL HE COMES

I n 1 Corinthians 11:26, speaking of the partaking of the Lord's Supper, Paul told the Corinthians that whenever they ate the bread and drank the cup, they were proclaiming the Lord's death "until He Comes." What was Paul telling the Corinthians? Was he saying Communion would cease at Christ's coming? Are we no longer commanded to proclaim our Lord's death and celebrate Communion after our Lord's return? Are we no longer to commemorate his body broken and his blood shed for our redemption?

With careful study, we might discover Paul was not telling the Corinthians that the Lord's Supper would cease, but would be observed in a New Way. In their observance of the Lord's Supper, Paul called them to commemorate Jesus' death, 'in remembrance of him', only until He had Come Again. At their Lord's Coming, they were no longer called to partake of the bread and wine in remembrance of his death; they were to take and receive it in celebration of his return, rejoicing in the restoration he promised the faithful remnant.

Observance of the Lord's Supper should no longer be a solemn remembrance of him in his absence, recalling his suffering and death, anxiously longing for his return. It should be a victory celebration with him at His Table, feasting with him in his presence, in his Kingdom. (1 Thessalonians 4:17)

Christ's faithful disciples dwelt with that promise; they comforted each other with the words 'Until He Comes'. At His Return, they would eat and drink with Him and commune with him in All His Glory with all who had served him in holiness. With their Lord present with them, they could celebrate and sing of his glory.

That is surely what many of the songs in our hymnals, the liturgy, and our prayers speak. We proclaim His Presence with us in our songs and prayers, but do we truly believe he abides with us? If He is with us and will never leave us, we do not need to await his return. He is here! The Lord's festive meal would have so much more joy and meaning if we acknowledged that we feast with him in his kingdom and abide in His Presence.

Paul did not say Communion's observance would cease at the Parousia; it would continue in a new way, just as the Passover took on new meaning after Israel entered the Promised Land. The original Passover, the type for our Communion, was instituted as Israel was leaving Egypt. They only observed it once in their forty year wilderness wandering. As Israel entered the Promised Land under Joshua, forty years later, they resumed its observance but it was no longer celebrated as a memorial of their deliverance from Egypt; it celebrated their victory over the Canaanites, their inheritance of the Promised Land and gratitude to their LORD for fulfilling all He Promised. This was a change of meaning, not a cessation of observance.

Did Jesus say the Supper would continue with a new meaning as the Passover had? At his Last Supper, before offering the cup, Jesus told his disciples he would not drink of the fruit of the vine from that day on until he could drink it new with them in his Father's Kingdom. (Matthew 26:29, Mark 14:25) Speaking of the Passover, he said he desired to eat the Passover with them before he had to suffer, but he would not eat of it anymore until it was fulfilled in the Kingdom of God. (Luke 22:18)

It is no wonder the early church longed for Christ's return. They longed to eat and drink with him in His Presence. They continued to observe the Lord's Supper in his memory, while he was away, but they eagerly awaited His Coming, longing for the time they could eat it in a new way, with Him in His Father's Kingdom.

This also implies continued life on earth after his return. We no longer observe Communion in memory of him in his absence. We feast with Him in his Kingdom. We can gather at His Table and observe it in his Honor, in his Glory, at his Side, in his Presence. It has new meaning, just as the Passover had new meaning after Israel entered the Promised Land. We observe the Lord's Supper in our Heavenly Promised Land. We celebrate, rejoicing in our Lord's completed sanctification, deliverance, redemption and restoration, exactly as he promised. We dwell with our Lord and reign with him in His righteousness. We celebrate Communion with him at his Table.

Before AD 70, the Lord's Supper commemorated his death and our deliverance from the bondage of sin; after AD 70, it became, and remains a glorious feast celebrating our inheritance in the Eternal Promised Land, the New Heaven and Earth. We eat and drink with him in His Presence, in his Glory at His Table, rejoicing in our deliverance from Spiritual Death, separation from the LORD our God. We celebrate with Christ and all the saints who have gone before us. Resurrected in Him, we stand, 'Anastasis', at his Table, in His Presence and praise His Name.

All things are made NEW! To God be the Glory;
Great things He Has Done.

Appendix 8

THE SHEKINAH GLORY—
THE ABIDING PRESENCE OF GOD

In Hebrew, Shekinah means 'The Presence of God,' describing God's presence in the Shekinah appearances. 'Shekinah', not found in any Biblical text, is first mentioned in the Jerusalem Targum, Aramaic paraphrases of the Hebrew Bible, written during Judah's Babylonian Exile. It is identified as God's abiding presence or the extended abiding of the physical expression of God amidst his people. The "Encyclopedia Judaica" defines Shekinah as 'the Divine Presence of God in the world, revelation of the Holy amidst the profane'. (Vol. 14 pp. 1349-51)

The image of the Shekinah Glory is revealed in fire and light. In "Yehovah's Shekinah Glory", John Keyser records the visions of God's presence are discovered in the Bible where 'shakan' is used. The glory of the LORD settled on Mount Sinai. The Shekinah Glory covered it six days. On the 7th day, God called to Moses out of the midst of the cloud. In their journeys, when the cloud was taken from the tabernacle, the people went on. (Exodus 24:16, 40:15) The cloud covered it by day; fire or light covered it by night. When the cloud was taken from over the tent, the people set out; in the place where it settled, the people encamped. (Numbers 9:16-18) Shekinah describes the mysterious Abiding Spiritual Presence of God. The Hebrew for tabernacle is 'ohel' or tent; 'Mishkan' is the dwelling place of the Shekinah, or Him who abides.

The light of God's presence is his Shekinah Glory. Ezekiel saw the glory of God coming from the east; his voice was like mighty running waters. The earth glowed with his glory. (Ezekiel 43:2) Many Rabbis believe that just as the Shekinah glory was seen on Moses' face as he came down from Mount Sinai, the angels in heaven and the righteous in the world to come, the 'olam-ha-ba', are sustained by the radiance and glorious presence of the Shekinah.

Isaiah 57:15 proclaims *"This is what the high and lofty One says: I live in a high and holy place but also with him who is contrite and lowly in spirit."* One who inhabits, 'shokeyn', is as close to the meaning of Shekinah that is found in the Bible. Shokeyn is the masculine participle, 'he who inhabits' or God, who inhabits heaven and human hearts at the same time. Shekinah, the Presence of God dwelling on the earth in the Mosaic dispensation, is the same word, only the gender is changed. Adding the feminine ending, shokeyn (shkn) becomes Shekinah (shknh). The masculine form of Shekinah appears in the Bible in this verse.

Isaiah 51:9-10 uses feminine pronouns. The KJV uses 'thou and it', but these pronouns are feminine in Hebrew. In Isaiah 51:9, '*the arm of the LORD*' describes the Messiah. Jesus was the Shekinah presence revealed in Old Testament events, explaining why the coming of the Messiah and the return of the Shekinah to the 2ⁿᵈ Temple are combined.

Zechariah speaks of the Shekinah's presence as it was revealed in Christ in the destruction of Jerusalem in AD 70. *"After he has honored me and has sent me against the nations that have plundered you, for whoever touches you touches the apple of his eye, I will surely raise my hand against them so their slaves will plunder them. Then you will know the LORD Almighty has sent me. Shout and be glad O daughter of Zion, for I am coming; I will live among you, declares the LORD. Many nations will be joined with the LORD in that day and will become my people. I will live among you: you will know the LORD almighty has sent me."* Zechariah 2:8-11

SHEKINAH   THE PHYSICAL PRESENCE OF GOD

Judaism is a monotheistic religion with a patriarchal God known as YHWH. "Shekinah, The Presence of Divinity" speaks of a maternal aspect of God that was present from the first day of creation and is still essential today. Shekinah is a Talmudic term describing the abiding presence of God on earth. Many Hebrews understand Shekinah as the 'mother' or feminine Presence of God, closely connected with the Sophia Wisdom of God found in Proverbs 1:20. *"Wisdom calls aloud in the street. She raises her voice in the public squares. At the head of the noisy streets, she cries out."* Jesus, our teacher of wisdom, was kindred to the Sophia tradition.

The Talmud calls Shekinah 'The Holy Spirit' or 'The Spirit of God', and is seen in the feminine form. Genesis 1:2 reveals Shekinah's presence from the beginning. *"The Spirit of God moved upon the face of the waters."* Shekinah's feminine nature is revealed in the Hebrew. The Gender of the subject in the Hebrew plays an important role in sentence structure. "The glorious Shekinah returned to bless us" does not reveal gender in English. In Hebrew however, verbs and adjectives have male and female forms, and suggest gender. In Hebrew, this sentence indicates three times that Shekinah is female. Judaism and Christianity understand God as Father, Lord and King. Everything we understand of our Bible reveals God is male. Hebrew writings however, reveal a feminine presence of God, not understood in our English translations.

An unknown Jewish Sage, living in Alexandria c. 50 BC., gives a poetic expression of the Shekinah Glory, the Spirit of God, revealed in feminine form. Though written by this unknown sage, authorship has been ascribed to Solomon. "The Wisdom of Solomon" may cause some to cringe at the thought of a feminine form of God but the words speak only praise and glory to the 'Spirit' who fills us in Communion with God who is All in All.

"THE SHEKINAH"
"THE WISDOM OF SOLOMON"

Shekinah is the Supreme Spirit devoted to the good of all people.
She shines bright in the bloom of ignorance. She is unfading.
She is seen by those who love her, easily found by those who look for her.
And quickly does she come to those who seek her.
One who rises early, intent on finding her, will not grow weary of the quest.
For one day he will find her seated in his own heart.
To set one's thoughts on her is true wisdom,
and to be aware of her is the sure way to perfect peace.
For Shekinah, herself, goes about in search of those who are worthy of her.
With every step, she comes to guide them,
In every thought she comes to meet them.
The true beginning of spiritual life is the desire to know Shekinah.
A desire to know her brings one to love her.
Loving her enables one to follow her.
Following her will is the sure path to immortality.
Immortality is oneness with God.
The desire to know Shekinah leads to God and his kingdom, a never-fading kingdom.
With all your thrones and scepters, you may rule the world for awhile.
But take hold of Shekinah, and you will rule the world forever.

This glorious presence was amongst his people as God's Shekinah Glory. God's Presence is normally invisible, however sometimes we are fortunate to envision his Glory. Exodus 13:21-22 says the Shekinah was a Pillar of Cloud and Fire. In 11 Kings 2:11, it was a chariot-throne propelled through heaven by winged creatures. In Psalms 104:3, we see the wonder of Shekinah. God stretched out the heavens, laying the beams of his chambers on the waters. The Clouds were his chariot.

The Shekinah was God's presence and blessing hovering in the Holy of Holies. When sin covered the land, the Shekinah Presence departed; the temple was left desolate. (Ezekiel 11:23) Shekinah was a medium of holy judgment toward unrepentant sinners, moving swiftly, executing God's sentence against them.

Throughout Scripture, images of the Shekinah Glory are often overlooked. Its image is complex, shrouded in mystery. Shekinah is seen in bright and dark clouds, in God's radiance, angels, lightning, rainbows, earthquakes, trumpet blasts, thundering voices and still small voices. It is revealed in blessing and protection but also judgment and destruction. Accepting its ever-changing reality, we can see its presence throughout Scripture.

Throughout Scripture we see visions of the presence of God, revealed in His Shekinah Glory. Genesis 1:2 gives us our first vision of the presence of God's Shekinah Glory. *"In the beginning God created the heavens and the earth. The earth was formless and empty; darkness was over the surface of the deep. The Spirit of God, God's Shekinah Glory, was hovering over the waters. God said, Let there be Light, and there was light."*

In the 1st moments of creation, the Spirit of God, the Shekinah Presence, hovering over the waters, overshadowed the deep. In the darkness, we hear the voice of God. "Let there be Light." At that moment, the awesome glory of God's Shekinah Presence gave the earth its first glimpse of God. God's Shekinah Glory shown down on the darkness, revealing God's Glorious Light.

At the Burning Bush, we witness the Shekinah Presence. Ancient Rabbis believe God's Shekinah appeared before Moses in the burning bush. The Angel of the LORD, the Shekinah Presence, appeared in a flame of fire, the Shekinah Fire. *"Out of the midst of a bush, the bush was burning but was not burned."* Exodus 3:2 This hovering, fiery presence was seen again by the children of Israel as they escaped slavery in Egypt. In their Exodus, God dwelt on Mt Sinai however, his Shekinah Presence was with the children of Israel, leading them through the wilderness as they journeyed to the Holy Land. In the Pillar of Fire by night and Pillar of Cloud by day, the Shekinah Presence guided them. At the end of their wilderness journey, they built a Tabernacle for the LORD where he would dwell. The glory of his Shekinah Presence indwelt the tabernacle, the very dwelling place of God.

Elijah saw the Shekinah Glory at Mt Horeb. God told him to stand on the mountain before him. The LORD passed by. A strong wind tore the mountain and broke the rocks; the LORD was not in the wind. After the wind, there was an earthquake; the LORD was not in the earthquake. After the earthquake, there was a fire; the LORD was not in the fire. After the fire, there was a Still Small Voice. (1 Kings 19:11-12)

The power of God's judgment was often seen in windstorm, earthquake and fire. Through the still small voice of God's Shekinah Presence, Elijah was told to return, to continue God's mission to his people. Elisha would carry it to the next generation. The Presence of the Shekinah Glory was revealed as a chariot and whirlwind of fire as Elijah ascended into the Heavens. A chariot of fire and horses of fire separated Elijah from Elisha: Elijah ascended in a whirlwind of fire into heaven. God's Shekinah Glory guided Elijah into the Heavens. (11 Kings 2:1)

Solomon knew God was not bound to earthly temples because of his abiding, eternal nature. Completing the Temple, he asked: *"Will God truly dwell on earth? Heaven, even the highest Heaven cannot contain you, how much less the house I have built."* 1 Kings 8:27

It is only in this immortal infinite way that Shekinah is known today. God indwells his people as a Spirit. *"This is what the high and lofty One says, he who lives forever, whose name is holy: 'I live in a high and holy place but also with him who is contrite and lowly in spirit, to revive the spirit of the lowly and revive the heart of the contrite'."* Isaiah 57:14-15

In Psalm 68:16-17, we see the Shekinah presence and realize the Messiah, the Shekinah Presence, indwells his people. *"Why gaze with envy, O rugged mountains, at the mountain where God chooses to reign, where the LORD himself will dwell forever? The chariots of God are tens of thousands, thousands upon thousands; the LORD has come from Sinai into his sanctuary."* Psalm 68:18 speaks of the Lord's resurrection and ascension resulting in the resurrection and indwelling of his people. *"When you ascended on high, you led captives in your trail; you received gifts from men, even from the rebellious, that you O LORD God, might dwell there."*

God's Shekinah Presence resided in the completed tabernacle, visible to the whole nation. The cloud covered the tent; the glory of the LORD filled the Tabernacle. On the day the tabernacle was set up, the Shekinah cloud covered the tabernacle. The tent of testimony was like a vision of fire until the morning. (Exodus 40:34) Number 9:15 repeats the glorious vision.

After entering the Promised Land, God's presence was manifest in the tabernacle and the Holy Temple. God promised that he would dwell in the house Solomon was constructing. If Solomon walked in obedience to God, if he obeyed his ordinances and kept his commandments, God would establish his word with him. As the Shekinah Glory, God would dwell with the people and would not forsake them. (1 Kings 6:11)

We find God's Shekinah Glory throughout the Gospel. In Matthew 1:35 the Shekinah overshadowed Mary, preparing her for the birth of our Lord. In Luke 2:9, the glory of God's Shekinah shone over the shepherds in the fields. In Matthew 2:10, the Wisemen searched for this king and God's Shekinah fire shone down on the house where the young king lived. In Acts 2, at Pentecost, the majesty of the Holy Spirit, God's Shekinah Glory, filled the disciples with the Fire of God's Shekinah Presence.

Christ possesses the glory of the Shekinah Presence as he reigns in majesty, wisdom and power in his people, in his Kingdom. Through all these verses, we see God's Power and glory revealed in His Shekinah Presence and sit in wonder when we see all he has revealed concerning the Presence of God's Shekinah Glory.

Departure of the Shekinah from Solomon's Temple.

With all the unholy acts of the Kings and their disobedience to God, the Shekinah Glory left Jerusalem's Temple in the days of Ezekiel. For refusing to follow their LORD's commands, the land was destroyed; the Temple was razed. The Shekinah Glory would not remain in the desecrated Temple. Prophesies of Shekinah's departure and return are seen in Ezekiel and Zechariah. Zechariah revealed an imminent restoration of what Ezekiel saw depart and predicted the return of the Shekinah to the Restored Temple.

The Hebrew words 'Kavod YHWH', the Glory of the LORD, and Shekinah are identical and refer to the hovering cloud and fire on Mt. Sinai, the Shekinah Presence at the dedication of Solomon's Temple and Shekinah's departure and return.

Ezekiel saw the departure and return of the Shekinah in two visions. He saw the promise of the restoration of the Temple, though at the time it was desolate and Jerusalem all but abandoned. Ezekiel 1 describes Shekinah's presence in the temple; in Ezekiel 10, he envisioned its departure. The glory of the LORD went up from the cherubim to the threshold of the house; the house and court were full of the brightness of the glory of the LORD. (Ezekiel 10:4) At that time the Shekinah indwelt the Temple, however Ezekiel continued. Lifting their wings and mounting from the earth, they went forth with the wheels beside them. They stood at the east gate of the house of the LORD; the Glory of the God of Israel was over them. He saw departure of the Presence of God from the Temple in Ezekiel 11:23. The Glory of the LORD went from the city.

Ezekiel saw himself return to the captives and reported the events. In Ezekiel 40-43, he saw a vision of the Shekinah's return to the restored 2nd Temple. Zechariah saw this happening in the days of Zerubbabel. (Zechariah 2:10) Zion was to rejoice; the LORD would come and dwell in the midst of his people. This verse was a promise, a vision of the imminent return of the Shekinah at the dedication of the Second Temple.

Ezekiel foretold the glorious future endlessness of the restored Shekinah revealed as 'That Day', beginning with the return of Shekinah to the time of the calling of the Gentiles. (Zechariah 2:11) Many nations would join themselves to the LORD and they would be his people. God would dwell in the midst of them. They would know the LORD of hosts had sent him to them. (Zechariah 2:8-11)

The Return of the Shekinah to the Restored Temple.

Zechariah began his ministry in Darius' 2nd year, four years before the Second Temple was completed and dedicated. The Shekinah Presence returned to the Temple at the Temple's dedication. Zechariah 8:3 promised: *"Thus says the LORD, 'I will return to Zion and I will dwell in Jerusalem'. Jerusalem will be called the City of Truth; the mountain of the LORD Almighty will be called the Holy Mountain."*

The Golden Age would follow the return of the Shekinah. After their desolation, Jerusalem and all Judea would be at peace in an age where people could grow old in a secure environment. The people of Jerusalem considered this a miracle, so great was the destruction and devastation they knew. Zechariah prophesied old men and women would again sit in the streets of Jerusalem with their staffs in their hands. (Zechariah 8:4)

The Departure of the Shekinah from the Restored Temple.

Jesus of Nazareth, the physical embodiment of God, lived in Israel while the Shekinah indwelt the Temple. Jesus prophesied that their house would be forsaken, abandoned. Their house, the Dwelling Place of the LORD, the Holy Temple of God, would be desolate, rejected. The Jerusalem Talmud says the Shekinah departed the Temple in AD 30 and it lay desolate until its destruction in AD 70. Scripture however, clearly says the Shekinah remained in the Temple through Jesus' life and the ministry of his apostles to the start of the War in AD 66.

Christians in the 1st Century, at the War of the Jews, were very interested in the Mount of Olives. Christian Jews knew the Prophets and knew Ezekiel prophesied the departure of the Shekinah to the Mount of Olives. The Glory of the LORD went from the midst of the city and stood on the mountain east of the city. This would have been the Mount of Olives. Just as the Shekinah departed Solomon's Temple at the desolation under Nebuchadnezzar and stood on the mountain on the east side of the city, they knew the Shekinah Glory which indwelt the Holy of Holies again left the sanctuary and abode on the Mount of Olives, hovering there through the years of the Roman War against Judea which ended in AD 70.

We learn of Shekinah's departure from the Temple from Eusebius, in "Proof of the Gospel." He revealed: *"Believers in Christ congregate from all parts of the world that they may worship at the Mount of Olives, opposite the city, wither the glory of the LORD migrated when it left the former city."* (Bk. VI, ch. 18) Eusebius says the Shekinah Glory left the Temple and hovered over the Mount of Olives from AD 66-70.

Eusebius was not the only observer who recorded the departure of the Shekinah Presence from the Temple before its destruction. In "Hope of Israel Ministries", John Keyser records that an eyewitness to Jerusalem's destruction, Rabbi Jonathan revealed the Shekinah Glory had left the Temple and abode on the Mt of Olives, hoping the children of Israel would repent. A 'still small voice' from heaven, the 'Bat Kol', cried *"Return, O backsliding children. Return to me; I will return to you."* When there was no repentance, the voice said: *"I will return to my place."* Hosea 5:15 says: *"Then I will go back to my place until they admit their guilt and they will seek my face. In their misery, they will earnestly seek me."*

Josephus recorded the Shekinah Glory departed the Temple in the Spring of AD 66. He showed three signs he believed revealed the Shekinah departing the Holy of Holies. He recorded that the brass gates of the temple opened of their own and twenty men were needed to close and secure them. The wise men understood this as God's displeasure with his people and understood this as his departure from the temple. He also recorded a Great Light shining over the altar a week before Passover, AD 66, and then departing.

The same Light that guided the children of Israel through the wilderness, abiding in the Tabernacle and Solomon's Temple, was seen departing the rebuilt Temple, leaving it totally desolate! Wise scribes understood this as a bad omen. They cried: *"It was like the*

Shekinah Glory leaving the Tabernacle in the wilderness as a sign to disassemble and transport it to another location."

Josephus also recorded at Pentecost, AD 66, the priests, on entering the inner temple courts, heard a great uproar and a voice of a great multitude proclaiming, *"Let us depart hence."* As these three 'signs' revealed, the Visible Presence of God, the Shekinah Glory had departed the Temple and the hosts of heaven, the vindicated Old Covenant saints, had departed Sheol. The presence of God no longer indwelt its gates. The once Holy Temple was without the presence that truly made it Holy.

In Zechariah 14:4-9, in the destruction of the Temple and Holy City, we read: *"On that day, his feet will stand on the Mount of Olives, east of Jerusalem. The Mount of Olives will be split in two from east to west, forming a great valley. Then the LORD my God will come, all the holy ones with him. On that day there will be no light, neither cold nor frost. It will be a unique day, without daytime or nighttime, a day known to the LORD. On that day, living waters will flow out from Jerusalem. The LORD will be king over the whole earth; on that day there will be one LORD, and His Name the only name."*

THE PHYSICAL, VISIBLE SHEKINAH GLORY.

Learning of the glorious appearances of the Shekinah Presence, we know there are many faithful believers who cannot envision this glory. They would assure us that the Fire and Cloud that led the Israelites was a Spiritual presence, surely not something we could literally see or accurately describe or record.

Ezekiel told his people that the Shekinah had departed the temple but would return to the rebuilt temple before Ezra and Nehemiah came to Jerusalem. The Shekinah remained in the 2nd Temple through the time of the temple's enlargement by Herod, starting in 18 BC. In Josephus' "Antiquities" we learn about Herod's project of enlarging and improving the Temple. His record of Herod's plans reveals the glorious power of God's Shekinah Glory and the physical, visible attributes of the LORD's Glorious Abiding Presence.

Herod was making plans to expand on the Holy Temple. He discovered all the sacred treasures had been exhausted. The people from all around the world, the whole of the Roman Empire, had sent an abundance of money for the project but much was still lacking. On careful examination, Herod discovered there was another source available for the resources he needed to complete his project.

Herod financed expansion of the temple by tapping David's sepulchre as the prime source to pay for his works. He used what Solomon laid aside for expenses of the 1st Temple for expansion of the 2nd Temple. *"Herod opened the sepulchre by night and went in. He endeavored it should not be known in the city and took only faithful friends with him. He planned to explore David's tomb to the limits.* Suddenly, in the depth of the sepulchre, a miraculous, glorious and terrifying appearance was seen. *Herod had a great desire to make a more diligent search and go further, as far as to the very bodies of David and Solomon when two of his guards were slain by a flame that burst upon those that went in, as the report was. He was terribly affrighted and went out and built a propitiatory monument of that fright he had been in and this of white stone, at the mouth of the sepulchre."* (Antiq. 14.7.1, 97)

While we are tempted to believe Scriptural appearances of the presence and departure of the Shekinah Glory were spiritually seen and understood, Josephus' record of Herod's accounting speaks clearly of a Physical Abiding Presence, a flaming Fire the people could see with their physical eyes. The faithful saints of the New Testament were assured of His Presence. They could see, possibly with Spiritual Eyes, but also with their physical eyes, the glory and majesty of God's Shekinah Presence.

They knew God's Shekinah Glory hovered over the Mount of Olives, not just because of Ezekiel's words but because they could see Him. We can be sure Herod saw as well, and at the sight of the Shekinah Flame that burst forth, killing his men, the fear of God terrified him and the men who survived the encounter. God's Shekinah Glory terrified them to the bone and scared them to death.

THE SHEKINAH PRESENCE INDWELLS HIS TEMPLE, HIS PEOPLE.

The Shekinah Glory no longer dwelled within the Temple. It indwells the Church, the body of Christ. Christ, the Shekinah Presence, indwells his Eternal Temple. The children of Israel had the Temple but the Presence of God departed its gates, leaving the Temple desolate. The physical Temple and City fulfilled their purpose. In God's eternal Kingdom, his people are the Very Dwelling Place of God. Christ dwells within his people. They are his Holy Temple, His Faithful City. (Isaiah 1:26)

Daniel prophesied that at Jerusalem's desolation, sacrifices and offerings would cease. History reveals there were no priests to serve and no animals to sacrifice. The true reason for cessation of sacrifices however, was because the Shekinah Glory no longer indwelt the temple. Sacrifices were no longer necessary or accepted. The Shekinah Presence was amongst his children. Jesus would forever dwell within his people.

Throughout Jesus' ministry, the Shekinah Presence indwelt him in all his glory. At his death, the Shekinah Glory, the Holy Spirit, dwelt within his servants, disciples and witnesses throughout the world to the ends of the earth. The Shekinah Glory indwelt the 'Body of Christ', the children of his heart.

After Pentecost, the Shekinah Glory was seen and felt in the power and fire of the Holy Spirit, indwelling and abiding over Christ's faithful witnesses, filling them with the power of the Holy Spirit, God's Shekinah Glory. At Christ's return, in all his glory, the Shekinah Presence was Spiritually seen indwelling the faithful witnesses and saints of the LORD. In his glorious kingdom today, in the 21st century and beyond, the LORD's Shekinah Glory indwells all who live and witness to the Glory of God.

Just before his death, Jesus was confronted by the Jews. Speaking of the Temple and the Mishkan, the presence that lit the Holy of Holies on Yom Kippur, he said *"Destroy*

179

this Temple and in three days I will raise it up." John 2:18 Jesus declared he was the Temple, the Mishkan, the Dwelling Place of God. When the Shekinah Glory came down like a mighty wind through the roof of the Holy of Holies, the Holy Presence manifested on the mercy seat after the blood was sprinkled. That was the Mishkan, the Presence Jesus said dwelt within him.

God's Shekinah Glory continues to dwell within the hearts of all believers. In 1 Corinthians 6:19, Paul asked the Corinthians if they did not know their bodies were a temple, a Mishkan of God of the Holy Spirit within them which they had from God. Christ's prime concern was for his children to dwell in him. In his kingdom, in his presence, we are changed, restored.

In Christ, we are, and forever will be the Image of God. His Spirit, his Shekinah Glory dwells within us. In the glory of his Shekinah Presence, we are the Temple of God, the Very Dwelling Place of the LORD. The Holy Temple, built with hands, has been set aside, replaced by God's Eternal Temple, His Holy People, His Royal Priesthood. God's Holy Temple stands today, eternal, indestructible. We are the Very Dwelling Place of God.

Speaking to the scattered saints in Asia Minor, Peter proclaimed, *"You are a chosen people, a royal priesthood, a holy nation, a people belonging to God. Once you were not a people, now you are the people of God."* 1 Peter 2:9 We are God's people, His Holy Temple, His Royal Priesthood, His Faithful City. Nothing man can build could compare to the Glory of God's Holy Temple where in his Kingdom his people reign with and in their Lord. As His Holy Temple, His Holy Nation, we are God's Chosen People, His Holy Priesthood.

THE SHEKINAH PRESENCE OF GOD INDWELLS THE KING ON HIS THRONE.

The Glory of God, the Glorious Presence of God, dwells with us and in us. In Christ, we rejoice in the Shekinah Glory of God in his Kingdom. The Shekinah Presence indwells Christ, the King. The Shekinah Presence indwells us, filling his faithful servants who serve him in his kingdom.

Looking carefully with Spiritual Eyes, we can see the Glorious Shekinah Presence shining within his people. Just as Adam was created in the Image of God, we, in Christ, are God's New Creation. We are the Very Image of God. His light shines in all who proclaim the Glory and Presence of God within them. We reign with the LORD in All His Glory. The LORD reigns in us. His Glory will have no end. All his people praise him.

Our rejoicing will have no end. We are the 'Body of Christ'. With the glorious Shekinah Presence dwelling within us, we must rejoice. God no longer dwells in a physical temple made with hands, a building that could be taken away or destroyed. He dwells within His Eternal Temple, His faithful people, an indestructible Temple that no one can take away from God. In Exodus 25:8, when the LORD told Moses, "Let them make me a sanctuary that I may dwell with them", we should understand God literally said:

"Let them make me a sanctuary that I may dwell In Them."

God's ultimate goal has always been to dwell within his people and have his Spirit dwell within us. Remembering his promise in Jeremiah 31:31-33, we are assured God would make a New Covenant with the house of Israel, All Israel. He would put his law within them and write it on their hearts. He would be their God, they would be his people. In Christ's Shekinah Presence, we are One with God.

"Behold, I tell you a Mystery!"

We are in Christ, God's Holy Temple; We are God's Holy Temple.
We are God's Eternal Kingdom; We dwell in God's Eternal Kingdom.
God's Eternal Kingdom dwells within us.

We dwell in God's Faithful City; We are God's Faithful City.
God's Glorious Shekinah presence indwells us, His Holy Temple.
God has made us a Holy Temple. He dwells in us; we dwell in him.
His Shekinah Glory will Forever Fill Us.

Christ is the Mishkan of God, the Very Dwelling Place of God. He is the Temple of God!
Christ is the Law, the Torah, inscribed in our minds.
He is the Covenant, written in our hearts.
He is the Promised Land! We dwell in Him; He dwells in us!
He is the Temple, the Very Dwelling Place of God!
In Christ, We Have Become the Very Dwelling Place of God.
God's Shekinah Glory Dwells in Us. We Dwell in God's Shekinah Glory.

We Are ONE in Christ, His Beloved Bride.
We Can Rejoice; We Must Rejoice; We Must Proclaim:
Christ is All in All! We Are One, Echad!

*"The Earth is Full of the Presence and the Glory of God,
The Kavod YHWH, the Shekinah Presence,
As the Waters Cover the Seas!"*
God has called us to Rejoice and Celebrate Forever!

In Conclusion

From Joshua 24, we learn of the last days of Israel's long journey to their Promised Land. Joshua, Yeshua, gathered Israel's elders, judges and officials together and presented them before the LORD. The LORD spoke of all they endured from the time of Abraham and how their ancestors worshiped the gods from beyond the Euphrates and the gods of Egypt. God took Abraham, through his grandson, Jacob, out of that pagan land and led him to Canaan, giving him many descendants. The LORD spoke of Jacob's sojourn in Egypt because of a famine and his people's years in bondage to Egypt's pharaoh. He spoke of Moses, his deliverer and Aaron, his High Priest, and how he afflicted Egypt for their oppression, bringing Israel out of the land of Egypt. He reminded them of their escape at the Red Sea and how Egypt's armies all died in the waters. He reminded them of their wilderness journey when they cried to the LORD, and he fed them 'Bread from Heaven' and 'Water from the Rock'. Their LORD brought them to the land of the Amorites and Israel took possession of the land the LORD had promised Abraham.

The LORD spoke of their crossing of the Jordan to possess the land. God gave their enemies into their hands; not by bow or sword but by the hand of God. God gave them a land on which they did not build; they ate from vineyards and olive groves they did not plant.

After the LORD spoke, Joshua said, *"Fear the LORD; serve him with all faithfulness. Throw away the gods your forefathers worshiped beyond the river and in Egypt; serve the LORD. But if serving the LORD seems undesirable to you, choose for yourselves this day whom you will serve, whether the gods your forefathers served beyond the river or the gods of the Amorites in whose land you are living."* Joshua 24:14-15 The LORD gave them a choice; they could serve the gods of their ancestors or serve the LORD who brought them out of Egypt, led them through the wilderness and delivered them from the Amorites, to the land promised Abraham.

Hearing their LORD, they swore *"Far be it from us to forsake the LORD to serve other gods. It was the LORD our God himself who brought us and our fathers out of Egypt, from the land of slavery and performed those great signs before our eyes. We too will serve the LORD because he is our God."* Joshua 24:16-17,18b

That first generation in the Promised Land assured Joshua and their LORD that they would follow the LORD and obey all his commands. They swore allegiance to the

LORD. Joshua made a covenant with them and drew up the laws and ordinances they were to follow. Joshua set it as a stone of witness near the holy place of the LORD.

The first generation of the *New Israel* in the *New Promised Land* heard the same message. Jesus, Yeshua, stood before the apostles and elders, speaking of their Assyrian and Babylonian exile and their suffering under Syria's oppression. He also spoke of all they endured under Rome. Yeshua, their deliverer and High Priest had delivered them from slavery to sin-death. In him, Israel and Judah, Jews and Gentiles were One. Their Lord, the 'Bread of Heaven', the 'Living Water' brought them to Abraham's Heavenly Promised Land. By the hand of God, not by bow or sword, they would dwell in the New Jerusalem, a Heavenly Land, a land they did not build; they could eat from vineyards they did not plant. Serving him in holiness, they drew all nations to him. Their Lord told them: "Abide in me, serve me in holiness, throw away the gods of Babylon, Syria and Rome; I will be your God."

Just as Israel's first generation was sure of their faithfulness, this new generation would remain faithful. Standing in his glorious presence, they witnessed all he did to bring them together in him as One. They swore *"We will not forsake the Lord our God; he has delivered us from sin-death and performed great signs and wonders before our eyes. Crossing the Jordan, covering us at Pella, he delivered us from the nations that sought our souls. In His Body we stand, Resurrected in His Holiness. We are his people; He is our God."*

Yeshua wrote up a New Covenant, binding its laws and decrees on their minds, writing them on their hearts. Christ, the Rock of their salvation was their witness. If they faithfully served him in his holiness, they would be his people; he would be their God. They would forever dwell with their Lord in his Presence.

Those first generations were truly faithful. They taught their children for many generations but as we know, time passed; new generations came; new beliefs were born and doubt crept in.

We stand in our generation and our Lord asks us the same questions. Will we serve the Lord; will we acknowledge his presence with us or doubt all he did to bring us together in him? The choice is ours. It always has been. What will we say when our Lord asks us if we have been obedient to Christ, the witness of his Covenant? Will we acknowledge he has fulfilled ALL he promised, or will we continue to doubt?

From this day on we are called to celebrate.
Every Day is a Holy Day to our Lord! 'Hallelujah!'

BIBLIOGRAPHY

Unless noted, all Biblical passages are from the Zondervan New International Version. Some websites may no longer be available for research.

Adams, Jay E. "The Time is at Hand" Timeless Texts, Woodruff, SC 2000

Administration of "Biblical Holidays" "Messiah in Purim" www.biblicalholidays.com

Aphrahat "The Demonstrations" AD 280-367 www.preteristarchive.com

Augustus Caesar "Res Gestae Divi Augusti" transl. by P. A. Brunt and J. M. Moore

Bell, William "What is the Abomination of Desolation" www.allthingsfulfilled.com

Bible Insight "God's Annual Holy Days in Prophecy" www.bibleinsight.com/annual.html

Bible Prophecy Studies "The Wedding and Marriage of the Bride of Christ" www.link. Jesus.com/introwedding.htm

Bible Studies for Growth in God "The Year of Jubilee" www.growthingod.org/uk/jubilee.htm

Blume, Mike "Adam Clark and Matthew 24" http://mikeblume.com/adamclarke.htm

Bray, John L. "The Man of Sin 11 Thessalonians 2

Bray, John L. "The New Heaven and the New Earth

Bushnell, Thomas "Res Gestae The Deeds of the Divine Augustus" Transl. Bushnell c. 2009

Charlesworth, James H. "The First Christian Hymnbook The Odes of Solomon" Cascades Bks. 2009

Chilton, David "The Days of Vengeance" publ. Dominion Press c. 2006

Christian Evidences "Scripture Prophesies of the Messiah's Birth by 7 AD" www. christianevidences.org/shilohs-coming-prior-to-7ad.html

Chumney, Eddie "The Season of Teshuvah, Rosh Hashanah The Seven Festivals of the Messiah"

Chumney, Eddie "The Seven Festivals of the Messiah" Destiny Image publ. Shippensburg, Pennsylvania 1994

Cook, Steven R. "The Hypostatic Union" www.christonly.com/hypostaticunion.htm

Cortright, Michael "The Birth of Jesus Christ" www.cortright.org

Cropper, Tyrone "Eschatology from a 1st Century Viewpoint" www.newjerusalem community.net/?c=1548ca=1948

Cropper, Tyrone "Where and When did the Train Derail the Tracks" www.newjerusalem community.net.?c=1548ca=1948

Crusade Church of God "Holy Day Festivals of the Bible" www.pointsoftruth.com/festivals.html

Dankenbring, William "The Mystery of Shemini Atzeret The 8th Day" www.hope.of.Israel.org.shemini.htm

Deem, Rich "How the Passover Reveals Jesus Christ" www.godandscience.org/apologetics/passover.html

De Lashmutt, Gary "Sejanus and the Chronology of Christ's Death" www.xenos.org/essays/sejanus.html

Dokter, Hilke "Messiah in Annual Feasts" www.members.shaw.ca/hdokter/annual.htm

Elliot, David "Abomination of Desolation" http://insight2bp.homestead.com/152.html

Epiphanes "Pella Flight" www.preteristarchive.com/Study/Archive/e/epiphanes.html

Eusebius "Ecclesiastical History" Book 111 Ch. V www.preteristarchive.com

Eusebius of Caesarea "Demonstratio Evangelica" www.tertullian.org/fathers/eusebius_de_book1.htm

Eusebius of Caesarea "The Proof of the Gospel of Eusebius of Caesarea" Bk. 7 www.preteristarchive.com

Evidence for God in Science "Phlegon Trallianus' Olympiades" www.godandscience.org/viewtopicphp?f=68t=34157

Fadeley, Gene "Hebrews Covenants in Contrast" Anchor Publ. 1996

Fadeley, Gene "Revelation Kingdoms in Conflict" Anchor Publ. 1995

Fangio, W. N. "Time of Transition, The Promise of Joel 2:28-32" c. 2004

Farmer, William Reuben "Maccabees, Zealots and Josephus" www.preteristarchive.com

Federoff, N., Peterson, T. "Talmudic Evidence of the Messiah in AD 30" www.windowview.org/hmny/pgs/talmuds.30ce.html

Fenley, Ward ""The Myth of Already but Not Yet Theology" www.preteristarchive.com

Ferrar, Frederick "Early Days of Christianity" vol. 2 pp. 82-83 www.preteristarchive.com

Ferrar, Frederick "The Fall of Jerusalem" www.preteristarchive.com

Frost, Samuel, Green, David, Hassertt, Edward, Sullivan, Michael "House Divided" Vision Publ. 2009

Glenney, Gary "The Doctrine of the Virgin Birth" www.portlandbiblechurch.com

Grace Tabernacle "Our Sabbath Rest, Fulfilled in Jesus Christ" www.thegracetabernacle.org/studies/gtsn_sabbath.html

Greenburg, Rabbi Irving "God's Nostalgia, Rejoicing to Prove a Point" www.MyJewishLearning.com

Guzik, David "God Instituted Passover Exodus 12 www.enduringword.com/commentaries/0212.htm

Holford, George Peter "The Destruction of Jerusalem" 1805 publ. Leonard Jackson 1830

Hall, Ph.D. L. Michael "Apocalypse Then, Not Now" E. T. Publications 1994

Hampton-Cooke, Earnest "The Christ Has Come" publ. 1891 B. A. London, M/ A. Cambridge

Harden, Dan "Split Decision Olivet Stands United" www.bereanbiblechurch.org/transcripts/eschatology/split-decision.htm

Hebrew Date Converter www.hebcal.com/converter

Henry, Jimmy "The Glorious Return of Jesus Christ" c. 2002

Hill, Glenn L. "Christianity's Great Dilemma" Moonbeam Publ. Lexington, Ky. 2010

Hunt, Keith "The Feast of Atonement" www.keithhunt.com/Atone2.html

Jacobs, Marvin E. "The Eternal Kingdom" www.preteristarchive.com/preterism/jacobs-marvin-9/01.html

James, Timothy "The Messiah's Return Delayed, Fulfilled or Double Fulfillment" Kingdom Publ. 1991

Johnson, Jerome "At the Right Time, Dating the Events of the New Testament" Bathkol Bks. 1999 Havre de Grace, Md.

Josephus, "Complete Works", "Antiquities of the Jews", "War of the Jews", "Against Apion" trans. by William Whiston, 1987 Hendrickson Publ. Peabody, Ma.

Kaplin, Rabbi Arjeh "Sabbath Rest, Sabbath of Eternity" Publ. OU/NCSY

Keathley 111, J. Hampton "The Ascension of Jesus Christ Seeing the Lord High and Exalted www.bible/org/ascension-jesus-christ

Keyser, John D. "Jehovah's Shekinah Glory" www.hope-of-israel.org/nz/glory.htm

Keyser, John D. editor "The Mystery of Shemini Atzeret The Eighth Day" www.hope-of-israel/shemini.htm

Keyser, John D. "The Second Coming of Jehovah God www.hope-of-israel.org/shekinah.htm

King, Max. R. "The Cross and Parousia of Christ Writing and Research Ministry c. 1987

Kiser, Greg "Kiser's Science" www.preteristarchive.com/Study/Archive/k/kiser-Greg-science.html

Larson, Frederick "The Day of the Cross" www.bethlehemstar.net/day/day.html

Larson, Frederick "The Starry Dance" www.bethlehemstar.netdance/dance.htm

Lazarus Come Forth "The Rich Man and Lazarus Parable or Prophecy?" www.lazaruscomeforth.com/bible-lazarus-and-rich-man/index.cfm

Leonard, R. C., Leonard, J. E. "The Promise of His Coming" Laudemont Press 1996

Lewis and Reinhold "Roman Civilization" Nov. 1990 Columbia University Press

Linden, David H. "The Day of Atonement" www.grebeweb.com/linden/Day_of_Atonement_revised_2008.html

McCallum, Dennis "Melchizedek and the Priesthood of Christ" www.xenos.org/essays/melchi.htm

Magath, Julius "The Legal Power of the Sanhedrin is Restricted 23 Years before the Trial of Christ" of the N. Ga. Conference Professor of Emory College Eighth Edition Oxford, Ga. 1911

Martin, Brian L. "Behind the Veil of Moses" The Veil of Moses Project c. 1982

186

Martin, Brian L. "You've Got to be Kidding" Fulfilled Communications Group www.FulfilledCG.com

Martin, Earnest L. "Birth of Christ, Recalculated" 1980 publ. Foundation for Biblical Research Pasadena, California

Martin, Earnest L. "The Lunar Eclipse of Josephus" www.askelm.com/star/star011.htm

Melanson, Arthur "The Second Coming, Postponed or Fulfilled? Publ. Joy of the Lord c. 1998

Mills Jr., Jessie E "Daniel, Fulfilled Prophecy" c. 2003

Missler, Chuck "Who Were the Magi?" www.khouse.org/articles/2003/497/

Missler, Chuck "Until Shiloh Comes" http://xwalk.ca/shiloh.html

My Jewish Learning "Shemini Atzeret Simchat Torah Theology and Themes" www.myjewishlearning.com

New Jerusalem Community "The Early Church and the End of the World" www.newjerusalemcommunity.net/?-508ca=1798

New Testament Greek Lexicon "Hegemon" www.searchgodsword.org/lex/grk/view.cgi?number=2232

Nickels, Richard C. "Holy Day Words" www.giveshare.org/HolyDay/hdwords.html

Noe, John "Beyond the End Times" IPA Bradford, Pa. c. 1999

Noe, John "Dead in Their Tracks" IPA Bradford, Pa. c. 2001

Paleo Times "Yahweh's Word from ancient Times" www.Paleotimes.org

Parsons, John J. "Hoshana Rabbah The Great Salvation" www.hebrew4christians.com

Parsons, John J. "Rosh Hashanah Awakening to Judgment" www.hebrew4christians.com

Payne, William L. "Who is the Jewish Messiah? Irrefutable Evidence" www.newgateministries.com/jerualemchronicles/evidence.html

Piper, John "Simeon's Farewell to the World" www.desiringgod.org

Preston, Don K. "How is This Possible?" JaDon Management c. 2009

Preston, Don K. "Prophecy Fulfilled The Regathering of Israel" www.eschatology.org

Preston, Don K. "Seal Up Vision and Prophecy" JaDon Management c. 2008

Preston, Don K. "Typology and Covenant Eschatology" www.eschatology.org

Preston, Don K. "We Shall Meet Him in the Air" JaDon Management c. 2009

Preston, Don K. "With the Sound of the Trumpet" www.newjerusalemcommunity.net/c=54&a=1449

Raines, Rev. Mark "Shekinah, The Presence of Divinity" http://northernway.org/shekinah.html

Reed, Doug "Herod's Temple and its Demise" www.newjerusalemcommunity.net/>=508a=1284 and 1285

Revilla, Juan Antonio, Keyser, John D. "Did Herod the Great Really Die in 4 BC? www.hope-of-israel.org/herodsdeath.html

Revilla, Juan Antonio "On the Year of Herod's Death" www.expreso.co.cr/centaurs/steiner/herod.html

Rickard, Ed "The Virgin Birth of Jesus The Prophesies of Genesis and Isaiah" www.themoorings.org/apologetics/VirginBirth/Isaiah.html

Robinson, John A. T. "Redating the New Testament" Wipf and Stock Publ. 2000

Russell, James Stewart "The Parousia" Kingdom Publications, USA 1996

Sampson, Robin, Pierce, Linda "What Happened to the Biblical Holidays" www.biblicalholidays.com

Selden, Murrell "Chronology for Passovers Associated with Ministries of Jesus and John the Baptist"

Setterfield, Barry "The Christmas Star" www.ldolphin.org/birth.html

Simmons, Kurt "Adumbrations The Kingdom and Coming of Christ in the Book of Daniel" c. 2009

Source Unknown "Genesis 49:10 Israel's Blindness" http://bible.org/illustration/genesis-4910

Sumner, Paul "He Who is Coming The Hidden Afikomen" www.hebrew-streams.org/works/judaism/afikoman.html

Sullivan, Clayton "Rethinking Realized Eschatology" Book Review Timothy James Mercer University Press 1988

Tacitus "Annals" XV:44, 2-8 and "Histories" Bk. V"

Touger, Rabbi Eliyahu "Timeless Patterns in Time" Publ. Sichos in English

TryGod.com "Introduction to the Jupiter-Regulus Conjunctions" http://try-god.com/view_page.asp>id=124

Verdicchio, Michael A. "Why Swaddling Clothes" www.articlesbase.com/religion-articles/why-swaddling-clothes=1592623.html

Wesley, Charles, Edson, Lewis "Blow Ye the Trumpet, Blow" www.hymnsite.com/lyrics.umh378.sht

Wierville, V. P. "Jesus Christ, Our Promised Seed" American Christian Press 1982 ch. 16 pp. 200-204 1982

You Tube "Jesus' Birthdate Decoded Jupiter Regulus Conjunctions" www.youtube.com/watch?V=WaKqpopZXOQ